D0622461

TERROR IN CHECHNYA

HUMAN RIGHTS AND CRIMES AGAINST HUMANITY
Eric D. Weitz, Series Editor

Echoes of Violence: Letters from a War Reporter by Carolin Emcke

Cannibal Island: Death in a Siberian Gulag by Nicolas Werth, translated by Steven Rendall

Torture and the Twilight of Empire from Algiers to Baghdad by Marnia Lazreg

Terror in Chechnya: Russia and the Tragedy of Civilians in War by Emma Gilligan

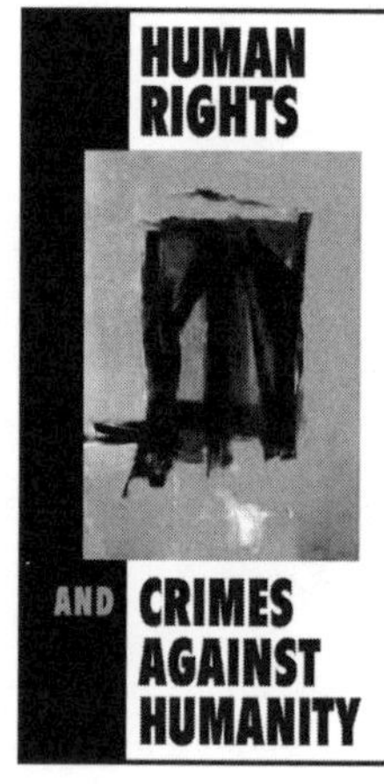

TERROR IN CHECHNYA

RUSSIA AND THE TRAGEDY OF CIVILIANS IN WAR

EMMA GILLIGAN

PRINCETON UNIVERSITY PRESS
PRINCETON AND OXFORD

Published by Princeton University Press, 41 William Street, Princeton, New Jersey 08540

In the United Kingdom: Princeton University Press, 6 Oxford Street, Woodstock, Oxfordshire OX20 1TW

Library of Congress Cataloging-in-Publication Data

Gilligan, Emma, 1967–
Terror in Chechnya : Russia and the tragedy of civilians in war / by Emma Gilligan.
p. cm. — (Human rights and crimes against humanity)
Includes bibliographical references and index.
ISBN 978-0-691-13079-8 (hardcover : alk. paper) 1. Chechnia (Russia)—History—Civil War, 1994– 2. Civil war—Protection of civilians—Russia (Federation)—Chechnia. 3. Human rights—Russia (Federation)—Chechnia. 4. Chechnia (Russia)—History—Autonomy and independence movements. 5. Russia (Federation)—Relations—Russia (Federation)—Chechnia 6. Chechnia (Russia)—Relations—Russia (Federation) 7. Russia (Federation)—Military policy. I. Title.
DK511.C37G55 2010
947.086'1—dc22

2009013381

British Library Cataloging-in-Publication Data is available

This book has been composed in Adobe Jenson Pro
Printed on acid-free paper. ∞
press.princeton.edu

Printed in the United States of America

1 3 5 7 9 10 8 6 4 2

For my mother

CONTENTS

ILLUSTRATIONS

ACKNOWLEDGMENTS

THERE ARE MANY PEOPLE who inspire and motivate one to complete a book. While it often feels like a solitary journey, it rarely is. I owe the greatest debt to my mother. While always acknowledging the complex problems that writing this book would entail and the criticism it may endure, she nevertheless urged me on and offered her assistance and opinion with great generosity. Her forbearance made it possible for this story to be told, and I truly honor and thank her for that.

For the past five years, the witnesses to the tragedy in Chechnya have been my shrewd and forthright guides. Candid testimonies came from those collated by Memorial, Human Rights Watch, Amnesty International, and Médecins Sans Frontières, and from individual interviews undertaken over four years. I am grateful to Anna Neistat, Jane Buchanan, and Diederik Lohman of Human Rights Watch, whose openness and candid assistance helped generate a book of greater depth and reflection. I am grateful to the many Chechens who offered views of, opinions on, and facts about the crisis, most notably Aset Chadaeva, Eliza Moussaeva, and Apti Bisultanov. I am grateful for their willingness to revisit a painful past for the sake of illuminating our knowledge of the scale of the tragedy.

This book has been shaped by a number of challenges, and I am grateful to all who attempted to assist me overcome them by providing interviews or information not readily available in the mainstream. These include members of the Council of Europe, the Organization for Security and Co-operation in Europe, the European Court of Human Rights, and the United Nations, Russian human rights activists Katya Sokirianskaia and Anna Kornilina, Chris Hunter of the Centre for Peacemaking and Community Development, Almut Rochowanski of the Chechnya Advocacy Network, Bill Bowring and Philip Leach of the European Human Rights Advocacy Centre, Karin Keil of Caritas (Vienna), Gillian Dunn and Mike Young of the International Rescue Committee, and Simon Panek of People in Need. I am grateful also to my mentor and friend, Edward Kline, president of the U.S. Andrei Sakharov Foundation and eternal giver of time and moral support to those most in need. I would also like to thank the Russian journalist Dmitrii Beliakov, who offered his photographs without charge. I appreciated our insightful and rich e-mail conversations. Finally,

I am grateful to all who granted interviews on the condition of anonymity. Many spoke frankly about the tragic human behavior they encountered in Chechnya with openness, anger, and sadness. Moreover, they provided essential empirical material that fundamentally transformed the tone of this book.

I am grateful to Brigitta van Rheinberg and Eric Weitz of Princeton University Press for their initial belief in the project, as well as to Dana Rowan for her meticulous final read-through of the text, a wonderful experience to share with such a dear friend. I am grateful to my family, notably Therese Grant, who urged me to stay calm and trust in the story, as well as to Philip Grant, who spent much of his summer Australian Christmas break reading a draft. I am grateful for the ever-joyous smiles and love of my nieces, Minna, Eilish, and Eden. I wish to thank my friends Robert Horvath and Dan Caner, who read the manuscript and offered invaluable feedback, and to two anonymous readers whose dedication to their scholarship greatly enhanced this book. Thanks also go to my colleagues Richard Wilson, of the University of Connecticut Human Rights Institute, and Shirley Roe, chair of the University of Connecticut Department of History, who provided moral and financial support that greatly assisted me in completing the manuscript and procuring the photographs. I am grateful also to Sheila Fitzpatrick, who provided me with a postdoctoral fellowship at the University of Chicago where the idea for this book was first conceived.

A Note About Transliteration

This book has adopted the Library of Congress Transliteration system, except in the case of the commonly known transliterated place-names "Chechnya," "Grozny," and "Ingushetia."

TERROR
IN
CHECHNYA

INTRODUCTION

> We are always finding, all across Chechnya, mass graves of civilians. Sometimes it's not even a grave but a heap of dumped bodies.
>
> —*Sergei Kovalev, Russia's former human rights commissioner, quoted in the* Moscow Times, *February 2003*

> You speak about the violation of human rights. Whose rights? Who exactly—give me first names, information, family names!
>
> —*President Vladimir Putin, to a* Le Monde *correspondent, October 2004*

FOR A LONELY BAND of human rights activists, Chechnya represents one of the greatest human rights catastrophes of the post–cold war era. In May 2001, the Committee on Conscience of the United States Holocaust Memorial Museum placed Chechnya on its Genocide Alert list, which had been created to sound warnings of potential genocides. Two years later, in Strasbourg, Rudolf Bindig, a German Social Democrat and Rapporteur to the Parliamentary Assembly of the Council of Europe, urged the council to support the establishment of an international war crimes tribunal for Chechnya on the model of the tribunals for Rwanda and the former Yugoslavia. Writing from Paris in May 2004, the outspoken French philosopher André Glucksmann despaired in the pages of the *Wall Street Journal*: "As the 21st century begins, the worst of the worst in terms of cruelty sprawls out in this desolate corner of the Caucasus, on the very shores of our Europe."[1]

Russia's first attempt to subjugate Chechnya in the post-Soviet era began with the destruction of Grozny, a city of half a million civilians during the winter of 1994–95. As Russian tank columns maneuvered through the Caucasus, massive artillery and aerial bombardment indiscriminately pounded the Chechen capital. The attack was a miserable military failure, but a success in human cruelty. From the streets of Grozny, Sergei Kovalev, Russia's human rights commissioner, appealed to President Boris Yeltsin: "Only you are in a position to stop this senseless war. . . . Every day, with our own eyes, we see planes bombing residential buildings. Every day, we see the corpses of peaceful civilians, fragments of people, some without heads and others without legs. Boris Nikolaevitch, I'm ashamed to answer the questions concerning this war. When will this stop?"[2] The explosive power unleashed on Chechnya that winter shocked both Russians and the rest of the world. Neither informed of a state of emergency nor prepared for evacuation, Grozny's civilian population was trapped in a city devastated by a conflagration not seen in Europe since World War II.

Five years later this onslaught was reenacted by a Russian government reacting to an incursion into Dagestan by radical Chechen separatists and to terrorist atrocities in Moscow. This second aerial assault ruined what was left of Grozny and rained bombs on some forty towns and villages from September 1999 through February 2000. This bombardment led to the mass exodus and displacement of over three hundred thousand civilians, a third of the Chechen population. Yuri Luzhkov, the mayor of Moscow, suggested building a wall around Chechnya to protect Russia from terrorists.[3] The proposed fortification, reminiscent not only of Berlin but of the more recent "wall of separation" erected on the West Bank, became known in more cynical circles as "the Great Chechen Wall."[4] A concrete wall was never built around Chechnya, but a bureaucratic wall sealed the region. As Anna Politkovskaia, the late Russian journalist, would lament, this small enclave in the Northern Caucasus had become "Russia's Chechen ghetto."[5]

Despite five months of bombing and guerrilla warfare, the situation in Chechnya remained largely ignored by the world. Western governments accepted the reassurances of Russia's new president, Vladimir Putin: "Today the situation in Chechnya has undergone a qualitative change, people are returning to normal life there."[6] Yet in February 2003 Sergei Kovalev arrived in the United States to speak before the Council on Foreign Relations and in U.S. Senate subcommittee meetings. He argued that a centrally organized system of death squads had been established in Chechnya, in line with a coordinated general policy.[7] He confirmed that the Russian security apparatus was employing tactics that included sweep operations (*zachistki*) in towns and villages, striking fear in the hearts of Chechen civilians. Russian troops were sealing off villages for up to three weeks. Civilians had been summarily executed in Novye Aldy, Staropromyslovskii, and Alkhan-Iurt. Lieutenant General Viktor Kazantsev, the commander of the Russian armed forces in the Northern Caucasus, had ordered the closing of Chechnya's borders to all males between the ages of ten and sixty. In the first four months of 2000, approximately ten thousand men and women had been detained,[8] many of whom were transported to Chernokozovo, an infamous detention facility. Greeted by guards, detainees were forced to run a gauntlet that saw them beaten with rubber batons, hammers, and rifle butts. "Welcome to Hell" was the routine greeting.[9]

Forcible disappearances became the enduring hallmark of the conflict in Chechnya. The Russian human rights organization Memorial estimated that between 3,000 and 5,000 people disappeared in the period 1999–2005.[10] In 2004, Human Rights Watch declared that the practice of enforced disappearances had reached such a magnitude that it constituted a crime against humanity under the extended definition set out in the Rome Statute of the International Criminal Court (1998).[11] Local officials in Chechnya have confirmed the existence of forty-nine mass graves containing the remains of nearly 3,000 civilians.[12] Some of the bodies had been blown up with explosives to conceal the identities of the victims.[13] Estimates of civilian deaths since 1994 resulting from the conflicts in Chechnya are highly inconclusive, but the most reliable approximation rests at a figure between 65,000 and 75,000.[14]

The human rights abuses in Chechnya pose a set of deeply troubling questions that require urgent examination. Chechnya is the site of one of the worst human rights catastrophes of the post-Communist era. And unlike the vast body of literature that has emerged on the crimes perpetrated in Rwanda and the former Yugoslavia, Russian scholars have devoted little attention to the carnage in Chechnya. There is no equivalent to Norman Cigar's *Genocide in Bosnia: The Policy of "Ethnic Cleansing"* (1995) or Jan Honig's *Srebrenica: Record of a War Crime* (1997). Accounts of Chechnya's recent history tend to journalistic or political narrative. All have expressed alarm at the human cost of the conflict, grounding their portrayals in personal experience and witness testimonies. Journalistic accounts, such as Anatol Lieven's *Chechnya: Tombstone of Russian Power* (1998), Anne Nivat's *Chienne de Guerre: A Woman Reporter behind the Lines of the War in Chechnya* (2001), and Anna Politkovskaia's *A Small Corner of Hell: Dispatches from Chechnya* (2003), have provided remarkable insights into the senseless destruction of these wars. Narratives like John Dunlop's *Russia Confronts Chechnya: Roots of a Separatist Conflict* (1998), Matthew Evangelista's *The Chechen Wars: Will Russia Go the Way of the*

Soviet Union? (2002), and James Hughes's *Chechnya: From Nationalism to Jihad* (2007) have charted the political landscape. No book, however, has captured the magnitude of the human rights abuses in Chechnya or sought to understand the motivation or rationale of the Russian government. No book has devoted adequate attention to the enduring consequences of Russia's Chechen campaigns.

In this book, the history of the human rights tragedy in Chechnya is a story of hubris, inordinate violence, and indifference. The idea of human rights has yet to sink deep roots into the policies of the Russian government. When Boris Yeltsin rose to power in 1991 after the collapse of the Soviet Union, Russia stood at the crossroads of its human rights history, on the edge of radical change. The language of human rights became prominent in public debates. And when Russia joined the Council of Europe in 1998, it seemed poised to embrace the values and principles of the council, with all its attendant regulations. Yet the Russian government failed to honor the commitments it made with respect to democracy and human rights reform when it was admitted to the European body. Chechnya is the tragic and enduring symbol of this failure.

This book is a contemporary account of war crimes and of crimes against humanity against a civilian population from 1999 to 2005. It by no means precludes the Russian side, but it is largely devoted to the Chechen victims. This is not because Russian soldiers and civilians have not been targets of reprehensible atrocities in the form of hostage-taking campaigns and retaliatory attacks, which will be addressed here, but because the sheer number of Chechen civilians affected and the extent of their suffering warrant particular attention. This book contends that the tragedy that befell the Chechens was not simply the unfortunate by-product of civil war. Russia had a concrete political objective in Chechnya, but the senseless cruelty that characterized the pursuit of this goal suggests another dominant explanatory factor—the role of racial prejudice. My approach to the history of human rights violations in Chechnya in the period 1999–2005 centers on three interrelated themes: the human rights abuses and the various attempts to expose them; the political conditions in Russia that gave rise to these atrocities; and the international dimensions of the crisis, against the background of the struggle against international terrorism.

* * *

What are the specific and most important questions that the tragedy in Chechnya raises? And why indeed should we focus on abuses aimed at a population of less than one million people in an obscure region of the Northern Caucasus? The first and most resounding reason is the moral tragedy of this war for the civilian population. The forced displacement of Chechen civilians, away from their historical place of residence, severely damaged the vital forces of Chechen society. The destruction of homes and cultural institutions dislodged and overturned the roots of a once strongly coherent and traditional culture. This campaign left a small republic of the former Soviet Union in physical and psychological ruin, forcing its intellectual elite abroad while aggravating the divisions within Chechen society. The Russian response to the independence claims of the Chechen people, legitimate or not, was wanton and disproportionate. The lack of moral restraint in this conflict was striking.

The Russian government has argued that what took place in Chechnya was driven by military necessity and that civilian victims were the unfortunate consequence of the government's campaign against international terror.[15] This argument is no longer sufficient or plausible. A public discussion should emerge about what took place in Chechnya and how to understand it. Was it genocide, ethnic cleansing, racism? How should the situation be interpreted according to internationally accepted human rights standards? It is clear that the Russian government's immediate aim was to enforce the subservience of the Chechen population by sustaining an atmosphere of fear within the territory. The Russian armed forces terrorized Chechen civilians in the hope of wearing down the material and psychological support base of the separatist movement. A principal objective of the Russian government was the subjugation of the population and the elimination of Chechnya's intellectual and political elite. The intent, it appears, was not to destroy the *entire* Chechen population but to exert control through fear and the military tactics of periodic summary executions, enforced disappearances, rape, torture, detainment, and humiliation. This, as one Chechen civilian claimed, was "worse than a war."[16]

The Russian Federation was undoubtedly striving to preserve its territorial integrity. The question is, at what cost and why? The most ignored question of this conflict is the role of racism as a deep motivating factor. The excessive violence directed at the civilian population of Chechnya was, in fact, collective punishment. I invoke racism not as a fashionable mantra but as one crucial fault line in understanding Russian motivation. The state-controlled media in Russia conducted a virulent propaganda campaign against Chechens as a group. What began in 1994 as a conflict with national separatists was in 1999 reshaped by the Kremlin spin doctors, led by Sergei Yastrezhembskii, into a war against international terrorism. Chechens were dehumanized with racially bigoted language that depicted the enemy as "blacks" (*chernye*), "bandits" (*banditi*), "terrorists" (*terroristi*), "cockroaches" (*tarakany*), and "bedbugs" (*klopi*).[17] The identity of the Chechen people was reduced to a few repeated phrases, images, and concepts embodied in the repeated image of the "bandit" or the "terrorist." The Russian propaganda machine was unfailing in its perpetuation of this image.

The Russian government selected international terror as its ideology of choice. And this ideology overshadowed all else: context, history, experience, and knowledge to frame the crisis in Chechnya. The reasons compelling the government to sell this image to the world were driven by more than the retaliatory attacks of radical Chechens. The chosen ideology was deployed not only to abstract and dehumanize Chechen identity but also to preclude the framework of international human rights and humanitarian law being applied to the crisis. The Russian state relentlessly pursued the line that what was taking place in Chechnya was not an internal armed conflict but an operation to eliminate terrorists. Igor Ivanov, Russia's then–foreign minister, even went so far as to claim that "The war in Chechnya is against international terrorism—not Chechens, but international bandits and terrorists."[18] Yet according to definitions of international law, armed conflict involves a party in revolt that possesses an organized military force and the deployment of a country's regular armed forces to fight that force. This is what took place in Chechnya. The Chechen separatist movement was substantial and organized enough to constitute a belligerent military force that itself was subject to international human rights law.

Therefore, the first category that can be applied to the crisis in Chechnya is one of war crimes. The Russian armed forces committed war crimes on a massive scale in the region, violating Article 3 common to all four 1949 Geneva Conventions on internal armed conflict and the broader definitions outlined in Article 8 of the Rome Statute of the International Criminal Court (1998). Although Chechnya remained, as former Czech president Vaclav Havel so aptly said, a "blackout" zone,[19] sufficient evidence has mounted to enable us to begin making some categorical claims on a pattern of human rights abuses. The fundamental principles underlying the laws of armed conflict—"distinction," "military necessity," and "proportionality"—were trampled upon in Chechnya. Under the accepted international definitions of war crimes, murder of all kinds was committed with reckless disregard for life, as well as rape, mutilation, torture, and other cruel treatment against both civilians and combatants.[20] Camcorder footage released in 2004 exposed the willful killing of Chechen combatants crammed into trucks without water and food. Severe beatings to the kidneys with rubber hoses and metal rods and the infliction of electric shocks in the mouth and the genitals were widely chronicled.[21] Individual testimonies cited threats of summary execution, of blowing up detainees with grenades who had been forced to kneel for hours with T-shirts pulled over their eyes, of the filing down of teeth and the throwing of stones at civilians, and of combatants detained in dug-out pits in the ground.[22] These acts were perpetrated by official representatives of the Russian armed forces and sanctioned by the Russian government under the 1998 federal law No. 130-FZ, On the Fight against Terrorism. And, despite the fact that the coordination between the Ministry of Defense, the Ministry of the Interior, and the Federal Security Service (FSB) in Chechnya was by no means consistent, the war crimes in the republic were the product of deliberate state action and an organized policy.

Financial exploitation is also a war crime. Economic incentives and massive human rights violations intersected to a remarkable degree in Russia's second war in Chechnya. Russian troops exploited the destruction of towns across the region and accompanying sweep operations with the undisguised objective of individual profit. Privately contracted Russian soldiers (*kontrakniki*), Ministry of the Interior (MVD) and Ministry of Justice (GUIN) troops, FSB operatives, the 41st Airborne Regiment, the 42nd Motorized Rifle Division, and operatives from the Main Intelligence Directorate (GRU) looted and pillaged; their actions ranged from small-scale demands for cash and jewelry to the wholesale transportation of furniture and electronic equipment in open trucks. Bribes at checkpoints across the region were commonplace. The extortion of money for the return of detained civilians or combatants—dead or alive—was routine. A Russian general telephoned the head of a Chechen village the evening before a planned sweep operation suggesting that money be collected before the arrival of the troops to guarantee a less brutal operation—for the sake of efficiency.[23] Direct evidence of the siphoning of oil and its transportation to surrounding republics by both the Chechen separatists and the Russian high command is difficult to obtain, but speculation is convincing.

This book does not preclude the crimes of the Chechen side. The crimes undertaken by the Chechen separatist movement also need to be categorized according to the laws of war, beyond the politicized and reductionist frame of terrorism. The practices of hostage taking and suicide bombing were no doubt strategies of war deployed by the separatists. And when one applies the strict terms of international law, they were war crimes. Nonmilitary objectives were targeted and premeditated acts of aggression were taken against Russian civilians. Although these strategies were deployed in response to the inequity of power, these were deliberate acts of aggression that forced the crisis outside the borders of the immediate war.

The next question is, why? Why did Russia pursue its second war in Chechnya? Why was President Putin, unlike Boris Yeltsin, incapable of negotiating with the moderate Chechen president Aslan Maskhadov before his death in March 2005? What was Putin's interest in perpetuating a war that cried out for a political solution? Was it a question of mere hubris? When the Russian armed forces killed Maskhadov in 2005 they also killed the only man with the stature to conduct negotiations with the Russian government. And this appears to have been their intention. The post of the moderate leader was replaced by Abdul-Khalim Sadulaev, a more fervent ideologue who worked openly with Shamil Basaev to establish a "Caucasus Front."[24] Although Sadulaev was killed in the town of Argun on June 17, 2006, his rise marked the death knell of a conciliatory end to the second Chechen war.

There are deep contradictions in the motivations of the Russian government, making it difficult for us to pinpoint one explanatory factor. And indeed there is no *one* dominant logic. Clearly the radical Chechen commander Shamil Basaev posed a genuine threat to Russia and to the safety of its citizens. The hostage-taking campaigns of Budennovsk (1995), Kizliar (1996), Dubrovka (2002), and Beslan (2004), and the bombings in Moscow's underground subway were acts that threatened the national security of the Russian Federation. In addition, the moderate Chechen president Aslan Maskhadov was unable to secure the territory and had struggled to guarantee Chechen civilians sufficient stability and security in the interwar period from 1997 to 1999. Nor had he been able to stop Basaev's incursion into Dagestan in August 1999. The Russian government claimed that if the crisis were not contained it could have a domino effect across the region. This too is legitimate, although less convincing than the first point. Some commentators have contended that oil was an important factor, but the amount of oil in Chechnya was negligible against the demands of the Russian economy—Chechnya produces 0.5 percent of the total output for Russia. So the question lingers—does realpolitik offer a sufficient explanation for the Russian government's actions in the Northern Caucasus from

1999? The answer appears to be a resounding no. Since the election of Vladimir Putin as president in March 2000, we have witnessed the rebirth of a strongly nationalist discourse on the part of the ruling Unity Party and a Russian parliament dominated by nationalist ideologues. The potential loss of Russia's last territory to the south generated a deep-seated attack of hubris, intimately connected to the rise of nationalist propaganda. And Russia's greatest post-Communist victory—freedom of expression—was undermined by the dominance of subservient, state-owned media outlets. The shallowness of democratic reform within the judiciary, the military, and the bureaucracy was apparent. Was the war in Chechnya therefore a means of keeping the Russian Federation in a state of perpetual crisis? Was it a way of appeasing a disgruntled army, vexed by its defeat in the first Chechen war? Were Chechens the ultimate scapegoat?

For most Chechen civilians, the motivations of the Russian government matter less than their consequences. Many claimed that what took place in Chechnya during the second war was genocide.[25] For them, the overarching impulse was racial. This argument cannot be discounted as the emotional reaction of a victimized group. If we look at the conflict in Chechnya from the vantage point of the 1948 UN Convention on the Prevention and Punishment of the Crime of Genocide, the acts committed by the Russian armed forces might well be framed under Article 2 of the convention.

> In the present Convention, genocide means any of the following acts committed with intent to destroy, in whole or in part, a national, ethnical, racial or religious group, as such:
>
> (a) Killing members of the group;
> (b) Causing serious bodily or mental harm to members of the group;
> (c) Deliberately inflicting on the group conditions of life calculated to bring about its physical destruction in whole or in part;
> (d) Imposing measures intended to prevent births within the group;
> (e) Forcibly transferring children of the group to another group.[26]

That there was a pattern of destruction directed toward a group of people—in this case a group defined by its religious and ethnic origins—is unequivocal. There was a clear mandate to target males between the ages of fourteen and sixty, both separatist fighters and civilians. Boys and men in both categories were detained, were tortured, disappeared, or were summarily executed. If torture was targeted at male genitals, as testimony confirms, there is a serious argument to be made that one of its outcomes would have been the destruction of the reproductive capabilities of Chechen males and thus of the ethnic group in part. Rape of female Chechens may be used to sustain the same argument. As one Russian soldier admitted to the journalist Maura Reynolds of the *Los Angeles Times* in 2000: "You should not believe people who say Chechens are not being exterminated. In this Chechen war, it's done by everyone who can do it."[27]

There is ample evidence to sustain the argument that the conditions of life inflicted on Chechens by the Russian armed forces caused serious bodily and mental harm. Many of these conditions were calculated, intentionally or not, to bring about the physical destruction of individual members of the group.[28] The detention of soldiers or civilians in pits in the ground, the mobile torture vans, and the temporary "filtration points" (*fil'tratsionnye punkty*) similarly caused bodily and mental harm. The conditions in which internally displaced persons (IDPs) were forced to live constitute a further serious attack on mental and bodily integrity. Likewise, the forced resettlement of Chechen IDPs from neighboring Ingushetia back into Chechnya in 2000 threatened a serious level of impoverishment for those unequipped to return.

Yet are we convinced that the *intent* of the Russian government was to destroy the Chechen population, in whole or in part? The question is of intent. There are no public documents or decrees to provide us with an adequate answer; evidence of this nature rarely exists. Such commands are most often hidden behind crude euphemisms or arguments of "military necessity," under the cover of war. Indeed, Hitler's Final Solution was an oral command, General Bogosara, the interior minister behind the Rwandan genocide, wrote a few planning notes in his daily calendar, and Pol Pot marked the "new people" for destruction.

The violence in Chechnya shifted in degree and scale over a period of six years. There was not always a logical consistency to the violence, the type of consistency that we have come to expect from genocidal regimes. It was not the intense and inexorable pattern of violence we witnessed in Cambodia, Rwanda, and Srebrenica. We did not have the RTLM radio broadcasts encouraging the killing of Chechens, nor the scope of concentration camps seen in Bosnia. The numbers of dead in Chechnya have been impossible to compute and have become the subject of fierce debate. And for these reasons we have witnessed a general reluctance to address the complexity on the ground, blanketing much of what we know and see in films like the Polish documentary *Murder with International Consent* (2003) and the remarkable footage produced by the twenty-two-year-old Russian sergeant released in 2004 from Northern Chechnya,[29] photographs of mass graves, and witness testimony under the rubric of an unfortunate civil war gone awry. Yet we cannot prove one of the key claims of the Genocide Convention—that a "substantial" portion of the Chechen people were targeted with the intent to destroy that population. Mistakenly or not, we now equate the intent of genocide with the number of victims dead on the ground or uncovered in mass graves, the unadulterated racist claims of its perpetrators, and wide administrative cooperation. This tradition has correctly grown out of the historical experiences and historiography of the Holocaust, Cambodia, Bosnia, and Rwanda and recent case law.

Semantic quarrels, of course, should never defuse the tragedy of human death. But such definitions and categories are essential on legal, intellectual, and moral grounds. One important charge that can be leveled at the Russian government and the Russian armed forces, I would argue, is the charge of crimes against humanity.[30] Two of the categories that form the foundation of humanitarian law—war crimes and crimes against humanity—intersected to varying degrees in Chechnya. A crime against humanity is a crime that is large scale, systematic in nature, state sponsored, and directed toward a civilian population during times of war and peace. The crucial factors here are that the acts are both "widespread" and "systematic." The victims in Chechnya were not only combatants who fall under the rubric of war crimes. This is surely bad enough—but it fails to encapsulate the entire landscape. Civilians too suffered on a massive scale. Genocide is conceptually linked to crimes against humanity, but unlike genocide, we do not have to prove the intent to destroy "in whole or in part" a particular group. A policy need not have been formalized. The perpetrators need not be fully conscious of their own intent or aware of the precise details of a state plan. Most important, a crime against humanity includes the crime of "persecution" intended to deprive an individual or group of their fundamental rights on political, racial, ethnic, or religious grounds.[31]

Crimes against humanity provide an additional framework within which to understand the scale of the violence in Chechnya. This framework also ensures that the racial component of the violence is not excluded. In the second Chechen war, the crime of persecution entailed the detainment, torture, and killing of the civilian population. Human rights monitors, journalists, and intellectuals were systematically denied freedom of expression, thought, conscience, and religion.[32] Refugees and IDPs were denied fundamental rights—the right to seek asylum, freedom from forcible return, freedom of movement, and basic economic, social, civil, and political rights. Moreover, one of the most striking crimes against humanity in Chechnya was the absence of measures to stop the ongoing impunity by punishing the perpetrators. The routine conclusions to investigations undertaken by the Military Prosecutor's Office were offered up to the world as "failure to identify individuals against whom proceedings could be brought,"[33] or "[the violations were carried out by] unidentified persons in camouflage uniforms."[34] As Rudolf Bindig concluded in a report to the Council of Europe, "I have by now come to the conclusion that the decisive factor in the equation cannot be inability—it must be unwillingness."[35] The second most striking crime against humanity was the crime of enforced disappearances. Men in particular disappeared with the support and acquiescence of the Russian government. Such measures were routinely accompanied by a complete denial of the existence of the disappeared or a refusal to pass on information as to their whereabouts. Those detained had no recourse to legal remedies or procedural guarantees.

Commentators have been reluctant to address the issue of crimes against humanity in Chechnya, preferring to bracket all violence outside the scope of the rules of warfare as war crimes. This response appears to have been driven by several factors. One argument is that Russians continue to live in relative peace with other ethnic groups still residing within the Russian Federation, thus making it difficult to conceive of racially motivated crimes of the magnitude displayed in Chechnya. This maintenance of relative peace, however, does not mean that racial and ethnic prejudice cannot be directed at Chechens or other minority groups inside Russia. It would be negligent to dismiss the historical memory of the Stalin regime's wholesale deportation of Chechens to Kazakhstan, Kyrgyzstan, and western Siberia in 1944, or, more vivid and contemporary, the razing of Grozny over the winter of 1994–95, as other than key landmark moments that demonstrated an ingrained racism toward Chechens.

A further argument is that the low morale of Russian conscript soldiers was not consistent with a propensity to commit racial crimes. Russian troops, however, were hardened by the Chechen wars. The appalling conditions within the Russian army are well-known; the lack of modern technology and equipment were ongoing factors that explain its often poor military conduct and the acceleration of racial hatred and revenge directed at Chechen civilians. Enlisted soldiers lived in a state of perpetual fear of ambushes and land mines. Guerrilla warfare has no frontline, and its absence has led to so much arbitrary violence. Indeed, high-ranking officers noted the breakdown of order within the army. One MVD officer concluded:

"Our forces in Chechnya have not been able to coordinate their actions during times of stress. The system is in utter disarray."[36] This lack of coordination under the Unified Group of the Russian Federation Armed Forces (OGV) of the Northern Caucasus and its toll on conscript soldiers have been well documented and were certainly cause for alarm. To counter these conditions, alcohol and drug abuse were widespread. General Vyacheslav Tikhomirov admitted in 2004 that the army urgently needed to hire more *kontrakniki*—professional soldiers working for bonuses—to undertake the serious combat work.[37]

These factors certainly elucidate the complex dynamic behind these wars, but they do not entirely explain the disproportionate violence directed at Chechen civilians and detained combatants. It also dismisses an important reality—the polishing of the Russian propaganda machine since 1999 under President Putin and its effect on both the Russian public and armed forces. The Russian Foreign Ministry took on the challenge of ideological manipulation to an alarming level, pumping out tired Soviet rhetoric wrapped with new trimmings. To dismiss its effect on the Russian public or the armed forces would be misplaced. This propaganda, of course, was also aided by the radical Chechen command under Basaev and his acts of retaliation in Moscow and surrounding republics. These acts merely consolidated anger toward Chechens among the Russian population. Chechnya's radical wing is also responsible for this growing hatred and its attendant consequences for the civilian population.

These historical moments prove a key argument in this book—that racial prejudice in Russia is by no means a stagnant phenomenon, and discourses about race occupied varying degrees of centrality in state institutions at different historical moments. The rise in nationalist rhetoric and anti-Chechen sentiment from the first to the second Chechen war was palpable. The attempts by the Putin presidency to restore Russian identity and status through a revived nationalist agenda were also arguments for seizing and retaining control over the state. As President Putin said in a meeting with the Federal Security Service a week after his election, "The FSB wanted to return to power. I am pleased to announce that we have succeeded."[38] It is no accident that the particular brutality of the second Chechen war coincided with this reassertion of Russian self-identity, matched by Putin's "management" of the oligarchs and internal strife. The search for national unity left little room for nuance or patience for persuasion. Even Russian civilians who questioned the direction of the Russian state or who happened to be in the line of fire during the bombing of

Grozny either in 1994–95 or 1999–2000 were given bare consideration. President Putin was not seeking an ethnically homogenous Russia but a compliant unified state that would not only offer little resistance to his goals but participate actively to enhance them. The Chechens were among the most brutalized victims of this quest for a new Russian destiny.

* * *

What is at stake for the international community today? Did the West's policy of unconditional support for Russian democracy turn out to be counterproductive? Was it not the human rights abuses in Chechnya—which Western governments failed to adequately condemn—that generated the retaliatory terrorist acts by radical Chechens? The deepening crisis pushed many Chechens to adopt the language of jihads and radical Islam. For the so-called black widows, revenge for the humiliations they had suffered became their raison d'être. As Akhmed Zakaev, President Maskhadov's special envoy to Europe, wrote in the *International Herald Tribune* in 2001: "How can anyone then be surprised that our youth—a brother whose sister was raped, a son whose father was tortured to death—do not heed our sermons of moderation, and join the ranks of desperate suicide avengers?"[39]

International indifference with respect to Chechnya increased after the September 11 attacks in the United States. Dismay at the backsliding in Russia's democratic transition was eclipsed by President Putin's support in the international war on terror. "After September 11, Chechnya ceased being a post-Soviet phenomenon," wrote Akhmed Zakaev, "and became an issue between the West and the Islamic world. We did not seek this role, it was bestowed on us by the West's policies."[40]

Although Putin explicitly reproached the West for not backing his "antiterrorist operation" in Chechnya in the immediate aftermath of September 11,[41] the United States and Europe did eventually align themselves with a government that was conducting a "dirty war." And Western governments clearly traded on Chechnya. Yet the United States could not maintain its claim to moral leadership while it traded its acquiescence in Russia's human rights violations in Chechnya for Russia's acquiescence in America's human rights violations in Iraq and at Guantanamo Bay, and the outsourcing of torture to Syria, Egypt, and Jordan. Nor can we dismiss the degree to which human rights discourse was and continues to be appropriated by the Russian government in a manner that strips the language of human rights of any validity. Russia continues to appoint its human rights commissioners, presidential human rights advisors, special human rights representatives to Chechnya, and an entire host of parliamentary committees, all with the words "human rights" placed strategically in their titles. The human rights mantle has been cleverly deployed, and the deliberate obfuscation of the discourse needs to be addressed publicly and more systematically by international governments.

The importance of this book rests finally with the question of punishment. It will assert the need for a nongovernment international commission of inquiry on war crimes in Chechnya, or a nongovernment war crimes tribunal. Indeed, such a commission should be the current aim of scholars, human rights activists, and politicians concerned about the implications of this conflict. This is a discussion long overdue.

✦ ✦ ✦

The aim of this book is to enable the specialist and nonspecialist reader alike to grasp the dimensions of the human rights crisis in Chechnya during the second war in the period 1999–2005. My aim in writing this book has been to put before the Western reader a broad picture of the human rights tragedy in Chechnya. Writing about human rights violations is a complex task. It is constrained by the craft of the writer as well, by the desire to convey the horror of human waste with a language that always seems inadequate. It is also made complex by the banality of repetition. For violence is often repetitive, banal, and crude. The words *murder, summary execution, rape, disappearance,* and *torture* wash over the reader as if they were all part of the same theater set. And in most cases they are. But how do we disentangle them to understand the human experience of tragedy and the motivating factors of those who commit these crimes? These demands are harder.

This book seeks to give some context to the crimes perpetrated in Chechnya, but it is not a quantitative analysis. So much research still needs to be undertaken before we can fully gauge the true scale of these crimes. Clearly it is also important to recognize that not everything in this war makes sense. The chapters will uncover, in narrative form, what I believe to be the landmark human rights violations that have characterized the second war on the basis of the information currently available to researchers.

There are several themes that will be considered in part 1, titled "The Crimes": the bombing campaign of 1999–2000, sweep operations, disappearances, and torture. Chapter 1, "The Bombing, 1999–2000," will privilege two major themes: it will offer a background to the Chechen crisis, seeking to elaborate the situation within Chechnya on the eve of the second war. It will then expand on the bombing of Grozny over the winter of 1999–2000—when Russia, under the direction of the prime minister, Vladimir Putin, relaunched its war in September 1999.

Chapter 2, "The *Zachistka,* 2000–2002," will illustrate the ways in which the war in Chechnya changed in scale and strategy. Beginning in the spring of 2000, the war was shaped by the sweep operation, or *zachistka*—one of the guiding motives of which was the humiliation and subjugation of the civilian population. Destroying the cohesion of the local communities was central to the larger objective of weakening resistance and the will of the people. Chapter 2 will argue that the *zachistka* also constituted collective punishment. It will highlight the most well-documented sweep operations, which occurred in Staropromyslovskii in December 1999–January 2000, in Novye Aldy in February 2000, in Sernovodsk and Assinovskaia in July 2001, and in the Kurchaloevskii district in July 2002. It will also focus on how torture and ill treatment were widespread in official and unofficial detention centers, at checkpoints, and during sweep operations.

Disappearances were clearly the most effective and expedient method for the Russian armed forces to eliminate their enemy. Chapter 3, "The Disappearances, 2002–5," elaborates on the ways in which the practice of enforced disappearances marked the final collapse of the judicial edifice in Chechnya. The legal question as to whether captured fighters, those placed hors de combat by sickness or wounds, and civilians were prisoners of war or criminal suspects completely vanished in the process. This chapter will highlight the changing nature of this practice and the increased involvement of pro-Moscow Chechen forces from the end of 2002.

Chapter 4, "Finding Refuge," is devoted to the Chechen refugees and IDPs. As the crisis in the republic deepened over the winter of 1999–2000, Chechen civilians were inevitably forced to flee. Five months of bombing led to the mass exodus of approximately 250,000 anguished civilians into the neighboring republic of Ingushetia. A tiny country of 300,000 people, Ingushetia was overwhelmed with the flood of displaced persons. Russian officials failed to honor their promise to establish exit corridors into Dagestan, Stavropol, and North Ossetia at the outset of the war. The driving motivation of this chapter is to illuminate the ways in which Chechen refugees and IDPs were denied the basic rights linked to their status—the right to seek asylum, freedom from forcible return, and freedom of movement, as well as basic economic, social, cultural, civil, and political rights. Moreover, the fate of Chechen refugees and IDPs became inextricably linked to the countless struggles by the Russian government to assure the West that the situation in Chechnya was returning to normal, and in its efforts to forcibly push IDPs back across the border from Ingushetia, the Russian government and the pro-Moscow Chechen administration repeatedly violated the UN Guiding Principles on Internal Displacement (1998).

Chapter 5, "Chechen Retaliation," marks the beginning of part 2, titled "The Response." This chapter addresses various campaigns undertaken by the radical wing of the Chechen separatist movement that in themselves constitute serious violations of international humanitarian law. The chapter considers in particular the hostage-taking campaigns at the Dubrovka Theater in Moscow (2002) and in the North Ossetian town of Beslan (2004). The importance of this chapter is to illustrate the extent to which the acts of the Chechen separatists, most notably the radical strain, are to be understood as violent and crude acts of retaliation that not only forced a measure of suffering on innocent Russian victims but did very little to advance the separatist cause.

Chapter 6, "Civil Society Reacts," proves that despite the prejudice emanating from the offices of the Russian ministries of defense and the interior, as well as from the FSB, the war in Chechnya did not pass uncontested by civil society in Russia. Many individuals stood up, most notably Sergei Kovalev, Oleg Orlov, Anna Politkovskaia, Andrei Babitskii, Svetlana Gannushkina, Alexander Cherkasov, Timur Aliev, Stanislav Dmitrievskii, and Lidiia Iusupova. This chapter deliberately spotlights the extensive efforts made by Russian and Chechen individuals and human rights organizations, in Moscow and in Chechnya, to stop the war and monitor the human rights situation.

Chapter 7, "International Failure," chronicles the international reaction. The importance of this chapter rests in highlighting the ineffectiveness of international statements of concern on Chechnya, and in tracing the gradual easing of statements by the United States after the September 11 attacks. In the nearly six years of the second Chechen war, Russia did not comply with UN resolutions calling for the deployment of UN thematic mechanisms, with the exception of the UN Special Representatives on displaced persons and on children and armed conflict. Time and again, those seeking access, including the UN Special Rapporteurs on extrajudicial, summary, or arbitrary executions, and on torture and other cruel, inhuman, or degrading treatment or punishment, were denied entry. Russia is the only member of the Council of Europe that refused to allow the council's Anti-Torture Committee to publish its annual reports on Russia. The committee was confined to issuing strong public statements condemning the use of torture.[42]

Chapter 8, "Seeking Justice in Europe: Chechens at the European Court of Human Rights," explores the emerging role of the European Court of Human Rights for Chechen civilians seeking justice and compensation. This chapter traces the struggle of the young Russian lawyer Anna Kornilina to prepare the first cases of human rights violations in Chechnya to be heard by the court. It also explores the intimidation of Chechen applicants by the Russian security apparatus, and the murder of the human rights activist Zura Bitieva, her son, husband, and brother in their home in May 2003, soon after Bitieva had submitted her application to the court. The central focus of this chapter is on several Chechen cases before the court and what this relationship between the European Court of Human Rights and the Russian government may tell us about the lengths the government is prepared to go to conceal its actions in the region.

In closing, this book explores how we might begin to understand what took place in Chechnya. It elaborates on possible scenarios for bringing Chechnya back onto the public's moral radar. It argues that international bodies should begin the process of publishing a detailed list of all current and past investigations into abuses. A database of these should be established and a survey conducted to begin the process of determining the number of civilians who have died in Chechnya since 1994. International foundations, like the Open Society Institute and MacArthur, should fund a systematic and comprehensive documentation project, staffed by Chechen, Russian, and Western experts, to consolidate and enhance the extremely diligent work already undertaken by Russian and Chechen non-government organizations. The documentation project should be catalogued, researched, and analyzed. An international commission of inquiry, like the Kosovo Commission led by Judge Richard Goldstone, should produce a document that illuminates the depth of the Chechen crisis. This concluding chapter will argue for the historical urgency of this project.

Given the contemporary nature of these events, the methodology of this book has clear limitations. This study is by no means definitive. Obviously the second Chechen war is a vast topic and what follows should be regarded merely as the beginning of a broader discussion. It is an attempt to bring together the sources we have available to make sense of them. Future scholars will surely recast much of what I have written. This book relies heavily on Russian and English-language newspapers, on interviews conducted in

Western and Eastern Europe and the United States over a period of four years, human rights and humanitarian aid reports, records of parliamentary hearings in the Russian Duma, and documentation from the Council of Europe and the Organization for Security and Co-operation in Europe (OSCE) archives. Documents such as the Ingush government's response to the IDP crisis were made available by the Kline Archive in New York, as were periodic information sheets from the Chechen NGO Lam. Documents from the Russian human rights organization Memorial and from Helsinki Watch were made available to me in Moscow.

PART ONE

THE CRIMES

1

THE BOMBING, 1999–2000

> You can see what a mess Russia is in. They can't bring any order to us. The only thing they bring is war, and I think the fight will last a long time.
> —*Chechen civilian, January 2000*

> I don't know why the sun comes back here, to a city used to the dark, to a people used to pain. Every night when darkness sets traps in the broken windows of the houses (like the toothless smile of an old woman) I solemnly swear that if the morning returns, I will leave this city forever.
> —*Mainat Abdulaeva, in Novaia Gazeta, September 2002*

The Prelude to War

Chechnya was a failing state in the interim period between the first Chechen war (1994–96) and the beginning of the subsequent conflict in September 1999. When Russia's armed forces entered the small republic for a second time that autumn, they were penetrating a politically fractured and economically deprived region, struggling to overcome its isolation. While the Chechen separatist movement had, for all intents and purposes, won the first Chechen war and elected a new president, Aslan Maskhadov, the question of Chechnya's status within the Russian Federation was still unresolved. The Khasaviurt Peace Treaty signed by Lieutenant General Alexander Lebed and Maskhadov in Dagestan on August 31, 1996, postponed discussion of this vital issue until 2001. The morass into which the country fell was a tragedy that had resounding consequences.

The new Chechen state of Ickheria struggled for a number of reasons. First, the radical wing of the newly formed separatist government—a faction led by Shamil Basaev, Movladi Udugov, and the ideologist Zelimkhan Yandarbiev—encouraged the adoption of an Islamic front that sought to repackage the political identity of the Chechen state and radicalize dissonant and disenfranchised groups. These groups and their private armies undermined President Maskhadov's call for a centralized and democratic order. Second, intra-clan (*teip*) rivalries diminished the effectiveness of the law enforcement agencies, whose officers were expected to respond to crime, regardless of *teip* allegiances, but who were in many cases frightened of the consequences if they did so. Finally, little international support was provided for the building of bureaucratic and administrative structures capable of providing care and services to the population under the guidance of appropriate specialists. Unlike the significant levels of attention and financial support devoted to Kosovo under the UN protectorate of June 1999, Chechnya was given neither. This was a country, despite its fragile victory, that had suffered a traumatic three years of brutal war. Recovering from this tragedy was a process that required time and support, fiscal as well as psychological. Chechnya was deprived of both.

The roots of Russian violence and Chechen retaliation in the post-Soviet era, however, should first be sought in two key moments: the political turbulence of the period from 1990 to 1994 and the patterns of violent coercion established during the 1994–96 Russo-Chechen war. The emergence of the Chechen separatist movement grew out of the "Popular Fronts" characteristic of the perestroika period. Led by the Vanaikh Democratic Party under Zelimkhan Yandarbiev, the so-called Chechen Revolution that followed in the wake of the "Velvet" Revolution in the Czech Republic in 1989 and the reassertion of independence claims in the Baltic Republics was marked by the first Chechen National Congress (CNC) and a "Declaration of State Sovereignty" in November 1990.[1] Chechnya's claim for independence was not uncharacteristic of the period. This call for self-determination was supported by Boris Yeltsin on the wave of his victory over former president Gorbachev in the lead-up to the collapse of the Soviet Union in 1991.

That support was short-lived. Internal problems in Chechnya soon grew evident. The Soviet air force major-general Dzhokhar Dudaev was elected chairman of the Executive Committee of the National Congress in 1991. And despite being a charismatic leader, capable of rousing nationalist sentiment, Dudaev soon displayed some problematic character traits. He dissolved the Chechen-Ingush Supreme Soviet under Doku Zavgaev and replaced it with a provisional government led by the Executive Committee of the CNC. He depended greatly on shady opportunists like Beslan Gantemirov and Ruslan Labazanov to provide financial and military support. And after his election as president, he formally declared Chechen independence on November 1, 1991.[2] Far from deferential, Dudaev quickly formed a National Armed Guard as the Russian government similarly armed its Chechen proxies. The Chechen president began withholding the payment of federal taxes, and thousands of ethnic Russians were forced to leave as a result of personal threats or blatant attacks on their apartments, or in response to the rapidly failing state sector. In asserting control over both the Baku-Novorississk pipeline and the main train route from Russia to Dagestan and Azerbaijan, Dudaev managed to make his intentions clear.[3]

Despite the Chechen president's autocratic tendencies, the evidence strongly suggests that Dudaev's ultimate aim was a constitutional secular state for Chechnya. The Chechen constitution approved in 1992 was a secular document with none of the Islamic references to Shariah law that would later dominate the political landscape or its attendant iconography.[4] His stubbornness in this fragile period from 1990 to 1994, however, proved to be a major contributing factor to the tragic events that followed. He categorically rejected a draft treaty on autonomy on the model proposed for Tartastan[5] and insisted that all negotiations be conducted at the executive level with Yeltsin personally.[6] On the Russian side, President Yeltsin imposed a cordon sanitaire, hoping to isolate the region economically and force the nationalist movement into submission. This policy was ruinous for the state sector. The Russian government, moreover, wavered dramatically between conciliatory gestures and bouts of arrogance in a negotiation process that could only be characterized as fatal to the future of Chechen life. The reasons were linked, in part, to the rapidly changing political circumstances taking place in the Russian Federation after the 1993 state Duma elections and the personal hubris of both presidents.[7] But no substantial negotiations ever took place. No meetings were ever convened between the respective presidents and both sides proved incapable of framing a set of negotiations capable of averting a crisis. By 1994, with the threat of an imminent attack, however, Dudaev did appeal to President Yeltsin on numerous occasions by telephone, letter, and through media interviews calling for negotiations[8] and apparently proposed in a meeting with Defense Minister Pavel Grachev that he was prepared to discuss a Tartastan variant.[9] His attempts were allegedly shunned.

On November 26, 1994, unmarked Russian tanks advanced to the center of the Chechen capital in the direction of the presidential palace. The Russian tank crews were attacked by forces loyal to Dudaev; some were taken prisoner while others were forced to retreat.[10] This set the tone for the following eighteen months. The troops had been hastily gathered together into untrained units. Photographs of eighteen- and nineteen-year-old boys with helmets askew and bewilderment in their eyes covered the front pages of Moscow's major newspapers. The first war in Chechnya could easily be depicted as a series of bungled errors, if it were not for the catastrophic consequences it produced. By the time of the full-scale bombing campaign against Grozny over the winter of 1994, a fondness for "ultimatums" was clear. And the decision makers in Moscow clearly understood each other. Characteristic leaflets air-dropped by the Russian armed forces on local villages threatened: "If there is open fire from your village, we will retaliate without hesitation with powerful missile strikes!"[11] Indiscriminate strikes became the preferred mode of warfare against a ground war the Russian armed forces were unfit to win. Civilians recall being unprepared, shocked by the indiscriminate bombing and the lack of warning to ensure safe evacuation. Thousands of people abandoned the city, but thousands, especially elderly Russians and Chechens, were stranded in Grozny[12] either with no relatives to help them move or too impoverished to move themselves. Many left for the mountains of Southern Chechnya or for the neighboring republics of Ingushetia and Dagestan.[13]

It is all too easy to reduce our memory of the first Chechen war to the incompetence of the Russian armed forces and the final victory of the separatists. Yet the first Chechen war was instrumental in establishing the patterns of violence that were later refined beginning in September 1999. In the aftermath of the indiscriminate airpower that struck Grozny over the winter of 1994, two actualities entered Chechen life. One was random detainment and the filtration point. The other was torture. Both features were soon tragically embedded into the routines of everyday life in the region. And while massive sweep operations were not of the scale later witnessed, the massacre of 103 civilians in the village of Samashki on April 7 and 8, 1995, was symptomatic of Russian privilege and immunity from criminal prosecution. Events like this, which spoke to the brutality of the Russian forces, gave Chechens valid reason not merely to fear the Russian troops but to justify the hatred that accompanied that fear. It only added to the growing sense that the new Yeltsin presidency was something alien and oppressive. As one civilian recalled, "Leaving the village for the hospital in

Grozny, I passed a Russian armored personnel carrier with the word SAMASHKI written on its side in bold, black letters. I looked in my rearview mirror and to my horror saw a human skull mounted on the front of the vehicle. The bones were white; someone must have boiled the skull to remove the flesh."[14]

Chechen forces under Shamil Basaev and Salman Raduev responded to Samashki with hostage-taking campaigns in Budennovsk and Kizliar illustrating the brutal tactics that they too were prepared to utilize. Yet Chechen men were fighting for disparate reasons in the first Chechen war; some were driven by a strong nationalist sentiment, others were responding to the bombing of Grozny, and many were fighting for the protection of their families and properties. It was this combination of motives that so enhanced the resolve of Chechen troops and explains the national unity that accompanied this first war. Fighting on their own terrain, with a high level of morale, they proved more astute at ground warfare than their Russian counterparts. They deployed strategies quintessential to guerilla warfare—spontaneous ambushes, sniper fire, and the destruction of Russian armored vehicles.

Indeed, it was the surprise assault on the Russian garrison in Grozny, led by Aslan Maskhadov, that finally convinced the Russian government to begin negotiations in August 1996. Other vital factors were the forthcoming presidential elections and the death of President Dudaev on April 21, 1996. Despite the signing of the Khasaviurt Peace Treaty that summer, it is doubtful whether the Russian government ever truly intended to grant Chechnya its independence.[15] But the Chechens saw it as their victory and responded by organizing presidential elections. The Russian blockade continued into the postwar period. And attendant economic, social, and political problems grew as a result, because of both the Russian blockade and the failure of President Maskhadov's government to establish a successful state administration. While de facto independence may have fed a national desire in Chechnya, the new government struggled to control the social changes unleashed by the war.

The hostage trade was a phenomenon that grew steadily in response to the burdens of the postwar period. And the kidnaping of locals and foreigners alike by Chechen criminal groups provoked legitimate alarm. The hostage trade expanded for a number of reasons. It was clearly an extension of the practices that had defined the exchange of prisoners of war from 1994 to 1996. Given that the 1949 Geneva Conventions were never applied to the first Chechen war, there were no rules regulating the exchange of POWs. An independent economy, run by intermediaries, grew up around the exchange of Russian prisoners for Chechen prisoners, and vice versa.[16] And the practice was merely criminalized in the interwar period. Criminal groups began to adopt the practice of taking hostages and demanding larger ransom payments for abducted civilians or foreigners. The hostage trade was then consolidated by an unemployment rate that stood at around 70 percent in 1998—creating a disenfranchised sector with little to do and little money to spend. And, finally, the middle-ranking commanders from the first Chechen war, unable to find a place in the new government or to face the demands of civilian life, established private armies that merely fractured already delicate political allegiances.

By 1999 the official number of those kidnaped stood at 560. The majority of foreign hostages detained in the years 1997–99 were released in exchange for ransoms. Among the hundreds seized was the Italian photographer Mauro Galligani, of *Panorama*, who was taken in February 1997 and was the first foreign journalist to be kidnaped. Three journalists from Radio Rossii and one from ITAR-TASS were taken in March, and Yelena Masyuk and her crew from the Russian television station NTV were seized in May. Humanitarian agencies like Médecins Sans Frontières, Campaign against Hunger, INTERSOS, and Equilibre were all targeted. Camilla Carr and Jonathan James, who had helped set up a rehabilitation center for traumatized children, were held for fourteen months.[17] Vincent Cochetel, the head of the Office of the UN High Commissioner for Refugees (UNHCR) in the Northern Caucasus, was held for eleven months.[18] The American missionary Herbert Gregg was filmed while his captors cut off his right index finger in an effort to hasten a ransom payment. Other aid workers, from Hungary, Poland, Sweden, and Switzerland, were also captured and freed. The Russian general Gennadii Shpigun and four employees of British Granger Telecom and British Telecom never emerged alive. On October 9, 1998, in what may have been the result of territorial rivalries between hostage-taking groups, Darren Hickey, Peter Kennedy, Rudi Petschi, and Stan Shaw were executed and their heads placed on the side of the road near the village of Assinovskaia, Achkoi-Martanovskii district, in a gruesome display of hauteur.

External factors undoubtedly contributed to the radicalization of Chechen society in the interwar period. Exactly how many radical fundamentalists arrived in Chechnya at this time is unknown. One training camp, the Caucasian Center of the Islamic Mission, which was located near the village of Serzhen-Iurt in the Shali district, was directed by the

Saudi-born Abu Ibn Al-Khattab and supported the austere form of Islam known as Wahhabism.[19] In his memoir, the Chechen surgeon Khassan Baiev recalls that the Wahhabis came to the region claiming that "our Chechen traditions contradicted the Koran. . . . I had been told that the Wahhabis offered young men what we considered large sums of money—from 100 to 200 a month—to join their movement, which distressed the elders, who ordered the Wahhabis out of the villages."[20]

The spread of the Wahhabi creed that extremist ideologues Yandarbiev, Udugov, and Al-Khattab propagated in the region during the interwar period can certainly explain the radical politicization of Islam in Chechnya. Yet even Dzhokhar Dudaev, Chechnya's first president, had admitted during his term (1991–96) that "Russia . . . has forced us to choose the path of Islam, even though we were not duly prepared to adopt Islamic values."[21] Both a kamikaze unit and a Jamaat Islam led by Ash-Shashani, a Jordanian Chechen, and later taken over by Al-Khattab were established during the first war.[22] By 1998, however, fighting units committed to a prescribed ideological agenda or bewildered youth in search of a political identity had found financial and moral support in the Wahhabi mission that had reached Chechnya after less successful appearances in Bosnia in the early 1990s. The Special Purpose Islamic Regiment (SPIR), commanded by Arbi Baraev, and two other Chechen terrorist groups led by Basaev and Al-Khattab—the Islamic International Peacekeeping Brigade (IIPB) and the Riyadus-Salikhin Reconnaissance and Sabotage Battalion of Chechen Martyrs (RSRSBCM)—emerged some time later.[23] SPIR, however, was a criminal organization headed by the extremely unstable Baraev, who had been stripped of his military rank after attempting to claim Gudermes, Chechnya's second-largest city, as his personal fiefdom in 1998.[24] Whatever Baraev's personal motives, however, his fighters were Wahhabi radicals.[25]

Many of the political and criminal rivalries that shaped this era of Chechen history on the eve of the second war with Russia are still in the shadows. Yet President Maskhadov was well aware of his predicament. "There are units that have been neither disarmed nor legalized," he admitted in early 1998. "A force stands behind each one and it is not that easy to serve them an arrest warrant."[26] By this time, the internal tensions in the Chechen government of Ichkeria had grown increasingly clear and distinct. Maskhadov spoke publicly about the divisions caused by Wahhabism, which directly challenged the moderate Sufi order that largely defined Chechen spiritual life. "The worst thing about it is the fact that it seeks to divide us according to our faith," he said, speaking on state-run television.[27] But by February 1999 the situation was volatile enough for the Chechen president to agree to the introduction of Shariah law in an effort to counter attacks by the radical factions that he was advancing "Muslim paganism" and "national Islam." Maskhadov made his announcement the day before the Wahhabi faction was to make a similar proclamation in an effort to discredit his government.[28] He agreed to the introduction of head scarves for women as a state policy and to public beatings, and engaged in a ludicrous public debate on the segregation of the sexes on buses. Perhaps he had little choice. Basaev was doing all he could to deprive Maskhadov of power, influence, and strength. To what degree Chechnya was threatened with a civil war is unclear, but a "cold" civil war had certainly begun between Maskhadov and Basaev, and secularism had been defeated in Chechnya.[29] And as James Hughes has poignantly written, the radical strain had successfully established a *parallel* authority that proved catastrophic for the future of the struggling republic.[30]

It would be wrong to minimize the ruinous effects of the radicals within the Chechen government. A Congress of the Peoples of Chechnya and Dagestan was convened in the capital, Grozny, in April 1999 to discuss the unification of the two republics into a caliphate. The proposal also called for an eventual alliance joining Abkhazia, Kabardino-Balkariia, Karachaevo-Cherkessiia, Ingushetia, Chechnya, and Dagestan—from the Black Sea in the west to the oil-rich Caspian Sea in the east—into a Confederation of the Mountain Peoples of the Caucasus.[31] And what followed was far from a defusion of the idea. An estimated sixty Chechen and Dagestani radicals crossed the border and entered the Babaiurt district of Dagestan, wounding eleven servicemen and two Dagestani policemen, one month later.[32] Russian aviation struck against radical positions in Chechnya for the first time since the end of the first Chechen war. A similar raid followed in June.[33] Highlighting the severe fracture in the Chechen separatist government, President Maskhadov was caught between radical Chechen extremists, the influence of foreign mercenaries like Al-Khattab as an ideological *point de repère*, and the proliferation of kidnaping for ransom. The president appeared in a nonstop televised broadcast on June 4, 1999, pleading for public support in a long-awaited declaration:[34] "They take the Koran . . . and find words in it that claim it is permissible to abduct people . . . that they can use them as a source of income. . . . Their calls for the immediate start of a war in Dagestan aim to pit Chechnya and Dagestan against one another."[35] Chechnya, he lamented, was on "the brink of civil and inter-*teip* war."[36]

It was precisely the activities of the radical forces that provided the pretext for the beginning of the second Chechen war. On August 7, 1999, an unknown number of fighters, led by Shamil Basaev,[37] crossed the border into neighboring Dagestan in pursuit of the proposed Confederation of the Mountain Peoples of the Caucasus. The incursion was aggression pure and simple. And the Russian government had legitimate reason to be concerned. In collaboration with local Wahhabi extremists, Basaev's troops surrounded the villages of Ansalta and Rakhata in the remote mountainous district of Botlikh and a third village in Tsumadi to the south. The local shura announced the formation of an independent Islamic Republic of Dagestan.[38] On September 4 a Buinaksk apartment block that housed Russian officers and their families was bombed, killing 61 and wounding 145.[39] In Moscow, two explosions blew up apartment blocks on September 9 and 13. Another apartment was blown up in Volgodonsk on September 16. Over 300 people were killed in the explosions. Although ethnic Chechens were never charged for the bombings[40] and many questions remain about possible FSB involvement, these events were decisive in shaping a pro-war agenda for the Yeltsin administration.

The extremists had trouble promoting the mass uprising they had hoped for in Dagestan. As Russian forces rained rockets and shells on villages to push the Chechen fighters back across the border, local women brought bread and food to the Russian soldiers, while Dagestani volunteers and armed forces provided military support to the troops.[41] Pamphlets with images of Basaev and Al-Khattab superimposed with a firing target were distributed bearing the slogan "Murder them!"[42] The fighting in Dagestan lasted for nearly two months with frequent periods of calm. The civilian cost was never satisfactorily tallied, but the Russian Ministry of Defense later reported that between August 2 and October 1, 118 soldiers had been killed, 281 had been wounded, and 32 were missing in action.[43]

Most would agree that pushing the radicals back across the border was a legitimate response to the barbaric harm the extremists had inflicted on innocent civilians in small villages across the region. Yet sympathy for the Russian government's predicament does not ipso facto justify the level of aggression that followed *inside* Chechnya. This was not a struggle against international terrorism but against radical elements within the Chechen government that had adopted a radical Islamist frame under the Wahhabi creed. Foreign influence was undoubtedly present, but it was not the core of the problem. The Chechens themselves were also responsible for the direction and shape of the radicalization of their own society.

The Russian government had clearly decided that it would realize its goal of subduing Chechnya as forcefully and as expediently as possible. Military intervention was the immediate response. And the question quickly grew into one of proportion. The acting prime minister, Vladimir Putin, backed by Colonel General Valerii Manilov, first deputy chief of the Russian General Staff, blatantly lied in the lead-up to the second war in Chechnya. "We are planning no large-scale military operation in Chechnya," claimed Putin as late as September 22 when bombs were already being dropped on Grozny. Such claims inevitably sought to counter the need for a state of emergency. No declaration of war was ever heard. As in November 1994, the civilian population of Chechnya was *again* abandoned to an impunity bereft of any of the customs of war for the sake of a public relations campaign—a strategy that sought to minimize both the scale of the conflict for public consumption and to deflect the application of Russia's international humanitarian obligations.

The Assault on Chechnya

By September 28 a full-scale assault on Chechnya was largely anticipated when Prime Minister Putin announced: "The whole world knows that terrorists must be destroyed at their bases."[44] Famously, he concluded: "Corner the bandits in the shithouse and wipe them out. There's nothing left to discuss."[45] This absolutist language set the tone for the state violence that followed for the next six years. This was by no means an uncomplicated affair for either the Russian government or the Chechen side under President Maskhadov, and for this very reason the strategies of nonmediation and uncensored violence employed by the Russian government proved disastrous for the region. This resort to violence powerfully underscored how Chechens were not seen as men and women deserving of negotiations but as a danger to Russian territorial integrity. The Russian government refused to engage with the complexities of the issue, to recognize Maskhadov's position, to acknowledge that the radicals were not popular among the Chechen population at large, or to sit at a table to negotiate, with or without international mediators. The result was that despite the divisions within its own ranks, the radicals and moderates within the Chechen government were forced to consolidate their forces against a common enemy, an alliance that would later prove disastrous for the civilian population of Russia. As the Chechen field commander Ruslan Galaev is purported to have said to the fighters within his division, "When you fall down a precipice, it's not important who it is who provides the hand that pulls you up."[46] As the war progressed, three strongly competing spheres of influence emerged in Chechnya: Maskhadov, Basaev, and by June 2000 the pro-Moscow Chechen administration strongly backed by the Russian government, first under Beslan Gantemirov, the former mayor of Grozny, and then under the Chechen mufti Akhmat Kadyrov.

The language that constructed this war was emblematic of a larger prejudice, however. All efforts were made to avoid using the terms "civil war" or "ethnic conflict." The first Chechen war had been euphemistically labeled the "restoration of constitutional order." This campaign was an "antiterrorist operation," conducted with tactical missile strikes, aerial bombardment, and the return of approximately 120,000 Russian troops to the region. On September 29, Prime Minister Putin announced, "Today we are a victim of international terrorist aggression. This is no civil war."[47] Displaying a deep commitment to ideological politics, the Russian Foreign Ministry vigorously pursued policies in three directions. The first direction was that what was taking place in Chechnya was an "antiterrorist operation," not an internal armed conflict. "Comments have been made," stated Igor Ivanov, Russia's foreign minister, "about the duties and obligations of Russia to resolve international conflict through peaceful means, but there is no international conflict with the Russian Federation. The war in Chechnya is against international terrorism—not Chechens, but international bandits and terrorists."[48] While international terrorism served as the key phrase of Ivanov's speech, ethnicity and religion were conspicuously marginalized. The second direction was that the Chechen campaign was by no means a racial war. In his address to the Parliamentary Assembly of the Council of Europe in 2001, Ivanov argued, "There is no nationalism in Russia, which is a multinational state. Any isolated manifestations of unwelcome nationalism that occur are dealt with appropriately. In no way," Ivanov assured the assembly, "do we consider the conflict to be interethnic or religious." And finally, on the question of proportion, the Russian government rarely relented, belaboring the same theme that the scale of the operation was "proportionate to the threat coming from bandits entrenched in the Chechen republic."[49]

The success of the campaign depended on avoiding the mistakes of the first Chechen war. Untrained troops, hastily gathered, would not form the central fighting force as they had done in December 1994. Yet this war also reflected Russia's longstanding military policy—the big-war paradigm—that continued to profoundly shape the Russian armed forces' approach to its task.[50] The Ministry of Defense deployed ninety thousand troops to the border, supported by an additional thirty thousand Ministry of the Interior (MVD) troops. It had tripled its number of ground troops from the first war. The violence began on September 21 with a massive bombardment with "Grad" and "Uragan" volley fire systems and air strikes. Each mobile rocket launcher was capable of launching twelve to forty rockets simultaneously. For six days the upper Terek region, a sparsely populated open steppe, was bombarded to clear the way for ground troops. To compensate for the low quality of its fighting units, the Russian military had designed a strategy that attempted to replicate NATO's actions in the Balkans in March 1999. It used massive firepower to assure victory without heavy Russian casualties. The Russian general Anatolii Kornukov, commander of the Russian Air Force, admitted: "The Kremlin is using the scheme NATO applied in Kosovo."[51]

The Ministry of Defense under Igor Sergeev was in charge of operations. Among those who directed the assault were forty-two-year-old Major General Vladimir Shamanov, Colonel General Valerii Manilov, Army General Anatolii Kvashnin, Lieutenant General Viktor Kazantsev, and Lieutenant General Sergei Makarov—all of whom had served and lost in the first Chechen war. The ministries of defense, the interior, and justice, as well as the Federal Security Service (FSB), were all joined under the Unified Group of the Russian Federation Armed Forces (OGV) of the Northern Caucasus, which was responsible for coordinating military strategy across the ministries. Within a week, Russian ground troops had entered the region and pushed the Chechen forces out of the district of Naurskii, northeast of Grozny, and further south toward the capital. A cordon sanitaire was established in the upper Terek region and Russian paratroopers were sent into the south in an effort to squeeze the Chechen forces into Grozny and the southern mountain range before the spring foliage formed a natural camouflage in the forests.

What followed inside Chechnya was the beginning of a collective trauma. And air power was the blunt instrument that first imposed it. The evidence available on the number of strikes is incomplete, but the current estimate is that more than four thousand combat sorties, of which the majority were strike sorties, were directed against Chechnya between October 1999 and February 2000.[52] The capital was first bombed on September

22 by Su-22 Fitter and Su-25 Frogfoot bombers designed to destroy ground targets during the day or night in all-weather attacks. Both bombers have the capacity to carry 4,000 to 8,000 kilograms of air-to-ground weaponry under the wings.[53] There is also ample evidence, including television footage, of the use of TOS-1 Buratino thirty-barrel multiple rocket launchers, fitted to ground tanks. These tanks moved through the cities and towns, firing flame rockets that released large clouds of flammable gas, causing massive explosions. The 1980 Geneva Convention on Prohibitions or Restrictions on the Use of Certain Conventional Weapons Which May Be Deemed to Be Excessively Injurious or to Have Indiscriminate Effects prohibits the use of such air-delivered incendiary weapons, the purpose of which is to set fire to objects or cause burn injuries to those on the ground.[54]

As the international human rights community was struggling to pass a universal ban on cluster bombs that winter, they were being deployed extensively in Chechnya.[55] They had been used in the first Chechen war in Grozny and the surrounds, notably Shali, Shatoi, Vedeno, Argun, and Gudermes. Renowned for dud rates up to 30 percent, the small bomblets send hundreds of shards of steel at ballistic speed over wide areas of terrain. Apart from the barbarity of the shards, the small canisters create unmapped land mines when they fail to explode on impact. After the village of Elistanzhi was attacked with eight cluster bombs on October 7, killing 48 and wounding over 100, it was the strike on Grozny's Centralnii market, made up of sprawling wooden stalls, Maternity Hospital No. 2, and the local mosque in the suburb of Kalinina, on October 21 with an estimated six OTR-21 Tochka ballistic missiles that garnered the most public attention. The missiles carried cluster-bomb warheads, and the civilian death toll reached 137, while around 400 civilians were wounded.

The purported official reason for the strikes on the market and surrounds—after many official denials—was that Centralnii was an arms bazaar or depot.[56] There was undoubtedly a small stall that dealt in arms, but it was one of many kiosks and stalls selling food, clothing, and home supplies. It was a market packed with civilians. As one observer recalled:

> There were a tremendous amount of people at the market, and not only those who were shopping. The Grozny market was also a place where you could meet your friends, exchange the latest bits of news, etc. At 4:30 P.M., the merchants were getting ready to take down their stands when the bomb was dropped. In a fraction of a second,

> the market became a blood bath. Pieces of flesh were strewn over the ground; there was screaming, and wounded and dead people everywhere. The wounded were taken to the hospital. I, myself, helped gather up a few mangled bodies. . . . We left Grozny during the night of October 24th–25th.[57]

The civilians reacted in horror against what was taking place. Thousands streamed across the border into neighboring Ingushetia and Georgia as the bombing continued into November. And the displaced soon joined a different battleground—the realm of competing realities. Unlike the first war when journalists and human rights monitors had traveled largely unrestricted in the region, they were blocked at the borders over the winter of 1999–2000, forced to join military press tours organized by the Russian armed forces or to travel illegally. The Russian government had learned from the first war. It now managed to streamline and orchestrate a highly polished propaganda machine that sought to counter the civilian testimonies coming over the border in the west and the south with its own language of "precision strikes," "humanitarian corridors," and "safe zones" for the civilian population. This effort began with an article in the government broadsheet *Rossiskaia Gazeta* by Aleksei Kulakovskii, the Russian government's representative in North Ossetia and Ingushetia. Kulakovskii argued that it was the separatist forces that were provoking the civilians, perpetuating an atmosphere of "public terror" and "hysteria" and chasing the population out to create the illusion of a humanitarian disaster. The civilians were "running from the terror of the bandit formations," he contended.[58]

While internally displaced persons (IDPs) were indeed leaving villages to escape fighting between Russian and Chechen forces, it was the ongoing bombing campaign that featured most strikingly in their testimonies. As one witness recalled, "We could no longer live like that, hidden away like rats, waiting for death to strike us from the sky."[59] For many displaced persons, the war had taken on a distinctly punitive tone: "During the first war, we lived north of Grozny. At that time it was still possible to stay in Chechnya, which is no longer the case. We can neither hide nor defend ourselves. What can you do against missiles fired from bases hundreds of kilometers away? The Russians have adopted the strategy of minimum risk for themselves against maximum damage to the population. To say that the fight was uneven would be a serious understatement."[60] According to a refugee who fled through the mountains to Pankisi Gorge in Georgia that November, "The Russians don't want a direct confrontation. To them, we don't even deserve the right to defend ourselves."[61]

As the bombing of Grozny continued throughout November, so too did the aerial attacks on the surrounding villages. As the Russian armed forces sought to blockade the capital before a full-scale attack, aerial bombardment and artillery strikes shaped a semicircle from the west, east, and south in an effort to pin Chechen forces inside Grozny and cut off access to their mountain bases. Apart from the bombers, the Russian armed forces used Ka-50 Black Shark, Mi-24 Crocodile, and Mi-26 Cow combat helicopters. When a fighter pilot who called himself Major P returned to the Mozdok military base in North Ossetia from a combat assault on Gudermes, he told the *Boston Globe* reporter Dmitrii Shalganov: "If you're asking whether I wasted any Chechens, yeah, I blew away a lot of them."[62] On November 12, a Russian flag was hoisted over Gudermes, twenty-one miles east of Grozny. And from Samashki, bombs and artillery struck Zakan-Iurt, Alkhan-Iurt, and Urus-Martan in the west, Argun and Shali in the east, and down to the Argun and Vedeno gorges, through Starye Atagi and Shatoi, to the "Wolves Gate" at the entrance to the mountains in the south.

While the response of Major P may be written off as hubris, it reflected the shared attitude of his superiors. Over the course of the next three months, the hawkish posturing of the Russian generals underscored this atmosphere of impunity. In the words of Lieutenant General Gennady Troshev, deputy commander of the Northern Caucasus Military District, "If we are fired upon from a house, we destroy that house, if we are fired upon from a settlement, we destroy that settlement."[63] "We will cleanse Chechnya of any scum," promised Lieutenant General Viktor Kazantsev, the commander of the Russian armed forces in the Northern Caucasus.[64] "If given the opportunity," he concluded, "I would finish the campaign within a week. I would bomb the whole republic, since I have enough force and means to do that."[65] Finally, for Lieutenant General Sergei Makarov, commander of the Eastern Group of Forces, Chechnya was simply "a nation of parasites."[66] For the army generals, the war was being waged to protect "Europe and the whole world" from the "terrorist abyss."[67] And such hyperbole was an accepted feature of this war.

Rumors circulated that General Anatolii Kvashnin, chief of the Russian General Staff, had threatened to resign if negotiations were proposed with Chechen president Aslan Maskhadov. Whatever the factual basis of this hearsay, forty-two-year-old Major General Vladimir Shamanov threatened that negotiations with the Chechen government would result in a "massive defection of officers of all ranks," with the country possibly "pushed to the brink of civil war" if they were not given the latitude to finish the job they had started in November 1994.[68]

It soon became clear that neither the Russian president, Boris Yeltsin, nor Prime Minister Putin would negotiate without conditions with Maskhadov. The Russian government publicly agreed to talks, but on terms that were not merely humiliating but sought to implicate the Chechen government in a series of acts for which there was no incriminating evidence of its involvement. Putin asked Maskhadov to apologize for the apartment bombings that had taken place in Moscow and Volgodonsk in September. "First the terrorists guilty of attacking peaceful villages . . . and bomb attacks on blocks of flats . . . must be extradited," Putin said. "Give us the men whose hands and arms are stained with blood and we will be prepared for full-scale talks."[69] Fully negating Maskhadov's identity, the Russian prime minister later declared that there was essentially no one left to talk with. He would not sit at a table with bandits, he concluded.[70] It is difficult to imagine just how Maskhadov could have handed over Basaev. It would not have been enough to take Basaev; he also had his followers. But Maskhadov did agree that Basaev and Al-Khattab would be dealt with once Russian troops had ceased military activity in Chechnya.[71] He sent a plan of settlement to President Ruslan Aushev of Ingushetia[72] and appealed to Pope John Paul II, U.S. president Bill Clinton, and Secretary of State Madeleine Albright. He appealed to the Russian government to work jointly with his government to combat the problems besieging Chechnya.[73]

These calls for a cease-fire, however, were countered by a new phase of bombing. In Grozny, graffiti on the walls read "Welcome to Hell: Part Two."[74] From the end of November onward, Grozny was subjected to a constant bombing campaign that saw the destruction of telephone, electricity, and gas infrastructure, water reservoirs, the airport, bridges, and roads. Throughout the day on December 6, Russian warplanes scattered leaflets on the city, warning citizens to leave. "People who stay in the city will be considered terrorists and bandits and will be destroyed by artillery and aviation," warned the Russian armed forces. "There will be no further negotiations. Everyone who does not leave the city will be destroyed. The countdown has started."[75] A five-day pause in bombing was promised to allow citizens to exit. This promise was broken the following day with resumed attacks. With television and radio stations off the air for the most part and the phone system down, civilians were unable to access information on possible routes out of the city.[76] Many of the estimated fifteen to forty thousand people remaining in the city either stayed in their basements or scurried to the cellars from their apartments once bombing began. With gas cut off, some had improvised wood-burning stoves and set up mattresses on damp concrete floors. Water had to be fetched from outdoor wells during lulls in the bombing. "I had nothing left to eat, not even canned pickles," recalls Shudin Taisumov. "I was terrified to go to the bathroom."[77] Occasionally the Chechen newspaper, *Groznenskii Rabochii*, would reach the city with news, or there would be access to the Russian-controlled radio station Free Chechnya—but these were rare instances.[78] And the leaflets distributed on December 6 were swept away in the winter wind, leaving the civilians abandoned underground.

Thousands of civilians remained trapped in the southern mountain villages. The districts of Urus-Martan and Shali, and the Argun and Vedeno gorges, the natural gateways to the mountains and the resting ground for the separatist forces, continued to be subjected to intense shelling. Wanting to cut off the supply routes from Georgia, the Russian forces targeted the southern gorges. Unable to leave because of the constant shelling in the daylight hours, many civilians left in the middle of the night, walking through the forests or mountain passes to Pankisi Gorge in Georgia, where a refugee population of some four thousand soon gathered. Many, however, remained in Chechnya. For those who tried to protect their communities from both sides of the conflict, the retaliation from radical fighters was fierce. Village elders and local representatives often appealed to the Russian forces to cease the bombing while simultaneously prohibiting Chechen fighters from entering their villages or pleading for them to leave. On Sunday, November 28, the elders and local administration of the village of Gekhi, southwest of Grozny, gathered over one hundred civilians in the local square to discuss the terms of a truce with the Russian armed forces. Seen as betraying the cause, however, radical Chechen fighters opened fired on the crowd, shooting two men in the legs and causing other injuries.[79] In Staraia Sunzha the villagers set up roadblocks in the east and the west. As in Gekhi, the Chechen fighters again fired at the civilians' feet. "We asked the fighters to leave," recalls Tahid Zagaev, "because they could do nothing against such a Russian division and if they fired on them the Russians would destroy our village."[80]

With a peacetime population of around nine thousand, Alkhan-Iurt, seven miles south of Grozny on the Rostov-Baku Highway, was subject to heavy bombing from November 6 onward, which killed an estimated 132

FIGURE 1.1. A local woman asks "Why?" as she prepares to leave the village of Vedeno after a bombing in December 1999. Photograph by Eddy van Wessel. © Eddy van Wessel.

civilians.[81] Numerous attempts were made by Haji Vakha Muradov, a village elder, to persuade the Chechen forces to leave their bases on the outskirts of the village: "I begged them on behalf of the village, 'please leave our village, this is not a place for you to fight.'"[82] The commander of the Chechen forces allegedly replied that they would not leave, saying, "We cannot retreat from Russian soldiers."[83] Entrenched in their positions, the Russian ground forces repeatedly failed to push the Chechen forces back. By some accounts the local fighters agreed to leave, while other foreign fighters insisted on staying. With a crude ultimatum similar to that presented to the elders of Samashki before the massacre in April 1995, the Russian armed forces promised to cease bombardment only if the elders convinced the Chechen forces to leave.

Russian forces finally entered Alkhan-Iurt on December 1. The first documented case of what became known as a *zachistka*, or sweep operation, took place in Alkhan-Iurt from December 1 to December 8, 1999. And the tactics that would later come to define the *zachistka* were crudely demonstrated here. By all accounts, it was Major General Vladimir Shamanov's 15th Battalion, part of the Western Group of Forces that surrounded the village with armored personnel carriers (APCs). In the course of house-to-house searches, around one hundred and fifty men and women were forced from their cellars and basements onto the street. The women were separated from the men and expelled to Kulary, a village about one mile west of Alkhan-Iurt. The men were detained for three hours on the outskirts and were checked for bruises on their shoulders and any other signs that they were fighters. According to witnesses, the *kontrakniki* (privately contracted soldiers) and conscript soldiers argued between themselves. The *kontrakniki* wanted to shoot the men, but they were eventually let go in the direction of Kulary. Yet tanks crawled along behind them, firing shells to their left and right. As one witness recalled, "The shells exploded around us on both sides of the road. We had to fall to the ground, and crawl until we could stand up again and run, then fall again. The Russians were 'teasing' us in that way."[84]

Alkhan-Iurt was blocked off until December 14. A twenty-two-hour curfew was imposed on the village and civilians were permitted to leave their basements and enter their yards only between the hours of 11:00 A.M. and 1:00 P.M. Many who were left in their cellars were attacked with live grenades, and houses were set on fire. Looting of the village began almost immediately. Ural trucks arrived and began to pack up rugs, refrigerators, televisions, and housewares. "When the soldiers realized we were registering the cars [license plates], they took to local transport—" recalled one witness, "tractors, trailers, wagons—and with these, they carted the things away."[85] From December 1 to December 18, eighteen to forty-one civilians were summarily executed in Alkhan-Iurt; the majority seem to have been shot for attempting to stop the soldiers from looting. The last to die was Aindi Altimirov, who was beheaded by Russian soldiers on December 18.

The final encirclement of Grozny did not prove easy. The Chechen forces filled trenches with burning oil, producing a thick smoke that gave off toxic fumes containing sulfur, mercury, dioxins, and furans.[86] While the problem of oil spills was the direct result of Russian bombardment of plants and refineries, there is no doubt that the burning trenches contributed to the environmental calamities that have since plagued the region.[87] The Chechen forces were also responsible for trapping civilians. They laid extensive antipersonnel land mines in apartment buildings and around the city, obstructing their exit from the capital. Designed to maim rather than kill, the landmine blasts inflicted extensive damage—blindness, burns, destroyed limbs, and shrapnel wounds. The Chechen forces moved easily at night once the bombing had ceased, ambushing Russian units. Using grenade launchers and sniper rifles as their main weapons, they traveled via underground passages beneath the city, attacking Russian lines from the rear.

President Yeltsin unexpectedly stepped down on December 31. His replacement, Vladimir Putin, visited Chechnya the following day. In a discussion with Russian soldiers in Gudermes, the acting president consolidated his nationalist agenda. While the Russian Foreign Ministry attempted to eclipse any discussion of an ethnic war, there was a consonant rise in nationalist rhetoric, and the two levels of political manipulation were radically reframed under Putin's administration in the lead-up to the presidential election on March 26, 2000. This nationalism sanctioned a strong revival in classic racial prejudice against Chechens, which already had a long history in Russian society. Putin sought to counter what he interpreted as a crisis of identity in Russia by resurrecting a national identity based on pride and an all-powerful state. "This is not just about restoring the honor and dignity of Russia," he said to the soldiers. "It is rather more important than that. It is about putting an end to the breakup of the Russian Federation. That is the main task, Russia is grateful to you."[88] Putin made it clear that he was not going to tolerate any "humiliation" to the "national pride of Russia."[89]

But January proved a difficult month for the Russian armed forces. The battles centered on the territory south of Grozny, 18.5 miles wide and 37 miles long, extending from Samashki in the west to Kurchaloi in the east. The separatist forces stationed in the mountains struck back forcefully on January 10. They conducted raids in Argun, Gudermes, and Shali. In Argun they attacked checkpoints and took two schools and the local administration building. They resumed control of the Gudermes-Argun-Grozny road.[90] The Russian forces were infuriated. Lieutenant General Kazantsev announced the closure of all administrative checkpoints in response to the raids. "Only children up to the age of ten, men over sixty and women will henceforth be regarded as refugees," he announced publicly.[91] The threat was not executed owing to international pressure, but the situation of indiscriminate force remained unchanged. Argun and Shali were again bombed in an effort to push the Chechen forces further south.

The turning point in the battle for Grozny came when Russian troops began to fight their way into Minutka Square. They moved through the Staropromyslovskii district on the northwest side of the city. It is unclear exactly when the district was secured, but toward the end of January it grew apparent that thirty-eight civilians had been summarily executed and their bodies mutilated by Russian forces during sweep operations from late December. It was here that news leaked of Russian soldiers forcing elderly Chechens to leave their basements to pick up the dead bodies of Russian soldiers to be used to protect the Russians from Chechen sniper fire.[92]

Early in the morning on February 1, the Chechen forces retreated from Grozny. Pushed out of the Zavodskii district, the Chechen units headed west of the capital toward the village of Alkhan-Kala. Hitting a minefield, allegedly planted by the Russian armed forces, they suffered heavy casualties. Russian artillery opened fire on the field, killing and wounding scores more. Two Chechen generals, Aslambek Ismailov and Khunkarpasha Israpilov, were killed, as was Lecha Dudaev, the mayor of Grozny. Shamil Basaev, the radical commander, had his left foot blown off. Pushed into the village, around three hundred fighters sought treatment in the hospital or were left lying wounded or dead in the snow around the clinic. Khassan Baiev, the surgeon who was treating the fighters, later recalled that the village was just waiting for the Russian ground troops to follow with a sweep operation: "Some forty men hid in the storage area under the vegetable depot. Relatives and volunteers around the village hid others under the floorboards." Baiev continues: "We loaded three buses with wounded fighters and several women and children, hoping to transport them to the hospital in Urus-Martan. Those fighters who wouldn't fit in the buses hid in the village."[93] But Beslan Gantemirov, head of the pro-Moscow Chechen militia, reneged on his promise to let the buses through the checkpoint if the fighters onboard gave up their weapons. Once they did so, Gantemirov handed them over to the Russian armed forces. The buses were rerouted to the village of Tolstoi-Iurt, the home of Chernokozovo, the infamous detention center.

Other Chechen fighters continued on via Zakan-Iurt, Shami-Iurt, Katyr-Iurt, and Gekhi-Chu. As the fighters entered the villages, they were blocked and air-bombed by Russian forces. Hundreds of civilians were still caught in the southern villages, with no planned evacuation routes. Katyr-Iurt had been declared a "safe zone," only to have artillery and air bombs dropped on the village on February 4. The estimates as to how many civilians were killed the morning of February 4 range from several dozen to over one hundred.[94] Those responsible for the attacks were Major Generals Vladimir Shamanov and Yakov Nedobitko.[95]

Retreating to the south, the separatists fortified themselves in the Argun Gorge. And it was the village of Starye Atagi, some two miles from the gorge, that essentially separated Russian and Chechen forces to form the

FIGURE 1.2. Separatist forces in Alkhan-Kala, February 2000. Photograph by Thomas Dworzak. © Magnum Photos.

new warring front. This small town of eleven thousand inhabitants had surrendered to the Russian armed forces on December 5. Over the coming years, Starye Atagi would suffer some of the worst punitive operations by Russian Special Forces.

* * *

There may be a paucity of available statistics with regard to the number of combat sorties flown that winter over Grozny, but the evidence of the violence lies most poignantly in the ruins of the city. By February 2000, the hollowed capital stood as a testament to the depravity of war—gutted and negated of life and identity. Even Lieutenant General Gennady Troshev, after touring the city on February 6, admitted: "The city is ruined."[96] As Dmitrii Beliakov, the Russian photographer, traveled through Chechnya with Russian marines in February, he captured the immensity of the damage. There is no way to avoid the historical evidence of the photographs, all of which confirm a picture of absolute destruction. Figure 1.3 shows two Russian soldiers with furniture looted from a bombed-out apartment sitting in Minutka Square in the aftermath of three months of bombing. In the background is a typical residential apartment block made desolate by air artillery. The looted tablecloth, the decorative room divider, the kitchen

FIGURE 1.3. Minutka Square after the bombing campaign, February 2000. Photograph by Dmitrii Beliakov. © Dmitrii Beliakov.

chairs—intimate objects of home—are all mocked by the makeshift Red Cross flag hanging from the traffic light.

Figure 1.4, also by Beliakov, shows the entrance to Lenin Street, now Prospekt Akhmat Kadyrov, one of Grozny's main thoroughfares. The shot was taken from the east, close to the Romanov Bridge, in February 2000. A gray blanket of dust hangs in the sky. The tire marks from the Russian APCs stretch out toward Minutka Square. The boulevard's trees are burned and charred.

The number of dead civilians from the first campaign against Grozny over the winter of 1994–95 was tabulated by the Russian human rights organization Memorial and recognized by Goskomstat, the Government Statistical Committee, as between 25,000 and 29,000. Memorial believes that it was probably closer to 50,000.[97] For the first nine months of the second war, between September 1999 and June 2000, Human Rights Watch estimated that between 6,500 and 10,000 civilians died. No concerted national or international effort has been made to calculate the number who died from the bombing campaigns, either in 1994–95 or 1999–2000, and serious questions remain about the tabulation of the dead and the accuracy of the figures. Yet one cannot deny the complete inconsequence of the civilian population. The quantitative difference in the estimated death

FIGURE 1.4. Lenin Street, Grozny, now Prospekt Akhmat Kadyrov, in February 2000. The shot was taken near the Romanov Bridge. Photograph by Dmitrii Beliakov. © Dmitrii Beliakov.

tolls from aerial bombardment in 1994–95 and 1999–2000 most certainly relates to the preparedness of the civilian population. While in 1994–95 some 40,000 IDPs crossed the border into Ingushetia, by 1999–2000 that figure had reached an estimated 250,000. Most important, it is testimony to the scale of the bombing campaign. In 1994–95, many civilians living in Grozny were able to seek refuge with relatives in the countryside; in 1999–2000 the breadth of the strikes across the region, south, west, and east of the capital, made this option impossible.

By what privilege did the Russian government have the right to kill thousands of civilians for the sake of an "antiterrorist operation" and why were the rights of the civilians so negligible in Grozny and its surrounds that winter? The Russian government argued on the side of necessity to defend its actions. How then do we weigh the threat as opposed to the response? The first issue rests in the dimensions of the war. Approximately 2,000 fighters were pinned in the capital and another 3,000 in the southern mountain districts, against 120,000 Russian troops with massive firepower. Aside from the asymmetry and the moral obligations that should indeed accompany such divisions of scale, the question of tactics lies at the heart of the first stage of the Chechen campaign. The largely unrestrained militarism that defines this period worked on a simple principle. Civilians, personal property, state institutions, and cultural and historical monuments would largely be killed, wounded, or destroyed in order to protect Russian ground troops and to avoid high casualty rates. The laying of antipersonnel land mines and a massive fire wall preceded any ground troop movement, and the photographs and testimonies show that the firepower was far from precise or accurate. The crucial principle of distinction between military and nonmilitary targets was largely ignored. Russia's defense minister, Igor Sergeev, admitted that Russian forces in Chechnya used the tactics of "remote war, beneficial for us and extremely unprofitable for the bandits."[98]

There can be little doubt that the bombing of Chechnya from September 1999 to February 2000 was a war crime according to Article 3 common to the four Geneva Conventions of August 12, 1949, Additional Protocol II, and the Rome Statute of the International Criminal Court (1998). The two most notable violations with regard to civilians relate to "violence to life and person, in particular murder of all kinds, mutilation, cruel treatment and torture."[99] The second violation relates to the bombing of population centers as elaborated and codified by the Rome Statute: "Intentionally directing attacks against buildings dedicated to religion, education, art, science or charitable purposes, historic monuments, hospitals and places where the sick and wounded are collected, provided they are not military objectives."[100] The most well-known instances were the attack on Centralnii market in Grozny, the strike on the mosque at Kalinina, and the attack on a Grozny maternity hospital on October 21, 1999; the bombing of a Red Cross IDP convoy on October 29;[101] the attack on the village of Elistanzhi; and the air raids on Novyi Sharoi and Samashki.

Humane treatment and proportionality are at the center of international humanitarian law. The Russian government refused to negotiate with or support Chechnya's only legitimate political leader, President Aslan Maskhadov, and instead chose the path of full-scale war. Instead of taking appropriate measures to protect the civilian population and winning the hearts and minds of a population itself exasperated by the radical Wahhabis, the Russian government instead resorted to massive air bombardment. Little was done to minimize suffering or to create appropriate conditions for the evacuation of the civilian population. The argument here is that there were less costly ways to accomplish the Russian government's military objective, regardless of how important its objective was. Only a political settlement could have relieved the mutual siege and prevented the tragic consequences that followed. Why were these means not taken? Was it part of a strategy to terrorize the population into submission? Or was it just a complete disregard for human life in pursuit of a political aim? It could have been both.

Proving intent is a difficult undertaking. But a policy need not have been formed; intent can now be inferred from the manner of the crime. We cannot be sure that the acts were directed *against* the civilian population or that they were the object of the attacks, but we can be sure of the results of the acts themselves. We can also be certain that a given human group was victimized and that the Russian armed forces and the Russian government were well aware of the attacks themselves and their potential consequences for Chechnya's civilian population. Under the Rome Statute, the bombing of Chechnya could be considered a crime against humanity under Article 7 (a): "'Attack directed against any civilian population' means a course of conduct involving the multiple commission of acts referred to in paragraph 1 against any civilian population, pursuant to or in furtherance of a State or organizational policy to commit such attack."[102]

Whether these actions were crimes against humanity is a jurisdictional category that must be contemplated here. Three months of bombing Chechnya was not an isolated event. It was repeated across the region, it was a widespread action, and it was part of a group plan or state-initiated policy. It was also, I would argue, an especially egregious crime on the level of its impunity. Even if one accepts that Russian forces had the right to bomb separatist forces, one cannot accept the scale of civilian life that was sacrificed for it and the negligence that accompanied this campaign. The level of seriousness of this crime has to be reconsidered.

The disproportionate treatment of Chechen civilians suggests something deeper about the motivation of the Russian government. The basic point is whether such negligence amounts to racial prejudice in this instance. Negligence may certainly be driven by apathy or incompetence, but it is underscored nevertheless by a certain motivation. I would argue that the negligence displayed from September 1999 to February 2000 undoubtedly had a racial underpinning. The disregard for human life in Grozny and across the region cannot be written off as an act of an incompetent, arrogant army seeking to restore the dwindling power of the state it served. The disregard for human life was too immense and the military threat too marginal to fully legitimate the scale of Russia's counterattack. Moreover, it grew clear sometime later that the Russian government had been planning to attack Chechnya since March 1999.[103] Preparations for a state of

FIGURE 1.5. A survivor of the Russian bombing campaign in Grozny, February 2000. This woman lost her husband during the bombing. Behind her is a Russian marine. Photograph by Dmitrii Beliakov. © Dmitrii Beliakov.

emergency and appropriate evacuation could have been instituted long before to ensure the safety of the civilian population.

The net result, therefore, has been a general underrepresentation of the bombing of Chechnya that winter as a mere factor of a civil war. This bombing campaign, I would argue, however, was the beginning of a racism of severe oppression that included the subjugation of the population and the elimination of the noncompliant intellectual and political elites. In addition, the bombardment undoubtedly served a larger political purpose. Vladimir Putin's rapid, violent response was central to consolidating his position as head of Russia's new government. And the implacability of President Putin's position—this failure to acknowledge or deal with Chechen nationalism—helped lay the foundation for a radical and violent response.

2

THE *ZACHISTKA*, 2000–2002

We will cleanse Chechnya of any scum.
—*Lieutenant General Viktor Kazantsev, January 2000*

Often the guys don't even know what to cleanse, where to cleanse, who to cleanse and so everyone is cleansed.
—*Russian soldier, July 2001*

THE ATMOSPHERE OF FEAR manifested by the winter bombing campaign took on a different shape beginning in the spring of 2000. Chechen civilians inherited a new stage of warfare, embodied in the ubiquitous *zachistka,* or sweep operation. Officially deployed to root out separatist forces in population centers—whether through killing or detainment—the *zachistka* and its side effects soon displayed all the traits of a collective punishment campaign.[1] The sweeps in the village of Alkhan-Iurt in December 1999 and in the Staropromyslovskii district of Grozny over December 1999–January 2000 illustrated how punitive and violent the sweep operation could be. From 2000 to 2002, the civilian population of Chechnya, those placed hors de combat by sickness or wounds, and fighters were neutralized and disempowered through summary executions, disappearances, torture, looting, and verbal abuse. Undertaken in revenge, anger, or trauma—motivated economically and sadistically—the sweep operations conducted by Russian Special Forces and privately contracted soldiers became the pervasive form of warfare for over three years.

The sweep operation embodied all the features of a standard counterinsurgency tactic. Formally it was defined as a "special operation aimed to check residence permits and identify participants of the illegally armed formations."[2] A sweep ranged in duration from one to twenty days. In the majority of cases, a village was encircled and sealed by heavy artillery, armored vehicles, Ural and Kamaz military trucks, and helicopters, preventing civilians from entering or exiting. The cordoning of the village was usually conducted by conscript soldiers. Federal Security Service (FSB), Main Intelligence Directorate (GRU) officers, or Special Rapid Reaction forces (OMON and SOBR) then entered the village from multiple directions—by foot or by military vehicle, or via paratroopers who were dropped down into the village by helicopter. The Special Forces conducted street-by-street searches of homes, often during the day but also in the early hours of the morning or in the middle of the night with no official witnesses or public prosecutors, no search warrants or legislative regulations. According to civilian testimony, the military servicemen and the policemen entering the houses during sweep operations rarely identified their rank, brigade, or affiliation; their faces were frequently covered by masks or blackened with soot to conceal their identity. The military vehicles normally had no designated registration numbers or the registration plates were deliberately covered in mud or painted over, making it almost impossible to determine who committed the atrocities.[3]

The *zachistka* embodied more than a military practice, however. It was a *mind-set*. And this was exemplified in the proliferation of the word itself. In the same way that the term *ethnic cleansing* (*etnicko ciscenje'*) was coined in the former Yugoslavia in the early 1990s, the term *zachistka* found a distinct voice in the Russian popular vocabulary and in the official addresses and speeches of military and government personnel. By late 1999, the use of *zachistka* in the press and everyday speech had reached an infectious and alarming level. From September 1999 to 2005, *zachistka* appeared 787 times in the headlines of Moscow's central newspapers in relation to the second war in Chechnya.[4] In the text of the papers, it appeared 10,730 times. From the verb *zachistit'*, *zachistka* was used in the literal sense to describe the cleaning of pipes, the sanding or smoothing out of metal, the cleaning of paint or corrosion from surfaces,[5] or the dusting away of sand or dirt to uncover archaeological objects.[6] It was also used to describe the sweeping up of objects—autumn leaves, snow, coal, or rubbish—into a corner. The prefix *za* suggests concerted movement and the stress is on *cleaning up* or *cleaning out* as the operative implication.[7] Within six months of the beginning of the first Chechen war, however, *zachistka* was being employed by the Russian armed forces as military slang. It was linked euphemistically to the idea of cleaning out *human beings*—in this case, suspected Chechen rebel fighters and their alleged civilian supporters. No longer neutral or inoffensive, *zachistka* became congruent with the practice of gathering or sweeping, in the literal sense, Chechen men and women into fields, factories, or schools to be checked, detained, or executed, usually on the outskirts of a targeted village. In this respect, the idea of harvesting or cleansing the land is reminiscent of the metaphor adopted in Hitler's Germany—that of *völkische Flurbereinigung* (cleansing of the soil), also adopted from agricultural terminology.[8] Versions of the word were linked to the cleansing of space, not the human body as such—the "gentle sweep" (*miagkaia zachistka*), the "total sweep" (*total'naia zachistka*),[9] the "continuous sweep" (*sploshnaia zachistka*),[10] the "repeat sweep" (*povtornaia zachistka*),[11] the "ethnic sweep" (*ethnicheskaia zachistka*),[12] the "military sweep" (*boevaia zachistka*),[13] the "fire/artillery sweep" (*ognevaia zachistka*),[14] and the "targeted sweep" (*adresnaia zachistka*).[15]

For many Russian intellectuals, human rights activists, and journalists, the normalization of *zachistka* in the public domain by December 1999 was a startling development. To the ear of the Russian speaker, the word summoned a picture of unrestrained violence with a resonant subtext of cleansing and purging—all undertaken with mechanical indifference. As Irina Levontina concluded in *Itogi*, "At first glance, the word is absolutely concrete, even technical, and completely deprived of any pathos. In essence, it is a powerful ideological tool."[16] "As a philologist, I am quite intrigued by the word 'zachistka,' which one hears so often on television," claimed writer Sergei Esin. "I always wonder how much life will be taken, along with this 'zachistka.'"[17] "The word 'zachistka' has entered our lexicon, it's shameful to say, without a trace of the horror or repugnance that accompanied its use in 1995–1996," concluded Russia's former human rights commissioner Sergei Kovalev. "It is now pronounced as something that goes without saying. The result, unfortunately, has been a very powerful and effective manipulation of public opinion."[18]

As we search for the linguistic roots of *zachistka*, its relationship to *purge* (*chistka*)—and, by extension, to the "Great Purge" (*velikaia chistka*) of the 1930s—as associative terms, is instructive. *Purge* was used to depict the periodic purging of the Communist Party (*chistit' partiiu*) of ideological "enemies" or "aliens." The 1919 operation by the Bolsheviks was the "first of several operations officially called purges" in which members were screened for suitability.[19] As Getty reminds us, "under no circumstances were operations, arrests or terror involving non-party citizens referred to as purges."[20] The modus operandi was to purge the party of enemies, real or imagined. *Chistit'* or *ochistit'* appeared regularly in Soviet reports on the quelling of the mass insurgencies during the Antonov rebellion of 1920, as the peasant "class enemy" revolted against the forced procurement of grain.[21] With regard to the dekulakization campaign of 1929–30, Soviet directives were given to "cleanse the collective farms from kulak and other counter revolutionary elements."[22]

Zachistka first appeared in its current form in the Moscow newspaper *Izvestiia* in 1995. It was used to characterize stage two of the first Chechen war as Russian troops spread out into rural villages and the smaller towns of Urus-Martan and Gudermes after taking the capital. The Russian human rights organization Memorial first heard *zachistka* deployed by Russian troops in relation to the attack on the Chechen village of Samashki on April 7–8, 1995. The sweep was conducted by the Ministry of the Interior (MVD) forces and Special Rapid Reaction Forces (OMON and SOBR), which used this military slang to characterize the nature of the attack on Samashki. The military explanation, later refuted, was that the village had to be sealed to cleanse out Chechen fighters.[23] The result was the massacre of 101 civilians and the burning and looting of their homes.[24] As Russia's defense minister, Pavel Grachev, stated in 1996, the operation to "liquidate the insurgents is continuing and the cleansing [*zachistka poselka*] of villages where the fighters remain hidden among the civilians."[25] But the deployment of the word was limited over the course of the first war from 1994 to 1996; by no means pervasive, it appeared a mere six times in *Izvestiia* throughout 1995.[26] In 1996 it began to appear more frequently, especially in relation to the sweep operations conducted in Vedeno, Shali, Grozny, Sernovodsk, and Samashki.[27] Almost without exception, it appeared in quotation marks or with the modifier "so-called"—suggesting ambivalence about its precise tactical meaning.

By 1999, however, it was firmly lodged in public discourse and attempts to challenge its meaning had largely disappeared. In December the Russian weekly *Moskovskie Novosti* published an article titled "Words of the Year" (*Slovo Goda*) in an effort to identify the most popular and symbolic catchwords of 1999, in the tradition of the German daily *Frankfurter Allgemeine Zeitung* (FAZ). The first word on the list was *zachistka*.[28] By October 1999, the Russian Ministry of Defense was using the term liberally in its routine press releases. Although it was never used in formal decrees or orders, regular updates in the ministry's broadsheet, *Krasnaia Zvezda*,[29] included characteristic announcements such as the following: "Sub-units of the Ministry of the Interior . . . conducted a passport check, took measures to cleanse [*po zachistke*] the population points and outlying areas of fighters."[30] No effort appears to have been made to counter its use in the military press. Besides *Krasnaia Zvezda*, the Ministry of Defense published numerous publications from the center to the regional military districts encouraging the use of the word not only in the popular political imagination but among military personnel reading *Soldat Otechestvo*,[31] *Voennyi vestnik Iuga Rossii*,[32] *Voin Rossii*,[33] *Na strazhe Rodiny*,[34] *Na boevom postu*,[35] *Armeiskii Sbornik*,[36] and *Voennyi zheleznodorozhnik*.[37]

The proliferation of *zachistka* was emblematic of a new way of thinking about the Chechen problem. It was symptomatic of an acceptance or tolerance of the impunity that reigned in Chechnya. As Emil Pain, the former Russian national relations advisor, commented, "By using professional military jargon in their reports, journalists lend the war an everyday flavor."[38] And this shift in language only reinforced the impunity on the ground. Many grew to accept the massive violations of the rules of war as the necessary cost of cleaning up "terrorist concentrations."

But Moscow was totally remote from the daily horrors of life for the average Chechen. Subject to a permanent sense of fear and capitulation, the Chechens were not wrong to see in the *zachistka* a collective action against them. The encirclement of villages, passport checks, house searches, and the detention of suspects were strategies practiced by militaries across the world. But it was the repeated and systematic abuse of these tactics that concerns us here. Alkhan-Iurt and Staropromyslovskii were the sites of the first well-documented sweeps that gave rise to an atmosphere of complete impunity. But it was the sweep operation in the village of Novye Aldy on February 5, 2000, that was the most shameful example of a *zachistka*. Paradigmatic of what was to come, the events that occurred in this village and the concurrent emergence of the infamous filtration point Chernokozovo in the village of Chernokozov (Naurskii district) set the tone of impunity that resonated throughout the rest of the ground war.

The Massacre at Novye Aldy

Local civilians had begun to flee Novye Aldy on the southern outskirts of Grozny once the bombing of the capital began on September 22, 1999. News of long lines of IDPs waiting to enter neighboring Ingushetia, the closure of checkpoint "Kazkaz 1," and the tragic firing on a Red Cross IDP convoy on October 29, however, convinced many to stay. In the same way that the civilians of Gekhi and Staraia Sunzha sought to protect their communities from both sides of the conflict, about one hundred locals approached the Russian position on February 3. Under the protection of a white flag, they sought to assure the Russian troops that the separatist forces had left the village.[39] As they approached the Russian position, the locals were fired upon. A Russian civilian from neighboring Chernorech'e was shot. The crowd was ordered to lie face down on the ground. The young man died before the crowd was permitted to stand up. The locals nevertheless met with Colonel Lukashev, commander of the 15th Motor Rifle Regiment. They asked him to stop the strikes and the dropping of cluster bombs,[40] insisting that there were no Chechen fighters in the village. "We explained that there were no fighters in the town, that it was safe to go in. 'If you don't take our word for it,' we said, 'you can detain us as hostages; or we can walk in front of you, as human shields.'"[41] Colonel Lukashev promised to stop the bombing. "He said he could stop the artillery," recalled Aset Chadaeva, a pediatric nurse, "but not the bombs—orders to drop bombs were always given the day before."[42] The bombing ceased the next day. On February 4, families began to emerge from their cellars, anxious to return home, hopeful that the bombing had ceased.

On the evening of February 4, 2000, poorly dressed and exhausted Russian conscript soldiers entered Novye Aldy.[43] Walking around the streets in groups of five and ten, checking passports, they warned the civilian population of a sweep operation planned for the following day. "We talked to them, offered them food, whatever there was . . . they warned us that the 'bloodhounds' would be sent in later," recalled Marina Ismailova.[44] Some soldiers were rude, others polite. But there were no killings or violence.[45] Aset Chadaeva recalled the soldiers telling her: "Don't stay inside." "'Don't stay in the basement' one of them said to me, 'they will unleash the dogs on you.'"[46] "Don't stay in your cellars, contract soldiers will come and throw grenades in," Raisa Soltakhanova, a thirty-nine-year-old cook, remembered the soldiers saying.[47]

Novye Aldy was surrounded by armored personnel carriers (APCs) on the morning of February 5. Pollution from the burning factories of the surrounding Grozny chemical plant and burning oil wells blackened the sky. That morning, a resident recalled, "two soldiers [were] running down the road shouting warnings that contract soldiers were coming. They shouted: 'If you have fighters, hide them. If you have young women, hide them or they will be raped.' I then saw contract soldiers coming with bandanas on their heads."[48] Snipers surrounded the village, and an estimated one hundred soldiers entered Novye Aldy around 9:00 A.M. Some were privately contracted soldiers, while others were members of the MVD Special

Forces and St. Petersburg and Ryzan OMON forces. According to one witness testimony, the soldiers told him that they were from the 245th Motorized Rifle Regiment, 6th Company.[49] It appears that the younger conscript soldiers were responsible for cordoning off the area and the Special Forces and contract soldiers conducted the sweep.[50] They walked around in groups of seven to ten. Chadaeva recalled that two of the men in the groups were always well dressed and clean shaven; some of the men were in uniform and others were in civilian clothes. "They looked like official men, FSB. . . . The others wore camouflage pants, some with white T-shirts, others with tattoos and no shirts, even in that cold weather. One had a fur hat with a fox tail. They had no military identification or insignias."[51]

Chadaeva further recalled, "My father and I went out into the street and saw the soldiers setting houses on fire. Our neighbor was repairing the roof of his house, and a Russian soldier took a gun and wanted to fire at him. I shouted, 'Don't shoot. He is deaf!' . . . The first words we heard from them, when they saw us, were 'Mark their foreheads with green iodine [*zelenko*] so that we'll have a better target to aim at."[52] One of the soldiers pointed a gun at Chadaeva's chest and shoved her against a metal gate. The officer in charge told the soldier "to leave me alone," she recalled. "He [the officer] told me to stay close to him and shut my mouth. And then he asked me how many people there were in Aldy. 'Thousands,' I say. 'What?' he says. 'What are you doing, bitch [*svoloch*]? Why don't you get out of here?' He was trying to avoid eye contact. He was shaking."[53] He told Chadaeva: "We have orders not to let a mouse escape from here."[54]

The officer allowed Chadaeva to gather her neighbors on the corner of Chetvertoi Almaznyi Lane and Kamskaia Street for a passport check.[55] She urged the residents of her street and the intersecting lanes to gather together on the corner. "I thought that if they [the Russian troops] saw that there were children, all of us together," she recalled, "then perhaps they wouldn't do anything."[56] The soldiers were pushing people into their homes, throwing grenades into basements full of civilians, and setting houses alight with people inside. Chadaeva remembered, "I ran back home, I took the hand grenade from the window sill in the kitchen in case they raped me, and I taped it under my left breast."[57]

Twenty adults and four children gathered on the windy corner of Chetvertoi Almaznyi Lane and Kamskaia Street. Males and females were separated. Chadaeva was ordered to move aside to have her bag checked. She had packed her things in a plastic supermarket bag. The soldiers discovered her blood pressure meter and medical kit. "Then the officer started screaming into the phone," she recalled: "'What are you doing? Have you gone mad?' he said. He grabbed me and said: 'See to it that all the dead are buried. Our chaps have killed your old men in their heated endeavor.'"[58] Learning that the soldiers were executing people, the officer in charge was anxious to get out and left the civilians standing at the corner. "They jumped on the back of the military truck and took our passports. I ran after them . . . and they threw the passports into the air."[59]

As the passports were being checked on Kamskaia Street, Chadaeva could hear screaming and shouting from Matasha Mazaeva Street, the main road through Novye Aldy. That morning, from around 9:00 A.M. to noon, Matasha Mazaeva Street was the first to be targeted as the Russian soldiers entered from the northern outskirts of the village and made their way toward the center. Raisa Soltakhanova and her mother lived at 183 Matasha Mazaeva Street.

> My mother and I were putting up plastic sheeting when the soldiers came at 9:00 A.M. The soldiers were wearing black scarves, some had knitted hats. They were wearing camouflage uniforms. They came from the beginning of the street, breaking the gates of unoccupied houses by shooting out the locks. They tried first with their feet; if it didn't yield, they then shot it out. A soldier ran into my yard. He shouted, "They are angry, they are killing everyone, go into the house." He was short with small eyes, about twenty-five years old. He had the same uniform as the others. It seemed like he was a conscript soldier. He made my mother and me go into our house and close the door.[60]

The soldiers then spread out, moving through the three main cross streets—Kamskaia, Ural'skaia, and Khoperskaia—into the back and side lanes, notably Fourth Almaznyi Lane, and Second and Fourth Tsimlianski lanes. The killings occurred in two main areas: along Matasha Mazaeva Street and on the corner of Voronezhskaia and Khoperskaia streets. Houses 112, 127, 140, 145, 152, 162, and 170 were targeted.[61] As the soldiers moved through the streets, small grenades were taped to the doors of several storehouses and to several gates, with trip wires leading into the yards.[62] The soldiers spilled kerosene from plastic containers to set the houses on fire. From the evidence available it is not possible to tell how many homes were destroyed in this way, but the aim to cause material as well as psychological damage was obvious. In this part of the city on February 5, 2000, fifty-six civilians were summarily executed, including five others on the other side of the dam in Chernorech'e.[63] On the same day, five civilians were killed on Podpolskaia Street in Grozny—one was a one-year-old child.

The next day, on February 6, the same contract soldiers returned to Novye Aldy. Never staying the night, they returned each day for the next week to loot the houses. Many civilians had left Aldy in early January and had stored their belongings together in several houses on Matasha Mazaeva and Voronezhskaia streets. Over the course of one week the soldiers returned each day to take away the goods: "When I was coming back from washing Zina's body," recalls one witness, "I saw soldiers loading looted things on to a truck on Voronezhskaia Street on February 9. My daughter accompanied me when we went to wash the bodies. When we came back it was 3:30 P.M. I saw two APCs and the soldiers taking out things and loading them. When the soldiers noticed us two women, they shot in the air. My daughter and I ran away quickly because the soldiers always killed witnesses," recalled a forty-one-year-old local, Zapiat Z.[64] On February 10 sixteen men were detained and loaded on a truck with looted property. They were taken to the edge of a ditch and made to kneel, their hands bound. They were forced to kiss the soldiers' shoes and beaten with rifle butts.[65] They were saved by the appearance of Russian journalist and Orthodox layman Viktor Popkov, who arrived in the village with a camera crew. Seeing the men kneeling at the edge of the ditch, he screamed at the soldiers on the streets. The soldiers quickly deserted the scene.

Torture at Chernokozovo

The men saved from detainment by the arrival of Viktor Popkov were fortunate. Illegal detainment became one of the dominant motifs of the sweep operations. At the same time that the *zachistka* was taking place in Novye Aldy, information emerged on the international news circuit about the existence of a filtration point called Chernokozovo in the village of Chernokozov. The Russian term "filtration point" (*fil'tratsionnyi punkt*) broadly characterized every type of detainment center, from legally based pre-trial detention facilities (SIZO),[66] like those in Chernokozov and Grozny, and temporary detention facilities (IVS)[67] to places with neither official status nor titles, like pits in the ground at checkpoints, a former reservoir, a quarry, factories, or fields on the outskirts of villages, all of which were established to detain real and suspected Chechen fighters.[68] The filtration point marked the creation of Russia's own "spaces of exception" in its war on terror. Originally established on the basis of the Ministry of the Interior Directive No. 247 of 1994, the unofficial detention points had no legal basis in Russian law.[69] As the Russian government continued to argue that what was taking place in Chechnya was not an internal armed conflict but an "antiterrorist operation," it was nevertheless bound by the legal provisions of the Russian Criminal Code and the Russian Constitution, the European Convention on Human Rights, the International Covenant on Civil and Political Rights, and the European Convention for the Prevention of Torture and Inhuman or Degrading Treatment or Punishment—*all* of which banned arbitrary detention and torture.

"Filtration" had two formal objectives. The first was to filter out the suspected fighters from civilians. It was therefore inevitable and even expected that civilians would be part of this process. The second objective was to filter the fighters out in order to transfer them to pre-trial detention centers that formed part of the broader Russian penitentiary system. An ever-increasing number of civilians were also swept up in the throes of an arbitrary process—men and women subject to the loose conception of who or what constituted the enemy. The problem rested not in the right of the Russian Special Forces to detain suspected fighters; this was a legitimate counterinsurgency tactic. The question rested in the character and scope of the detentions and what this may suggest about broader motivation. While the arbitrariness may be explained by the chaos within the Russian armed forces or by the absence of targeted intelligence information, the practice of arbitrary detention constituted too widespread a phenomenon to dismiss a deeper meaning out of hand.

The filtration points were never subject to normal due process between 1999 and 2005, and the Russian armed forces defied any attempt to regulate their existence. As one member of the Russian Special Forces confessed: "The only way to struggle against lawlessness is with lawless ways."[70] The fundamental issue, however, rested not only with the existence of the filtration points but with the *treatment* of those detained within them. The detainment of civilians on administrative infractions or passport irregularities, as well as genuinely suspected fighters, suggests contiguous factors during sweep operations—some legitimate, others motivated by material gain and a desire to inflict collective punishment. Yet the ritual practices of torture used by the Russian Special Forces were unequivocal in their intent.

Allegations of torture[71] and of cruel and inhumane treatment at the pretrial detention center Chernokozovo first reached the international news circuit via an article in *Le Monde* on February 4, 2000. While on the border of Ingushetia at checkpoint "Adler 20," Sophie Shihab, a French journalist, was passed a letter by a Chechen IDP.[72] Allegedly written by a Russian guard serving at Chernokozovo, where an estimated 750 detainees were being kept, the letter explained: "I cannot describe the exotic methods being used to break the human spirit, turning a human into an animal. I finish writing this trifle, but if on this earth there is some force, help these people. I am disappointed in my government, its lies, cunning and duplicity. Well, I am not that literate, if anything is not right."[73] Verifying the authenticity of this letter is difficult, but the facts outlined in the appeal are impossible to dispute—they were fully supported by other testimony, including that of the well-known Russian journalist Andrei Babitskii, who was detained in Chernokozovo from January 16 to February 2, and of tortured detainees who crossed the border into Ingushetia in the middle of February.[74]

The Ministry of the Interior presided over Chernokozovo from January 11 until early February. It later grew clear that Chernokozovo had once been a correctional facility, IS-36/2, and although in a state of disrepair it was being used, according to government sources, as a "reception and identification center" by Russian troops at the time of the second war.[75] It is impossible to determine which MVD divisions served in the facility and perpetrated the abuse. Fearing identification and possible future retribution, Russian soldiers in Chechnya frequently wore camouflage uniforms with no division patches or pins that could identify them. However, six interviewees testified that the Rostov OMON supplied the guards and commanded the facility during this period before it was handed back to the Ministry of Justice in February and officially given the title SIZO No. 2. As one detainee recalled:

> They took us to the camp "Chernokozovo." About fifty soldiers in camouflage uniform, in masks and with truncheons in their hands met us. They quickly dispersed to form a corridor which they forced us to go through. As soon as we stepped into line, blows from the truncheons started falling on our backs, heads and other parts of the body. . . . It turns out that on this first day I had several broken ribs. Then they took us into a separate space and ordered us to undress. The corporal punishment continued. They beat all of us; some because they screamed out, others for silently tolerating the blows.[76]

The human corridor cynically framed what awaited the detainees inside Chernokozovo. Prepared to inflict severe pain and suffering to obtain information or forced confessions, the Russian troops' desire for signed confessions appeared important, but not necessarily paramount. "They tried to make me sign confessions that we were wahhabis, fighters, that we were supporting the fighters. I did not sign," recalls one detainee. "They used electric shock to make me sign, but I did not do it. I was forced to put my back to the wall. . . . There were two cables, and they held the cables to my body. . . . They splashed water in my face. Two or three times during the interrogation, they electrocuted me."[77] The rituals included forcing detainees to crawl on the ground: "They ordered me to crawl along the corridor, which was twenty meters long. I tried to crawl and one of the soldiers was kicking me in the kidney, and another in the shoulder."[78] "They would make us say 'Comrade Colonel, let me crawl to you.' . . . After they beat us, they made us say 'thank you.'"[79] Genital beatings or electroshock was inflicted to force confessions, but testimonies also suggest an intent to inflict irrevocable damage to reproductive organs: "You will leave here half a man. . . . Do you want to have children? . . . It was February 7, late at night. I was lying on the floor, two guards held my legs while another kicked me in the testicles. . . . They would beat me unconscious and wait until I came round: 'He's woken up,' and they would come in and beat me [again]."[80]

Two witnesses spoke of being physically branded at Chernokozovo. The threat of marking foreheads with green iodine (*zelenko*) was first heard of in Novye Aldy. Victims detained during the sweep in the village of Shami-Iurt in February 2000 were taken to Tolstoi-Iurt. During transportation, a Russian soldier warned Dashaev and another man named Viskhan[81] that if their noses were marked in red, they were being branded for summary execution. He cautioned that it would be better if they were covered in green iodine. Whether this warning was used as a psychological weapon or had legitimate strategic value is unclear. But both Dashaev and Viskhan were later covered in green iodine and released.[82] The full extent of this practice is unclear.

The Russian government rejected the reports of torture at Chernokozovo. Over the course of 2000, the West was chastised for "information terrorism,"[83] and a chorus of high-level representatives voiced their displeasure. The deputy minister of justice, Colonel General Yuri Kalinin, concluded: "The accusation that the detained are being tortured and beaten is just sheer lies and slander."[84] Valerii Kraev, first deputy head of the Ministry of Justice's Corrections Department, said: "All the isolators existing in

Chechnya operate in complete observance of all the international conventions."[85] Sergei Yastrezhembskii, President Putin's spokesman for Chechnya, said: "Routine work like in any other detention center is going on there."[86] The prosecutor of the Chechen Republic, Vladimir Kravchenko, claimed that all the reports of violations and misconduct in Chernokozovo were unsubstantiated rumors.[87] Memorial received a reply from the Prosecutor's Office in June 2000 stating that "facts that the employees of the detention center exceeded their powers were not confirmed in the course of an investigation."[88]

Although the Russian government refused to acknowledge the use of torture at Chernokozovo, it was not immune to the damage the testimonies had inflicted on its public image. Acting president Putin quickly appointed Vladimir Kalamanov, the former head of the Federal Migration Service (FMS), as the Special Representative of the President of the Russian Federation on Human Rights and Freedoms in the Chechen Republic to manage the growing objections. Kalamanov later organized the release of over two hundred detainees at Chernokozovo, but over the next two years he never exposed the extent of the human rights violations in Chechnya. And despite the testimonies of Memorial, Human Rights Watch, Amnesty, *Itogi*, *Versiya*, *Novye Izvestiia*, and *Le Monde*, he concluded on March 29 with regard to Chernokozovo: "None of the delegations have confirmed rumors of torture or humiliation," and he attacked Western human rights organizations for their "very aggressive approach to the Russian authorities."[89] The head of the Presidential Human Rights Commission, Vladimir Kartashkin, who in the 1970s had vilified Russian dissidents in the pages of the journal *International Affairs*, responded to U.S. State Department spokesman James Rubin's critical comments on Russia's conduct in the war with what was by then a typical reaction to any criticism of Russia's strategy: "James Rubin," he wrote, "is calling global attention to Russian soldiers maltreating Chechen civilians. . . . As they are, Mr. Rubin's charges appear sheer and unreliable propaganda."[90]

Temporary Filtration Points

Chernokozovo was not an aberration. While those detained in the winter months were swept up at the height of the bombing campaign, it marked the beginning of a broader set of practices. By the summer of 2000, the partisan war had begun in earnest. Chechen forces began to ambush Russian garrisons at night and to target APCs and military bases with remote-controlled bombing devices. In response, the sweep operations grew in number, reaching a peak in 2001 and continuing throughout 2002 and early 2003. After the massacres at Alkhan-Iurt, Staropromyslovskii, and Novye Aldy, the pattern of public executions was replaced by enforced disappearances. Detention, torture, extortion, and looting also became the main features of the *zachistka*. The analogies to Argentina's "dirty war" were by no means unfounded. The tactics grew increasingly reminiscent of those of Jorge Videla's military government from 1976 to 1983. As conditions in Chernokozovo gradually improved as a result of international pressure, the violence shifted away from the notorious detention center to *temporary* filtration points on the outskirts of Chechen villages, to the boarding school in Urus-Martan, and to the military headquarters at Khankala and Tangi-Chu.

Torture was a routine practice at the temporary filtration points. Unlike at Chernokozovo, torture was practiced in specially equipped wagons,[91] in tents, or in fields. The torture wagons were the ultimate symbol of impunity—they were linked to neither a legal detention point nor possible witnesses. The most common forms of torture practiced included the following: electric shocks to the genitals, toes, and fingers with a field telephone (later a rectifier was used, an electric device that has an adjustable power output); asphyxiation with plastic bags;[92] cutting off ears;[93] filling mouths with kerosene;[94] setting dogs on the legs of the detained; knife cuts; and carving crosses in the backs of detainees.[95] According to witness testimony, the code name for the practice in which the dog was deployed either to incite fear or for physical torture was allegedly "Lawyer" (*Advokat*), and the dogs were trained to respond to the word *Nokhchi*, meaning *Chechen*.[96] Some detainees had electrodes attached to their ears or were beaten directly on the ears with a rubber cane. Beatings to the ribs, liver, kidneys, and genitals with bludgeons, hammers, rifle butts, soldiers' boots, or plastic bottles filled with water or sand were the most common.[97] Stress positions were employed—forced squatting for long periods of time, standing with arms outstretched or above the head, or the "ostrich" position, holding one leg up in the air for extended periods of time.[98] In the winter, men were often stripped and made to stand in the cold for twenty-four hours; in the summer months they were forced to lie face down in a field in the sun. According to witness testimony, mock executions were common.[99]

In this way, federal forces tried to get information about who in the village was supporting the Chechen forces and where weapons were hidden.

Witness testimonies have reiterated that the questions asked were often vague and undirected. The Russian Special Forces forced the detainees to sign confessions stating that they were Chechen rebel fighters or—after being tortured—they were forced to sign a document saying that they had no grievances about the way in which they had been treated. The filtration points were also used as places to recruit informers. The majority of detainees were released after detention.

July and August 2000 were brutal months for those left to languish in the southern villages. Punitive sweeps were common. On the outskirts of the village of Shuani, an APC was blown up at 4:00 A.M. on July 24. "Black Shark" helicopters started circling and firing on the village. Special units entered the region and forced people out of their basements. Men and women were again separated and told that if the civilians did not identify who was responsible for blowing up the APC then five Chechens would be shot for every soldier in the village.[100] Ten men were taken away and beaten until they were rescued by a group of women who followed them. Two weeks later, in Gekhi, an APC hit a land mine. Soldiers again surrounded the village with so-called Predators, covered Ural trucks used for torture, and detained fifty-seven people. The men were taken to a temporary filtration point in a field next to the cemetery. They were beaten and tortured under a tarpaulin called the "Hall of Mirrors" (*komnata smekha*) and threatened with further torture by *Gestapovtsi,* members of a so-called Gestapo group.[101] Whether this was a psychological threat or a more brutal torture unit existed is unknown. Men were no doubt tortured in such a way as to prevent them from fighting and were literally *defaced* by brutal attacks. Forced to lie in the open field on their stomachs, some were released after twenty-four hours, others after three days.

The village of Chernorech'e, across the reservoir from Novye Aldy, was closed for three days between August 30 and September 1. Young men and women were rounded up and held in massive empty cisterns near an automobile refueling station or in the basement of the station. Exactly how many were detained is unknown, but one witness testified that forty-seven people were held in one cistern. A nineteen-year-old boy was attached to the back of an APC and dragged to the outskirts of the village in front of civilians. His father recalled: "They dragged him along the road tied to the back of the APC and up to the edge of the forest. They filled his mouth with paint, tried a live wire that failed, then took him to the refueling station and dumped him there."[102] Other men were severely tortured by beatings and electric shock. One practice was to pour water over a detainee and then attach wires by means of a metal clip to an ear, the tongue, or the genitals. This method was known as "calling Maskhadov" (*zvonkom Maskhadovu*) or "calling a lawyer" (*zvonkom advokatu*).[103] The detainees were released with burns, bruises, and knife wounds. Some family members had paid bribes or given up weapons to ensure their release.

The political landscape shifted in the summer of 2000. Akhmat Kadyrov, the Chechen mufti, was appointed head of the Temporary Administration in Chechnya by the Russian government in June. While Kadyrov had supported the Chechen separatists in the first war, his growing concern about the rise of extremist groups compelled him to change sides in 1999 to lead the so-called team of pro-Moscow protégés. He was a member of the Benoi, one of the most influential *teips*, and the Russian government was keen to install a Chechen-led administration to counter the anti-Russian sentiment on the ground. Positioned in Gudermes, the administration had only a marginal influence until 2003. Kadyrov's appointment, however, marked the beginning of Russia's new political policy of Chechenization (see chapter 3).

The sweeps continued into the winter of 2000–2001 and into the spring. The public outcry was strong. Lieutenant General Vladimir Moltenskoi, acting commander of the Unified Group of the Russian Federation Armed Forces (OGV) of the Northern Caucasus issued Order No. 145 on May 30, 2001, in an attempt to rein in the impunity. The intent of the order was to regulate the sweeps by insisting that commanders cooperate with the local administrations, the military, and the heads of the local enforcement bodies. Regional prosecutors were also obliged to be present. But the outcry had little effect. In Kurchaloi, 120 men were rounded up and held in a warehouse that stored agricultural fertilizers. Mairtup, Chernorech'e, Chiri-Iurt, and Tsotsin-Iurt were similarly targeted. And villages like Alkhan-Kala and Starye Atagi were subject to repeated sweeps, sometimes conducted by Ministry of Defense troops with FSB forces and then by special forces of the Ministry of the Interior (MVD).[104] Turf wars between OMON, SOBR, and Ministry of Justice troops (GUIN) appeared routine.

But it was the punitive operations that took place in the western villages of Sernovodsk and Assinovskaia in 2001 that garnered the most public attention. A police UAZ truck was blown up in Sernovodsk, a village close to the border with Ingushetia, killing five policemen. On July 2, Russian troops entered the village, looted and threw grenades into seven homes. Several hundred local inhabitants (estimates range from three hundred to

FIGURE 2.1. A soldier from the Ministry of the Interior (MVD) unit "Vityaz" during a sweep operation in Alkhan-Kala, April 2002. Photograph by Dmitrii Beliakov. © Dmitrii Beliakov.

six hundred) were detained and taken to a field between Sernovodsk and Samashki.[105] Some of those rounded up managed to bribe their way out of detention by paying anything from 200 to 1,000 rubles.[106] Others were tortured with electric shock, beaten, and hounded by dogs in tents, in the basement of an unfinished building nearby, in a mobile torture wagon, and in a concrete pit used for storing food for cattle (*silosnaia yama*) closer to Assinovskaia.[107] While the majority of detainees were released, an estimated one hundred were transferred to a temporary detention center under the Ministry of the Interior in Achkhoi-Martan. In violation of Order No. 145, the operation was not conducted in cooperation with the local administration. Moreover, Vakha Arsamakov, head of the village administration, and Khizir Vitaev, head of the administration for the Sunzhenskii district, were locked up by servicemen for the duration of the *zachistka*.

On July 3 around 4,000 civilians walked or drove into neighboring Ingushetia to escape the violence. South of Sernovodsk, in the village of Assinovskaia, a sweep occurred from July 3 to July 4. An estimated 600–800 locals were detained, including Nazarbek Terkhoev, head of the regional administration. As Terkhoev later recalled:

> Early in the morning of July 3, with the support of aviation, military servicemen, and Ministry of Interior units, military vehicles entered the village from three sides. Russian troops had already enclosed the village with a solid circle of tanks and other heavy military vehicles. The first troop action was to block the administration and the local police precinct, after which police officers of the precinct were disarmed and taken to the filtration point at the temporary base of the troops. The head of administration was then disarmed and taken to the base of the troops.[108]

The detainees were interrogated and beaten in a deserted building close to the River Assa. In the evening, they were released and walked to a forest near the village of Chemul'ga.

Beginning in November 2001, the behavior of soldiers during sweeps became even more brutal. And the agony that accompanied this uncertain environment continued. Although symbolic attempts were made to counter these violations, the actions were officially tolerated. This tolerance for the impunity was later confirmed by the lack of accountability and criminal punishment for the perpetrators. Lieutenant General Moltenskoi, under significant pressure from human rights groups, signed another special order, Order No. 80, stipulating new rules for conducting the sweep operations on March 27, 2002. Aware that violations were ongoing, his specific aim in issuing this order was to "lessen the [number of] unlawful acts committed against the local population and to increase trust between the soldiers and the civilian authorities." The order mandated that all special operations were "to be conducted not only in the presence of procurators but also of the local authorities and the organs of internal affairs."[109] Russian presidential spokesman Sergei Yastrezhembskii admitted that this "unprecedented document" contains "an honest analysis of the established facts of unlawful actions by soldiers during the conducting of special operations."[110]

Clashes continued with separatist forces. Remote-control mines and explosives, as well as frequent attacks on checkpoints and military headquarters, created a tense environment for the Russian forces fortified in towns and villages.[111] The position of the Russian ground forces was by no means enviable. One example was the frequent, small-scale clashes that took place around the village of Tsotsin-Iurt during 2002. Yet the counterattacks on the village were striking acts of perversity that illustrate the chaos of motives that drove the sweep operations. Tsotsin-Iurt was targeted in January, February, March, July, and September 2002. In January,

FIGURE 2.2. A man is detained by a soldier from the MVD unit "Vityaz" during a sweep operation in Kulary, Chechnya, April 2002. Photograph by Dmitrii Beliakov. © Dmitrii Beliakov.

around one hundred men were detained in a half-demolished old repair shop on the outskirts of the city. They were made to stand in the freezing temperatures, some for up to two days. Approximately eighty-nine of the detainees were released. Five were summarily executed and six disappeared. Many were hardly able to walk as a result of the beatings and torture they had endured. Some were dumped back in the village by Russian forces in APCs.[112]

Eyewitness testimonies recount particular cases of harassment and insults toward women in Tsotsin-Iurt. But no testimonies of actual rape were given. Only a small proportion of survivors in Chechnya are likely to have admitted to having been sexually tortured and major difficulties have persisted for human rights groups seeking to document rape cases. Yet Memorial believes that rape was widespread. Acts of rape and sexual violence were recognized as forms of torture in the *Prosecutor v. Dusko Tadic* judgment in 1997 as part of the International Criminal Tribunal for the former Yugoslavia. It was not until an English organization, the Medical Foundation for the Care of the Victims of Torture, released its report in April 2004 that a sample case could be used as a basis for considering the possible scale of sexual torture in Chechnya. The foundation discovered in its treatment of nineteen women that sixteen had been raped, as had one man. Two of the victims were ethnic Russians. In 85 percent of the cases, the perpetrators were Russian troops or police and 15 percent were Chechen fighters.[113]

The stigma associated with rape appears to be the main reason for a shortage of statistics. One of the victims mentioned that her cellmate had committed suicide after being raped; another victim testified that she knew that suicide was often preferred to living with the shame. The occurrence of rape differed for each victim from one to "many" instances over various time frames; from once to everyday for a month. The number of perpetrators also ranged from "one" to "many" to "over ten." Rape was often accompanied by other forms of physical and psychological torture: kicking, punching, and being hit with a gun butt or slapped. Four women described "being made to cook, clean, and iron clothes for Russian troops." Most continued to suffer not only from headaches and musculoskeletal pain but from anxiety, nightmares, sleep disturbance, and recollections of the trauma.[114]

By July 2002, the villagers of Tsotsin-Iurt were enduring their fortieth sweep.[115] After an exchange of fire on July 24 on the outskirts of the village, the locals understood that there would be a sweep operation the following day. Under the cover of darkness, those who were not registered in the village, young men, and local people, frightened that they would be detained and beaten by the Russian forces, left the village by foot and car (several separatist fighters were likely among them as well). While leaving the village, they were ambushed by Russian troops who opened fire on them. A car was blown up with three people in it and others were caught by machine-gun fire. Those who survived headed back to Tsotsin-Iurt. Local women ran out of the village to pick up the abandoned remains of those who had been killed. The women were fired upon and forced back to the village. The soldiers gathered the dead bodies up and took them to Kurchaloi. They would later demand weapons from the locals in exchange for the corpses.[116]

The sweep continued for four days. Units of the Kurchaloevskii district department of the Ministry of the Interior (ROVD), which had been in Tsotsin-Iurt in January, took part. They prohibited the Chechen militia from entering the village. Around sixty people were detained, taken to the old repair shop, and subjected to torture. By July 27 and 28 the looting had increased. The same unit returned shouting, "Armed robbery!" Never seeking to conceal the fact that they had been there in January, they said: "'Remember

FIGURE 2.3. Graffiti on a wall in Grozny, "Better a terrible end, than terror without end!!!" Undated. Photograph by Natal'ia Medvedeva. © 2008, IPV News, USA.

us? We'll show you!'" recalled one eyewitness. In an international appeal, the local elders displayed the extent of their despair: "We . . . propose that you not kill us so slowly and cruelly. If we are being handed over to the harsh treatment of Russia, then kill us immediately, in one day, in one hour, everyone together. At least in this way you will alleviate our suffering and resolve all of our problems."[117]

* * *

Torture was an official state policy in Chechnya. Organized and encouraged by the military elite, by early 2000 it was an unexceptional feature of the armed conflict. Punishment was used to gather evidence and it was clear that civilians, suspected or otherwise, were tortured for information. The rituals of torture served several functions. Gathering information or confessions was the formal motive for violence, but it was not its only purpose. In actuality, it was used to assert the *dominance* of the Russian forces, to create a broader landscape of fear, and to neutralize potential fighters or those who were hors de combat. In the torture, we can see that there was not only a very broad definition of the enemy group in Chechnya but that torture was used to reinforce the powerlessness of the victim, either civilian or separatist fighter, and to undermine personal security or certainty.

Power is important here. Asking detainees to crawl on the ground or to kiss a soldier's boots is an example of an attempt to exert absolute rule over the detainees and to ensure compliance; it served no purpose other than humiliation. Mock executions served the same function. The fact that the majority of detainees were released after detention and torture, without being charged, further underscores this claim.

The personal and ideological motives of the Russian armed forces were multifold. A desire to exert state power and self-image were certainly among them. The contract soldiers were well aware of the fear they evoked in civilians and Russian conscript soldiers during sweep operations. The bandanas, the fox tail hanging down the back of the neck, singlet tops, sunglasses, and tattoos—all of these were emblems of their status and self-aggrandizement. Pure sadism and macho pride were factors, private agendas that both the Russian military and the Russian government were prepared to indulge. The role of ideology in the behavior of Russian troops, however, is more difficult to determine. The ideological agenda of the Russian government was the protection of national borders from international terrorism, as well as ostensibly protecting the United States and Europe. This agenda gave legitimacy and license to its actions. It was matched by a growing nationalism, led by President Putin, which sought to reassert Russia's national identity, both internally and abroad. The Russian Special Forces may have seen the civilians as either interfering with their ultimate goal—the elimination of the terrorists and terrorism—or as accomplices to the separatist movement itself and therefore worthy of punishment. How they justified their own actions and to what degree they believed that their actions were contributing to the fight against international terrorism or protecting Russia's national security remain questions that require further investigation.

The war was undoubtedly seen as an opportunity to redeem the Russian armed forces, as Algeria had been to the French after its defeat at Dien Bien Phu in Vietnam.[118] The shame that accompanied the defeat of the army in the first Chechen war (1994–96) and the severe budget cuts for the Ministry of Defense reduced the army to a shadow of its former self. In April 1995 General Kvashnin had said, "We will beat the Chechens to a pulp, so that the present generation will be too terrified to fight Russia again."[119] Unsuccessful in his initial endeavor, Kvashnin returned in 1999 as the chief of the general staff, number two after the defense minister, with a new resolve. The uncompromising position of the Putin administration with regard to negotiations proved timely for the ministry in terms of

FIGURE 2.4. Russian troops on an Armored Personnel Carrier traveling through Grozny. Undated. Photograph by Natal'ia Medvedeva. © 2008, IPV News, USA.

restoring its reputation. And this desire for a heightened military profile perfectly matched the nationalist narrative and statism that was defining the Putin presidency. The military elite were also well aware that there would be little of the vacillation President Yeltsin had exhibited; it could be assured of support. Statists, like President Putin, were also disappointed by the military's failure to protect the integrity of the state in 1994–96. In 2000, Putin declared military reform a national priority and substantially increased the budget.[120] "I do indeed believe that the rebirth of the army will begin with the North Caucasus Military District," asserted General Viktor Kazantsev, Presidential Envoy to the Southern Federal District, "and that the revival of the country will begin with the south. All the prerequisites for this exist in our highly abundant, highly fertile region. The south is Russia's 'solar plexus'. If we organize normal life [there], we will flourish."[121]

The degree to which the antiterrorist ideology was interwoven with racial prejudice is less complex. Whether or not the Special Forces and Russia's military elite believed that all Chechens were terrorists, the category itself served a particular purpose and concealed a *deeper* prejudice. The racial labeling and slurring as told by Chechen torture victims included references to "apes," "bandits," "cattle," and "blacks," as well as "chechmeki" and "chernomazye," both insulting terms for "blacks."[122] When Kazbek Khazmagomadov asked why they were being beaten, the Russian soldiers replied: "Because you are Chechens!"[123] The types of threats toward civilians that have been recalled in witness testimonies include: "We are going to purge you all by springtime and then we are going to send you to Siberia."[124] "Get out before we slaughter you all."[125] "We killed you in the past and we are going to carry on killing you."[126] "They smashed a partition in the corridor and then started shouting that we were all bandits."[127] The walls of School No. 18 in Argun were, as Politkovskaia reminds us, a "vivid textbook of ethnic hatred," the kindest comment being "All Wolves Deserve a Dog's Death."[128] Graffiti on the walls of Grozny included "We have come back to fuck you Chechen fighters"[129] and "Welcome to Hell: Part II."[130] By the second war in Chechnya, racial prejudice against Chechens as a long-perceived construct in Russian life was, without doubt, strategically placed at the forefront of public life—diffracted through the prism of political manipulation. The racial question was by 2000 repackaged under "terrorist," the dominant category by which Chechens would be identified.

The concept of cultural difference also figured prominently among the troops. As Arkady Babchenko, an officer of the second Chechen war and veteran of the first war, recalled,

> Quite apart from anything else, our soldiers resent the Chechens because they wash themselves after doing their business, rather than using paper. In each house there are special jugs with long spouts made from some silvery metal, and inscribed with ornate Arabic script. At first our boys couldn't figure out their purpose and used them for making tea. When someone finally told them, they freaked out. The first thing they do now when they occupy a house is kick these jugs outside or fish them out with sticks. Actual faith doesn't matter one bit to us, be it Allah, Jesus or whoever, since we ourselves are a godless bunch from birth. But these jugs embody the difference between our cultures. It seems to me that the political officer could distribute them instead of propaganda leaflets and we'd rip Chechnya to shreds in a couple of days.[131]

While Babchenko gives little credence to the religious difference between Sunni Muslims and Orthodox Russians, he does see portent in cultural symbols, rituals, and purported divisions of values. "I have nothing to do with Chechnya," he writes, "and I don't give a damn what it is, because it doesn't really exist. Because completely different people live here who speak in a different language, think differently and breathe differently."[132] To suggest that someone breathes differently is indicative of the remoteness and spatial distance, both psychological and cultural, that was heightened during the course of the war. Babchenko does not identify the Chechen civilians as "terrorists" but simply as "different." Seeing the Chechens as alien, the Russian troops sense that they are occupying foreign territory, not their own. Whether Babchenko and his fellow soldiers see in the jugs a claim to Chechen superiority or the complete opposite, inferiority—for their failure to follow Russian traditions—is unclear. Yet undoubtedly it is the intimacy of the act itself that inspires such vitriolic rage. Such personal moments embody a cultural division that confirms for Babchenko and his troops the gulf that divides them and certainly legitimates, on some level, the violence that follows.

Situational and economic factors also explain the behavior of Russian troops. And all of these factors clearly intersected, defying a simple rubric of understanding. One factor was stress and frustration, especially among recruits who were hired as contract soldiers with little experience in warfare. The extent of drug abuse and alcoholism was evident in the growing number of contract soldiers discharged in 2003.[133] A fear of ambushes and the desire to avenge the death of friends played decisive roles. Hazing and brutality were common among the Russian armed forces. According to Babchenko, "Not once in the whole war had anyone explained a mission to me in a normal civilized manner."[134] Talking about his superiors, he writes, "A stinking nobody in the outside world, he is top dog and master of souls here."[135] The torture exerted by the Russian forces was no doubt a form of control and a way to assert freedom and autonomy in an environment that lacked certainty within the army, within Chechnya, and within Russia more broadly in the aftermath of the collapse of the Soviet Union. It most surely enhanced already declining feelings of self-worth.

The other objective was clearly *economic*. And this aspect of the detention of Chechen men was entirely self-serving. The desire for material gain was symptomatic of a broader social and economic crisis both within the Russian army, which struggled to pay wages, and within Russian society more generally. The extortion in human bodies, dead or alive, was a brutal and cynical practice that targeted the very livelihood of Chechen civilians struggling to survive. What the testimonies tell us is that Chechen men were deliberately detained for money—countering yet again the hegemonic narrative of the Russian government over "normalization" in Chechnya. In the village of Tsotsin-Iurt the sweep lasted for five days, November 7–12, 2001. Of the thirty men detained, sixteen were released for ransom payments of 5,000 rubles each.[136] In the southeastern village of Mairtup, civilians were held at gunpoint in their courtyard in June 2001. On discovering young men in the group, the Russian soldiers threatened to detain them. They offered the family the chance to pay them before being detained.[137] In Alkhan-Iurt, the village elders organized a reserve fund to be used for paying off the military in exchange for promises to ease the scale of a sweep operation, thereby reducing the number of men detained.[138]

The use of state power for personal plunder was ubiquitous. After the *zachistka* in Alleroi in August 2001, which lasted for nine days, Russian soldiers tried to sell the carpets they had stolen in the market in the neighboring village of Novogroznenskoe.[139] While one unit detained suspected fighters or civilians on the outskirts of the village, the other unit would remain in the village to loot the houses. In Tsotsin-Iurt in October 2000, soldiers raided the mill and drove around selling stolen flour back to the local villagers. "The soldiers took all the flour. Sugar and jars of preserves from our home. What they couldn't carry, they smashed. They caught all the chickens in the yard," recalled one witness.[140] Another eyewitness, from the village of Chechen-Aul, stated: "First they would look around a building without committing any offense. Then they would ask the owners to sign a statement that no offenses had been committed. Then, often, the same people would go back a second time and take whatever they wanted."[141] Looting included material damage. In thirty-four of the eighty-nine sweeps researched here, soldiers blew up or set fire to homes, shops, and places of business. And there are many instances of gratuitous violence—setting alight haystacks put aside for the winter in the case of the operation in Tsotsin-Iurt in October 2001, destroying goods and property that had not been looted, smashing windows, and turning houses upside down.[142] In Alleroi and Tsotsin-Iurt, soldiers killed cattle and defecated on carpets in mosques.

The sweep operation in Chechnya ranged in scope from punitive massacres, looting expeditions, and exercises in torture and humiliation to standard passport checks. The systemic impunity, however, clearly undermined the legitimacy of the counterinsurgency operation for the Russian armed forces. The sheer number of testimonies of beatings and torture, in all their gruesome detail and the broken bodies they produced, contradicted time and time again the Russian government's claims that its goals in the region were purely military.[143] The Russian government created a space in which brutal practices were both permitted and encouraged. Memorial has estimated that for the period from the summer of 2000 to the end of 2004, for the 25–30 percent of the territory they were able to monitor, 5,000–10,000 people died as a result of cleansing operations.[144] If this was not a formally orchestrated military strategy, it was certainly a *tolerated* one. And while the motives may have been multi-causal, the overriding motivation was a deeply held sentiment of collective guilt—expressed time and time again in the *zachistka* itself.

3

THE DISAPPEARANCES, 2002–5

> Destroying the insurgents under the cover of night is the most effective strategy in this war. They are scared of it. And they don't feel safe anywhere—neither in the mountains nor at home.
>
> —*Russian officer*

> I was in the kitchen. I quickly opened the window and saw that he was being dragged into the car by his collar. . . . There were four of them, without masks, Chechens.
>
> —*Chechen civilian witness*

> I want to know where my son is detained and why. . . . I don't even know where he is and how he is. It's winter, my child went out in a T-shirt and barefoot.
>
> —*Rashan Alieva, December 2000*

THE VISUAL HALLMARKS OF THE SECOND CHECHEN WAR manifested in the *zachistka*—the sealed villages, trucks laden with looted property, and temporary filtration points on the outskirts of villages—began to diminish by the summer of 2003. Under growing pressure from the Council of Europe, the Russian government was forced to ease the large-scale sweep operations in an effort to rein in the impunity. The worst appeared to be over. But this picture of growing calm was highly misleading. Large-scale sweep operations were gradually replaced by an increasing number of targeted sweeps (*adresnaia zachistka*), nighttime abductions, and disappearances.[1] As one military intelligence officer admitted in the pages of *Izvestiia*, "Large operations are no longer necessary. We need night operations, directed and surgical. . . . Normal people are not disappearing in Chechnya. It's the scum who are disappearing, who should be destroyed, cleaned out."[2] Witnesses began to speak of masked men, in groups of six to thirty, arriving in camouflage or black uniforms during curfew times—11:00 P.M., 1:30 A.M., 3:00 A.M., 5:00 A.M., and 9:00 A.M. Arriving in APCs and military trucks, so-called *tabletka* minivans, UAZ jeeps, and VAZ-2107s, the Russian Special Forces entered private homes, pulled men and women, civilians and those placed hors de combat, from their beds in the middle of the night and took them away.

The Early Cases

Disappearances had long been a distinguishing feature of the second Chechen war. Shifting in character and scope over the course of six years, they had taken place across a range of sites—temporary filtration points, during house-to-house searches, at or near roadside checkpoints, and, less frequently, during targeted operations.[3] The available evidence suggests that those who disappeared in the early period between 1999 and 2000, were more likely to have been picked up randomly on suspicion rather than through credible military intelligence in an effort to rein in suspects or recruit informers. Cases such as that involving three young men from the village of Aslanbek-Sheripova detained in the spring of 2000 at the checkpoint between Chiri-Iurt and Duba-Iurt were emblematic. While transporting wounded women and children after the bombing of the village, two cars, a red Niva and a white VAZ-21099, were stopped at a checkpoint; the detained men were separated from the wounded and then disappeared. A month later, twelve men were arrested at the same site while making their way by foot from Ulus Kert to Chiri-Iurt. While their wives were released, the twelve men subsequently disappeared.[4]

Because human rights monitors had only limited access to the region, tracking cases from 1999–2001 was highly problematic. But the bodies of the disappeared began to turn up near the sites of detainment or in graves across the region with clear signs of violent death—hands bound, ears cut off, multiple skull fractures, bruised and broken fingers. The examples were numerous: a dumping ground close to the Khankala military base, where fifty-eight bodies were discovered in February 2001; a grain elevator in Argun, where several bodies were discovered after a sweep in December 2001; and fields in Avtury and Tangi-Chu. It was indeed the raw investigatory work undertaken by human rights monitors that allowed the vital link to be made between the corpses and those detained earlier by Russian troops. If there had been any illusion about the strategies of the Russian ground forces, the discovery of these corpses only underscored the willingness of the military to summarily execute detainees suspected of backing the separatists.

A consistent approach to the problem of suspected fighters or sympathizers had emerged by the early months of 2001. Cases began to grow in number as evidence accumulated. Examples like those of Sultan Isaev, a forty-one-year-old welder from Alkhan-Kala, became commonplace. When visiting his parents on April 21, 2001, Isaev went to use the steam bath at the house of his neighbors, the Magomadovs, which was situated in a small building in the courtyard.[5] His wife, Khamila Isaeva, and their four children were living in the village of Voznesenskoe in Ingushetia as IDPs and did not accompany him on the visit. A sweep operation with APCs and helicopters took place in Alkhan-Kala early that afternoon. Isaev's father recalled:

> I began watching through the window out into the street. Two APCs drove up to the same house where my son was bathing. . . . About ten more people came out of the APCs; two of them stayed in the street and the rest went into the courtyard. There were about fifteen people. About half an hour later they came out quickly, and I saw two civilians, that is, the owner of the house, Mr. Sherip Magomadov, who was dressed, and my son, who was half-naked, being shoved into the APC. . . . When they drove off, I immediately ran to the house where my son had been, and there I saw the broken door to the bathhouse and my son's clothes—his jumper, shirt, trousers and shoes. The owner of the house wasn't there; things were strewn all over the place, on the floor.[6]

Isaev was one of ten men detained in Alkhan-Kala that day. One month later when the village was subjected to a further large-scale sweep operation, Russian soldiers informed several local women that a corpse was floating in the Sunzha River, which ran alongside the village. On retrieving the corpse, the women discovered it had no head, only one leg, and several stab and gunshot wounds. It turned out to be Aburakhman Lorsanov, one of the ten men detained on April 21. The other nine detainees were disappeared. No custody records or official trace of their whereabouts or fate was ever discovered.[7]

Daytime abductions during sweep operations grew increasingly routine. A middle-aged man, Abuzar Saidtselimov, describing the abduction of his brother, said that the Russian security forces entered the village of Tsotsin-Iurt on May 7, 2001, between 11:00 and 12:00 P.M., detained his brother Vakhid Saidtselimov in the courtyard of the family home, pulled his shirt over his head, and took him to a nearby APC. Four other men were detained that day, cruelly beaten, and dumped several hours later at a gas station on the outskirts of the village. Saidtselimov's whereabouts were never determined.[8] Similarly, the village of Alleroi was completely sealed in January 2001. As Zulai Edilova was making her way to her parents' home around 11:00 A.M., Russian soldiers began conducting house-to-house searches. She arrived to discover several APCs parked close to her parents' home. In the courtyard stood Taji Talkhadov, her seventy-two-year-old father, waiting to show his documents. He returned to the house after the village imam called the *adhan*, summoning the village to mandatory prayer. An APC approached the gate and some twenty masked soldiers ran through the courtyard, into the house, and grabbed Talkhadov from the floor. When his wife attempted to intervene, a soldier hit her in the shoulder with his rifle butt. While running behind the APC in the hope of determining where they were taking Talkhadov, the family were blocked by soldiers at the edge of the village. The next day, a village demonstration was obstructed by Russian soldiers, preventing the group from making their way to the military base situated between Alleroi and Tsenteroi to protest Talkhadov's detainment.[9] He subsequently disappeared.

By the end of 2002, the number of disappeared had risen significantly. Memorial calculated that for that year alone, 540 individuals were abducted. Of those, 81 were later found murdered, 91 had been released, and 368 had disappeared. The rise in numbers of abducted over the course of 2002 is indicative of the growing emphasis that human rights groups placed on tracking disappeared cases and the interview campaigns they undertook in neighboring Ingushetia with relatives. Yet the rise in numbers may also reflect an improvement in military intelligence. While testimonies speak of attempts by the Russian armed forces to recruit informers during large-scale sweeps, the rise in disappearances may likewise be explained by the growing success of this strategy.

While human rights monitors investigated the cases, it was the families of the disappeared who played the most fundamental role in exposing the scale of the problem. Time and time again, they fractured the measured discourse of "normalization" that was filling the airwaves and print media in Russia and abroad in a crude attempt to convince international bodies that life was returning to normal in Chechnya. From the outset, they visited police stations, hospitals, military bases, morgues, and detention centers, held vigils outside the Khankala military base, and stood on the outskirts of villages at temporary filtration points demanding the release of the detained or—at the very least—knowledge of the charge and the location of detention. Mothers, sisters, wives, and husbands appealed to the local police precincts and local administrations, or filed complaints with the Procuracy of the Chechen Republic and Vladimir Kalamanov, Special Representative of the President of the Russian Federation on Human Rights and Freedoms in the Chechen Republic. On the eve of the constitutional referendum of 2003, a small group of Chechen civilians gathered on Victory Boulevard (Bul'var Pobedy) in Grozny on March 22 to demonstrate against the disappearance of their relatives. They held up slogans inscribed with messages in English, Russian, and German—"Give Us Back Our Sons," "Give Us the Right to Life," "Peace and Justice."[10] Three large placards with pictures of the disappeared were held up. In rows alongside, women in head scarves held up individual photographs.

Unlike the looting that had defined the *zachistka*, however, economic exploitation took on a different form for the families of the disappeared. So-called middlemen, both Russian and Chechen, appeared in villages on the pretext of providing information or assistance, or promising the release of the detained in exchange for cash. Trading in information on the disappeared soon ranked among the highest modes of economic profit in Chechnya and later grew to encompass an entire range of issues from housing compensation repayments to extortion in human corpses. The wife of Sultan Isaev, the welder from Alkhan-Kala, and the families of the disappeared from the village were told that their relatives were being held at the main Russian military base at Khankala. They were advised to collect US$1,000 per detainee to secure their release. In the interim, they paid the middleman 1,000 rubles per day to pass on to the guards of the allegedly detained men. Soon after, the middleman explained that he was unable to secure the release of the detainees. The relatives offered him US$1,500 per person. He returned to explain that two men, Sultan Isaev and Sherip Magomadov, would be released. The relatives arrived at the military base and were told that the deal was off.[11]

The protest on Victory Boulevard on March 22 saw the families of the disappeared border a strange line between the consolidation of two regimes in Chechnya—the Russian government and the pro-Moscow Chechen

FIGURE 3.1. Chechen women hold photos of their disappeared children during a protest in Grozny on Saturday, March 22, 2003. Photograph by Musa Sadulaev. © Musa Sadulaev/AP Photo.

administration. The March 2003 referendum marked the beginning of a new political campaign by the Russian authorities to ensure not only that Chechnya remain an integral part of the Russian Federation under the pretense of a democratic referendum but that the pro-Moscow Chechen administration in Grozny begin to assume responsibility for the country's political fate. While subsequent reports spoke of the empty polling booths on March 23, making official claims of a 98 percent turnout highly specious, the referendum was the first of a series of events that sought to institutionalize the new political doctrine.[12]

Five weeks before the 2003 referendum, Sergei Kovalev, Russia's former human rights commissioner, arrived in Washington, D.C. He spoke openly before the American Foreign Policy Council and in closed-door meetings at the U.S. Senate on death squads in the tradition of Latin America in the 1970s working inside Chechnya. Whether or not a formal official policy existed, the evidence showed that there was unspoken consent among the major decision-makers to employ death squads. Although it was obvious that the Russian armed forces were involved in perpetrating these crimes, identifying the perpetrators was as difficult here as it had been in bringing to justice those who had conducted the large-scale sweep operations. Which departments were instrumental—the Ministry of the Interior (MVD), the Federal Security Bureau (FSB), the Main Intelligence Directorate (GRU), or the 42nd Motorized Rifle Division, permanently stationed in Chechnya—remains unconfirmed.[13] By the end of 2002, Chechnya had become the Caucasian counterpart to the countries of the Southern Cone, if not in scale, then certainly in tone. It was not long before the appropriate label of "dirty war" was being applied to the conflict.

Chechenization

The rise in targeted disappearances in 2003 signaled a shift in the political as much as the military landscape. Moscow's Chechen protégés began to cooperate with the Russian Ministry of the Interior, the Ministry of Defense, and the FSB beginning in late 2002. And although it was widely held that the Russian Special Forces were responsible for disappearances for the first three years of the war, by 2003 witness testimonies revealed the presence of men speaking Chechen, or mixed Chechen and Russian, arriving either alone or with Russian troops in silver VAZ-2199s. One Russian military intelligence officer working in the mountainous region of southern Chechnya observed, "Thirty percent are kidnapped and killed as a result of criminal rivalries between Chechens themselves. Twenty percent are on the conscience of the insurgents who destroy those cooperating with the federal authorities. And fifty percent we destroy. There is simply no other way with our sold-out court system."[14] These statistics were well-known and clearly disseminated by Russian forces as a means of undermining the role of both Russian and pro-Moscow Chechen forces in the escalating pattern of disappearances. According to one human rights activist, the suggestion that 50 percent of the disappearances were the responsibility of Chechen separatist forces was, for all intents and purposes, a "complete fabrication."[15]

By tenuously shifting power back to the fragile world of Chechen *politik*, however, the Russian government submerged Chechnya in a political identity torn between radical fighters under Shamil Basaev, moderates under Aslan Maskhadov, and a pro-Moscow contingent under Akhmat Kadyrov, head of the Temporary Administration in Chechnya —with seemingly violent ties between them all. The face of the Chechen conflict changed dramatically. While Kadyrov had switched sides in 1999, it was not until the end of 2002 that most of the key bureaucratic and administrative posts were occupied either by his forces or by those of Beslan Gantemirov, the former mayor of Grozny. With the authority to appoint local heads of district administrations and members of the Chechen government at his own discretion beginning 2002,[16] Kadyrov also consolidated Chechnya's most violent and powerful security agency, the "Kadyrovtsy," headed by his twenty-eight-year-old son, Ramzan Kadyrov, in order to deal with his own internal threats. Made up of former separatist fighters amnestied under a guarantee from Kadyrov, by 2004 the Kadyrovtsy had become the most terrifying armed contingent in Chechnya.

"Chechenization" was a simple enough idea. It was nothing more than the tried-and-true method of "divide and rule." Anxious to establish a monocentric regime, the modus operandi of the Russian government was to strengthen local organs of power and security structures with civilian and pro-Moscow personnel, adopt a constitution that would ensure Chechnya's status as part of the Russian Federation, and elect a regional president. Yet transferring powers incrementally to Kadyrov also meant establishing a growing dependence on the new Chechen administrative structures. Kadyrov managed to create a local space that was almost impossible for those on the outside to penetrate. And in creating an armed force that understood the social texture of Chechen society, he established a more effective, although no less brutal, structure than the Russian armed forces. The political culture changed irrevocably.

Kadyrov's ultimate aim was to force the separatist fighters to *change sides*. For the Chechen leader, the key to the success of Chechenization was to recruit Chechen fighters back into the local police force and administration. And various methods were employed to achieve this. Kadyrov sought to strengthen his growing sphere of influence by offering separatist fighters the opportunity to surrender. No formal amnesty was available until September 2006, despite a weak attempt in October 1999 to amnesty those reluctant to fight. Yet the terms driving the surrender were highly problematic. Each ex-fighter was forced to join Kadyrov's newly appointed law enforcement agencies or combat units to fight the Chechen separatists. It later became known as the "Grey," or "Kadyrov," amnesty. The message was unambiguous. By appointing ex-fighters well aware of local realities, customs, and *teip* allegiances, Kadyrov sought to build a network of *dependent* former fighters bound by blood to his clan, the Benoi, in an attempt to close the door firmly on the past. Many fighters did not, however, agree to surrender. They were captured on the basis of local intelligence. And the methods employed to force them to join Kadyrov's forces were as brutal as those adopted by the Russian armed forces at the filtration points—torture, threats, and coercion were customary.[17] As one victim recalled:

> Five or six people, all Chechens in camouflage and masks, entered the room. They checked my documents. Then they said: "Dress warmly." I got dressed. They put my hat low over my eyes and fixed it with scotch tape. . . .
>
> They put me in a car and drove for a while. They were silent. We arrived at an unknown house, walked up the stairs and through some low entrance. Then they put me on a bench, attached wires to my two big toes and started questioning me. All the time the hat was over my eyes. "When was the last time you went to Baku? When was the last time you saw Doku Umarov or Akhmed [Zakaev]? Where are your children?"
>
> My answers did not satisfy them. No matter what I said, they would beat me with sticks. Although they spoke Russian, they were all Chechens. Sometimes, I answered something in Chechen, but they pretended not to understand. They continued to speak Russian. There were a few of them—how many exactly, I don't know. They beat me on the back, in the heart area. They had different sticks. . . . My scalp still burns.
>
> This continued for about an hour. Then, I was taken first outside, then down the stairs, then to a cold basement. When we were walking down, the one who was escorting me told me in Chechen: "Someone has reported you. We will check it, and if everything is normal, we will let you go. And we will punish the one who told on you." It was the first time that someone spoke Chechen to me.[18]

Some fighters did manage to negotiate their release and were able to return to civilian life without criminal punishment or forced recruitment into Kadyrov's own private army.[19] Other victims simply disappeared.

By the end of 2003, it had become clear that Chechen forces were working with Russian Special Forces, contributing to a centrally orchestrated policy of abductions by providing much-needed military intelligence and personnel. Far more systematic raids began on private homes at night, and the abducted, predominantly Chechen males between the ages of fifteen and fifty, were picked up on roads, in cafés, or in markets.[20]

The brutality of Kadyrov's forces deeply undermined Chechen identity.[21] Although this sense of self-identification had already been acutely challenged with the radicalization of layers of Chechen society since 1991, Kadyrov had once been a loyal supporter of the separatist cause, fighting the Russian armed forces under Aslan Maskhadov during the first Chechen war. While Kadyrov could not sanction the radicals nor attempt to appease them as Maskhadov was trying to do, many felt that his treatment of moderate separatist forces was an alarming development. And it no doubt dramatized the changing contours of Chechen interrelations. By 2003 the Chechens were responsible for killing and torturing their own people, taking their own initiative to seek out those placed hors de combat, destroying any notion of an organic society bound by its own internal traditions. No longer were the Chechen separatists united in their opposition to the Russian state; they were killing each other, moderates and radicals alike in a new period of invisible violence.

This lawless disregard for international law continued undeterred on both sides. The policy of disappearances extended to abducting the relatives of separatist fighters as hostages. Vladimir Ustinov, Russia's prosecutor general, suggested that the Russian parliament adopt a new antiterrorist law that would allow "counter hostage taking"—detaining rebel fighters' relatives in order to force the fighters to surrender. The initiative was supported by Chechnya's second pro-Moscow president, Alu Alkhanov, who promised the implementation of such a law, should it be adopted. Although the prosecutor general subsequently retracted his proposal, and the general consensus in the Russian media about Ustinov's plan was extremely negative,[22] Ramzan Kadyrov said on NTV in June 2004: "We will punish their relatives according to law. They help bandits. . . . We will punish them according to law. And if there is no such law, we will ask for it, we will turn to the Russian State Duma and they will pass such a law so that it becomes possible to punish."[23] This practice, however, was by no means new—Akhmat Kadyrov had already proposed such a strategy and the houses of separatist fighters had been bombed and set on fire since 2000. Yet with the assassination of Kadyrov in a bomb blast in May 2004, the kidnapping of family members grew more systematic. At least twelve people who disappeared over 2004 were relatives of rebel fighters, including eight of Aslan Maskhadov's relatives. The family was released three months after Maskhadov's death in March 2005.

One of the few cases of hostage taking that received publicity in 2004 was that of the family members of Magomed Khambiev, Chechen field commander and minister of defense of the Chechen Republic of Ichkeria. According to various estimates, between February 29 and March 1, forty members of the Khambiev family were kidnaped from different settlements across Chechnya. Mass detentions were carried out in the villages of Meskheti, Benoi, and Turti-Khutor. In Grozny, Aslambek Khambiev, a first-year student at Chechen State University Medical School, was kidnaped. Through intermediaries Magomed Khambiev was delivered a message with a demand to surrender immediately and "voluntarily." He did so to save his relatives. This was a massive blow to the morale of the Chechen separatist movement.

The policy of disappearances in Chechnya by now displayed a more *obvious* coordination that was integral to the success of the Russian armed forces. It was a strategy that evoked fear in suspected and actual separatist fighters. Yet fostering this uncertainty also had a massive impact on the general population. The courage that had defined the Chechen civilians who spoke to human rights organizations in neighboring Ingushetia or their local "fixers"[24] on the ground during 2000 and 2001 shifted with the rise of Ramzan Kadyrov, Akhmat Kadyrov's son. The Kadyrovtsy was formally liquidated after the assassination of Kadyrov senior, and its units were integrated into the Chechen Ministry of the Interior: the Spetsnaz battalions "Vostok" and "Zapad," which are part of the 42nd Motorized Infantry Division of the Russian Ministry of Defense; the Second Road Patrol Regiment of the Police (PPSM-2); and the "Oil Regiment" that guarded the oil refineries, oil pipes, oil products, and other industrial sites and the "antiterrorist centers" (ATCs).[25] While some units were legalized, others were organized into paramilitary formations. Ramzan Kadyrov was appointed vice prime minister on May 9, 2004. Two years later, at the age of thirty—with his renowned brutality—Kadyrov junior became prime minister of Chechnya, bringing Chechenization to its completion.

Frightened of both the Kadyrovtsy and the Russian Special Forces, civilians were no longer willing to talk when Human Rights Watch finally went into Chechnya without permission. "The situation changed dramatically after Ramzan Kadyrov took control," observed Anna Neistat, former director of the Moscow office of Human Rights Watch: "Chechens were extremely brave in 2001. I rarely heard 'What are we going to get from you?' They just said that they wanted the world to know. By 2004, they were just terrified."[26] And the effect of this prolonged state of anxiety was to create a situation in which some grew reluctant to lodge their complaints. "I searched [for him] everywhere, but did not write a petition. . . . Here, many who write petitions 'disappear.' . . . I was afraid. . . . I have two other sons at home. If I were to tell someone, [they] might take them away as well."[27] In a 2005 survey, 30 percent of the victims of human rights violations in rural Chechnya refused to provide details on the crimes, and nearly 80 percent in Grozny refused to give detailed information.[28]

This climate of fear led to a partial social withdrawal. As one civilian confessed, "People inform on each other, they disappear in the night and never return. No one trusts anyone else anymore, because Putin had a stroke of genius: he let Ramzan Kadyrov do the dirty work. Now it's Chechen against Chechen."[29] For those whose daughters were suicide bombers or their sons open separatist fighters, it led to social isolation and punishment. As Seierstad recounts in her book, "There are certain families no-one visits. . . . Former best friends no longer say hello. . . . There are certain people you shouldn't show feelings for or sympathize with. Having contact with these families can lead you into darkness."[30] By 2008, the homes of twelve families with sons suspected of supporting the insurgency had been set ablaze. Parents were being forced onto public television to beg their sons to leave the movement. Armed men arrived in the middle of the night, removed families from their homes, and set homes on fire in front of them. Muslim Khuchiev, the mayor of Grozny, threatened physical torture: "The evil which is done by your relatives in the forest will return to you and your homes. Each of you soon will feel it on your skin."[31]

From 2003 to 2005, 1,265 individuals were abducted.[32] Given the small amount of territory that human rights groups were able to cover, the overall estimate of disappearances between 1999 and 2005 is 3,000–5,000.[33] The disappearances ultimately contributed to the political success of pro-Moscow Chechens who were gradually seeking more power in the region. And the practice of enforced disappearances began to occupy a strange place in the human rights rhetoric of both the Russian and the Chechen governments. In March 2003, the Chechen president, Akhmat Kadyrov, had blamed the Russian armed forces for the abductions.[34] One month later, Rudnik Dudaev, secretary of the Chechen Security Council, ap-

FIGURE 3.2. Chechen women hold photographs of their disappeared children during a protest in Grozny. Undated. Photograph by Musa Sadulaev. © Musa Sadulaev.

peared on local television claiming that 215 Chechens had been abducted so far that year. Used to more cautious statements by the pro-Moscow administration, many found these to be surprising confessions.[35] Others went further. Alu Alkhanov stated in October 2004 that "according to the prosecutor's data, up to seven people a day . . . 'disappear' in the republic."[36] But these statements were entirely disingenuous. In an effort to secure votes for the forthcoming presidential elections, in October 2003 and then again in August 2004, Kadyrov and Alkhanov had, respectively, displayed an unsettling level of hypocrisy and political game playing that distorted the truth of who was involved in the abductions. In denouncing the measures of the Russian armed forces, both leaders sought to falsely perpetuate a public image of innocence that placed the blame on the Russian government. Clearly keen to establish a political persona *distinct* from Russian forces, the pro-Moscow administration did not want to give the impression at home that it would passively submit to the dominance of the Russian military.

The Civilian Prosecutor's Office in Chechnya began opening criminal investigations into cases of the disappeared as early as 2001. And these investigations may well have been undertaken with genuine concern and legitimacy, and with the intent of bringing the perpetrators to justice. But if

FIGURE 3.3. Slogan for the presidential campaign of August 2004: "No to sweep operations! No to terror! No to the war!—Alu Alkhanov." Photograph by Musa Sadulaev. © Musa Sadulaev.

cases were opened with justice in mind, the majority of the investigations resolved neither the question of the whereabouts of the disappeared nor the question of who was responsible. And despite the oppositional stance of the families, they were ridiculed in their quest for answers. Taus Dzhabrailov, the chairman of the State Council of the Chechen Republic, which ostensibly performed the duties of the republic's parliament, claimed that the Chechen Prosecutor's Office had opened 1,814 criminal cases into the abductions of 2,540 people that had occurred from 1999 to 2005.[37] For 2004, the prosecutor had stated: "Seven members of law enforcement agencies were found criminally responsible for crimes related to abductions." No details, however, were ever provided on these cases. By 2007, Memorial concluded that out of the 1,650 cases in their files the majority of cases had been suspended for lack of evidence.[38] As in the majority of cases concerning the actions of the Russian armed forces, investigations were dutifully opened but case files were shuttled *back and forth* between the civilian and military prosecutors in a routine exercise of evasion. Unable to question military personnel or carry out investigations at military sites to collect evidence, the Civilian Prosecutor's Office, legitimately or not—subject to intimidation or not—was paralyzed in its work. This dual system of jurisdiction protected the Russian military and the pro-Moscow Chechen administration from punishment time and time again.

Summary Executions and Mass Graves

Disappearances undoubtedly marked the final collapse of the judicial edifice in Chechnya. The legal question as to whether captured fighters, those placed hors de combat, or innocent civilians were prisoners of war or criminal suspects completely vanished in the process. Some of the disappeared were later discovered in unmarked graves across the region. The most well-known case was the discovery of a mass grave in the abandoned summer-cottage village of Dachnyi in February 2001. The grave was astonishing for its location: a heavily guarded area situated just a few hundred yards away from the Russian military headquarters at Khankala, where many had been detained and imprisoned since the base had been established on January 25, 2000, on the Grozny-Argun road. In February 2001, relatives of the detained arrived at Dachnyi to find bodies scattered among deserted summer cottages—in cellars, on verandas, or in the bushes. Magomed Musaev discovered his sixteen-year-old son, who had been detained in the village of Raduzhnoe, lying face down in three inches of snow with gunshot wounds to his right lung and heart.[39] Abdurashid Metaev found his brother Odes "in a half collapsed country house at the entrance on the porch. When I found him, he was lying on his stomach . . . his hands were bound with cord . . . two of his digits were missing on one of his hands . . . one of his ears was missing, he had been blindfolded. Odes' ear had been removed when he was still alive, because his face was covered in blood."[40] Fifty bodies were found at Dachnyi, although several had been ransomed back to the families before the forensic experts or human rights organizations were allowed in. Adam Chimaev's family had ransomed their son's body back on February 15 for the equivalent of US$3,000. How many others were ransomed before an official forensic investigation was completed is not known.

Vsevolod Chernov, the civilian prosecutor of Chechnya, visited the site on February 24. The area was closed until March 2 and the bodies transferred to a Ministry of Emergencies site in numbered body bags. Although the bodies were on display for identification, thirty-four unclaimed bodies were buried in a field near the village on March 10.[41] Of the fifty bodies, seventeen were identified by Memorial as having disappeared during sweep operations conducted by the Russian armed forces during 2000 and early

2001 in Raduzhnoe, Dolinskii, Grozny, Alkhan-Iurt, Alkhan-Kala, and Urus-Martan. The central question with regard to the graves was whether those discovered in them had been separatist fighters killed in combat. At first, Chernov alleged that the corpses were separatist fighters dumped after an internal struggle. The majority of victims when discovered were blindfolded, or had their hands tied behind their backs with cloth or wire, and their bodies were mutilated (heads scalped, noses cut off). They all had been shot in the chest, stomach, or head. They were not shot in combat. The fact that their bodies were mutilated strongly suggests that they were detained, tortured, and then summarily executed with no due process.[42] Of the four women discovered at Khankala, "the hands, legs and eyes of most were bound with wire or cloth, most bore gunshot wounds in the stomach and chest area, and in the head, several had been scalped."[43]

The astounding feature of the Dachnyi mass grave is that no effort was made to conceal the bodies. The corpses were not buried at one grave site but strewn across an area as if it were a dumping ground. The bodies were examined by forensic experts, but there was no evidence that there were conditions available in Grozny for a comprehensive forensic examination. According to Memorial, the Grozny public prosecutor lacked the essential equipment and the apparatus necessary to gather photographic and video evidence of the bodies or the site where they had been found. The thirty-four corpses buried in the field, with the bullets still intact, cast some doubt on Chernov's claims that a thorough examination had been undertaken.[44] The forensic experts, however, were successful in determining the cause of death and the approximate time of death, and were able to identify the nature of the wounds.

But Dachnyi was just one of many graves; it just happened to receive the most publicity. A total of forty-nine graves were recognized by official sources in Chechnya from 1999 to February 2002. A thirty-page confidential draft report from the Department of the Search for Missing Persons, stated the following:

> On places of Mass Graves of Civilians on the Territory of the Chechen Republic [Spravka] from February 26, 2002. Information from the Ministry of Emergencies of the Chechen Republic. Signed by Sh.B. Abdurakhmanov, head of the Department of the Search for Missing Persons of the Chechen Republic.
>
> Central cemetery of Grozny (260),
> Cemetery of the 12 *uchastke* of Grozny (141),

Prigorodnoe (106),
Sovkhoz 60 octoberia (109),
Goiskoe (699),
Proletarskoe (17),
Alkhan-Kala (35),
Aldy (22),
Tolstoi Iurt (9),
Urus-Martan (13),
Berdikel' (5),
Chechen-Aul (6),
Pervomaiskoe (13),
Staraia Sunzha (13),
Shali (9),
Karpinskii Kurgan (10),
Belgatoi (2),
Starye Atagi (2),
Goiti (5),
Achkhoi-Martan (3),
Ingush Republic (9),
Pobedinskoe (4),
s/z "Rodina" (1),
15 Mol. Sovkhoz (2),
Valerik (2),
Gekhi (2),
Butenko (10),
Assinovskaia (3),
Lermontovo (1),
Shalazhi (1),
Borzoi (1),
Orekhovo (1),
Kirov (3),
Alkhan Iurt (2),
Petropavlovskaia (2),
Berkat Iurt (5),
Katyr Iurt (1),
Bratskoe (4),
Novye Atagi (1),
Argun (2),
Nozhai-Iurt (1),

Andreevskaia Dolina (1),
Germenchuk (1),
Novogroznyi (1),
Khasav Iurt (2),
Kulary (1),
Shelkovskoi raion s. Kobi (1),
Sernovodskaia (2),
Dachnyi poselok n.p. "Khankala" (43)
Total—2,879[45]

One aspect of this report was in question, however. The 699 corpses found in the village of Goiskoe were mostly Chechen fighters killed in March 2000 in the battle for Komsomolskoe. The report was no doubt authentic, but it was incomplete. An exact calculation of the number of graves in Chechnya has never been completed. There was no mention of a grave that contained 74 bodies, discovered in June 2000 in the vicinity of the Urus-Martan-Tangi-Chu road. Nor has the discrepancy in numbers between Memorial's figure of 50 corpses discovered at Khankala, and the 43 mentioned in the list, ever been disputed. Information was also later disclosed on 10 smaller graves, containing two to ten bodies each.[46] All the aforementioned graves contained the bodies of those who had been detained earlier by the Russian armed forces. Beginning approximately in the spring of 2001, Russian troops began to blast the corpses of their victims in forests or gardens, making it increasingly difficult to discover the remains. Human rights groups began to suspect that many of the corpses were being eaten by wild or feral animals. Two examples of such places where remains have been found were Michurin, a collective farm close to Urus-Martan, and the Chernorechenskii forest near the road leading from the Rostov-Baku Highway into the village of Goiti.

* * *

The hallmark of a disappearance is that the state authorities neither accept responsibility for the disappearance nor account for the whereabouts of the victim.[47] While the Russian government continued to deny allegations of torture, it openly acknowledged that the practice of abductions and "missing" persons was a problem in the region.[48] At the end of 2004, a representative of Russia's prosecutor general stated that 2,437 persons had been abducted since 1999 and that the fate of 2,090 remained unknown.[49] But there was a stark refusal to accept responsibility for the act itself by identifying the perpetrators. The Russian government was well aware of the international advocacy campaign against enforced disappearances since the "dirty war" in Argentina in the 1970s and, more recently, the disappearances in Lebanon or Palestine suspected to have been perpetrated by Syrian security forces. While the Russian armed forces could frame the violations that occurred during sweep operations as inadvertent, it was difficult to argue around the deliberate, orchestrated nature of targeted disappearances. The Russian government clearly recognized that human rights organizations were framing the systematic nature of the disappearances as a crime against humanity. The Russian delegation at the UN suddenly became skeptical about the idea of an international Convention for the Protection of All Persons from Enforced Disappearances that had been gaining rapid ground since 2000. Beginning in 2003, the Russian delegation began to systematically torpedo every provision of the convention, openly obstructing and marginalizing the debate, along with the United States and Algeria.[50] In an effort to take the onus off of state actors, the Russian delegation proposed including private actors in the convention, which not only would allow states to blame disappearances on individuals or alleged non-state actors but would defy the intent of the convention. The mark of an enforced disappearance is that it forms part of a *state* strategy to deal with alleged or real enemies. In addition, the delegation opposed defining enforced disappearances as a crime against humanity.[51] The crescendo of the Russian opposition was a vicious personal attack on the chairman of the working group challenging his authority. Despite the slander, in December 2006 the convention was passed, ending a twenty-three-year advocacy campaign by relatives of the disappeared in Argentina.

The logic at work in the policy of disappearances in Chechnya was twofold. It was clearly designed to serve the military aims of the counterterrorist operation by providing an easy solution to the problem of how to capture suspected or real enemies. And disappearances often form a blurred picture: responsibility could be apportioned anywhere—between the Russians and the Chechens, non-state actors, intra-Chechen rivalries, vendettas, or economic infighting. The practice of disappearances also alleviated the problem of having to deal with the question central to the second Chechen war—how could this war be categorized under international humanitarian law? Human rights organizations argue that the majority of the disappeared were most likely persons who were placed hors de combat by sickness, wounds, or any number of causes.[52] But whether the men or women were civilians, those placed hors de combat or separatist fighters, and whether or not the abducted and disappeared had any ties to the separatist movement is irrelevant. They should have been arrested, charged, and given a lawyer—the normal patterns of habeas corpus should have been followed. Moreover, as the United States pursued its policy of rendition, abducting terrorist suspects off the streets of Germany and Italy and holding them in Guantanamo, Jordan, or Syria, abductions were already being sanctioned by some Western elites. As the conflict in Chechnya endured, however, Chechenization allowed the blame for human rights violations to be transferred from the Russian armed forces to local structures. During the debates on the Parliamentary Assembly of the Council of Europe (PACE) Resolution on Chechnya of October 2004, the Russian delegation insisted that responsibility for the disappearances and hostage taking be *shared* by the Russian and Chechen forces.[53] Moreover, when the Chechen Constitution had been adopted following what was believed to be the rigged referendum in March 2003, all responsibility for the protection of human rights was officially transferred to the local structures.[54]

The Russian armed forces certainly sought to build on the notion that disappearances were *organic* to traditional culture in Chechnya. This was directly linked to the history of kidnaping that defined the interwar years. If human rights organizations succeeded in organizing a war crimes tribunal, then blame could be apportioned to Chechens killing each other. In addition, disappearances diminished the number of testimonies on the wide-scale use of torture taking place in the region. And this may explain the subsequent practice of blowing up corpses with explosives in regional forests.[55] Strategically, it was far simpler for the Russian government to acknowledge to international audiences that disappearances were indeed occurring. It was much harder to counter accounts of torture taking place in Russian detention centers run by the Ministry of the Interior and the Ministry of Justice.

When thinking about motivation and the disappearances, the parameters of understanding do indeed shift during this period. There were some cases of plunder during the abductions, although extortion appeared less of a motivating factor. Certainly, intra-Chechen rivalries may have been connected to economic issues around oil, distribution of budgets, or business. Yet we do not witness the same economic motivation driving the act itself. As with much of the second Chechen war, it would be a mistake to see the racial prejudice in isolation from wider social and military relations. Of consequence here is that the early extermination of Chechen separatists undertaken by the Russian armed forces suggests higher degrees of racial motivation. By the time the pro-Moscow Chechen militias became involved, *political* identities had grown into more significant categories of identification than earlier observed. The ideas about racial prejudice, almost certainly after the involvement of Chechen forces, shifted here. In gaining more power, the Chechen forces were able to narrowly focus the target of attack to suit both their own military agenda and a *teip*- or class-based allegiance within their own elites. In doing so, they forced a larger turn away from the collective punishment that defined 1999–2003 to a concentrated political goal.

President Putin ended up with Ramzan Kadyrov—his thuggish tactics perpetuated an atmosphere of violence of an order far larger than that associated with Aslan Maskhadov. Pacifying Chechnya therefore meant giving legitimacy to a man who adopted the same tactics as the Russian armed forces and on whom they could rely. Displaying an equal indifference to the pain of the Chechen civilians, Kadyrov's forces continued to torture in the Ministry of the Interior's Operative Search Bureau (Operativno-Rozysknye Biuro) (ORB) No. 2 in Grozny and perpetuated a culture of personality politics. Once again the Chechens were left with a political identity that only deepened the differences between Chechens instead of bringing them closer together. While Chechen society reached a level of relative *external* stability, the undercurrent of violence remained an unresolved reality.

4

FINDING REFUGE

We dread for our lives if we return to Grozny, particularly for the lives of our sons.
—*Female Chechen IDP, Znamenskoe tent camp, Chechnya, June 2002*

Nobody is standing with a gun to my head, forcing me to leave. But they are telling me that the school will be closed tomorrow, that they will turn off the electricity and gas here in two weeks. Now, you tell me if my decision to return is voluntary.
—*Chechen IDP, Satsita tent camp, Ingushetia, February 2004*

Legally? How would I come legally? There is absolutely no way to enter through the border without paying bribes. Those times are gone.
—*Chechen asylum seeker, Ukraine*

THE BOMBING CAMPAIGN over the winter of 1999–2000 resulted in the displacement of more than 250,000[1] Chechen civilians across the border into neighboring Ingushetia. This mass exodus quickly brought into question the very *nature* of the Russian government's "antiterrorist operation" inside Chechnya. Claims of precision strikes directed at terrorist bases were undermined by the presence of thousands of civilians, in cars, in trucks, and on foot, waiting anxiously near the village of Assinovskaia. The displaced population of Chechnya soon became the most important source of information for journalists and human rights monitors, who were prohibited from entering the region without official sanction. Yet it was the sudden emergence of rows and rows of tent camps in Ingushetia run by the Russian Ministry of Emergencies (EMERCOM), the UN Refugee Agency (UNHCR), the Danish Refugee Council (DRC), the International Committee of the Red Cross (ICRC), Islamic Relief, and the Czech organization People in Need (PIN) to shelter the rapidly growing IDP population that posed the greatest challenge to the Russian government. Over five consecutive winters, the tent camps and the battered train wagons in which people sought shelter stood as testimony to the defiance of the civilian population—*physical* reminders that the war across the border was far from over. Every day brought new evidence that the violence continued, and thousands of IDPs preferred to eke out an impoverished and miserable existence on humanitarian aid than to face an uncertain future in Chechnya. The very presence of the IDP population in the villages of Karabulak and Sleptsovskaia proved to be a complex problem for the Russian authorities. How could the government legitimate its claims that the "antiterrorist operation" was over when thousands of IDPs refused to move back to Chechnya because they feared for their personal safety? The result was that the displaced of Chechnya soon found themselves the victims of a series of political maneuvers that not only denied them an appropriate legal status but sought to force them back across the border under the government policy of "normalization."

Evacuation Routes

The long and tense relationship between the Russian authorities and the displaced population of Chechnya began with the failure of the Russian government to provide safe evacuation routes out of the war-torn republic. Denied the protection of a state of emergency, Chechen civilians struggled to find safe refuge well before 250,000 displaced crossed the border into Ingushetia. Unlike the first war, when Sergei Kovalev, Russia's human rights commissioner, and his colleagues from Memorial, went from house to house organizing lists for the evacuation of civilians in buses organized by the Ingush government, *no* evacuation routes or safe transport were provided at the outset of the second war. When the bombing began on September 22, civilians started leaving Grozny and the surrounding regions of Urus-Martan and Achkhoi-Martan. The first main route was along the Rostov-Baku Highway through checkpoint Kavkaz 1 and into Ingushetia. Miles of cars were backed up on the highway and civilians were eventually permitted across the border by foot. The second main route was north of Grozny into Stavropolskii Krai, through the Oktyabr'skii checkpoint, and into Mozdok, North Ossetia.[2] Several thousand civilians also traveled south by foot, through the mountains of Chechnya into Georgia, with some finding refuge in Pankisi Gorge while others moved further on to Turkey and Azerbaijan.

Other borders were simply closed, such as those to Dagestan and Kabardino-Balkariia.[3] "It's impossible [to allow them in] after what has happened, after Chechen bandits sought to take over our land," declared Mukha Aliev, Dagestan's parliamentary speaker.[4] When the Russian journalist Anna Politkovskaia questioned Zamir Kalov, head of the Migration Ministry of Kabardino-Balkariia, as to why his government had not made public its refusal to accept IDPs and perhaps it should do so, he answered flatly, "No, what for?"[5] Russian major general Vladimir Shamanov ordered all Ministry of the Interior (MVD) units to *block* the exit of Chechen civilians through Ingushetia in a telegram dispatched on September 25, 1999.[6] This order was not uniformly applied, but the exchange of money for personal safety was. Forbidding civilians from passing through checkpoints for no other reason than personal whim or failure to pay a bribe was a constant and barbaric feature of the second war. Bribery was ubiquitous both at checkpoints inside Chechnya and at border checkpoints Kavkaz 1 and Oktyabr'skii. The price list was published by *Novaia Gazeta* on December 6—one person on foot was 100 rubles, a light vehicle was 500–600 rubles, and the transfer of a corpse was 1,000 rubles.[7] According to the Chechen surgeon Khassan Baiev, "I passed the time walking along the lines of cars to the border post, which was manned by Russian troops and Ingush police. I watched with disgust as the Russian soldiers turned back the refugees unless they produced a bribe. Most of the drivers paid up without protest."[8]

It was the closure of Kavkaz 1, however, that testified to the determination of the Russian authorities to control the flow of civilians. The surface-to-surface missile attacks that hit the Centralnii market in Grozny, a maternity hospital, and the local mosque in Kalinina on October 21 produced a mass exodus of civilians. Eight days later Russian air artillery struck an IDP convoy with five clearly marked Red Cross cars, killing at least twenty-five civilians and two Red Cross workers when the line of cars and trucks was forced to turn back from the closed border. A "humanitarian corridor" had been announced on RTR and ORT television broadcasts, but no formal process was implemented to regulate the evacuation. The civilian population, many of whom were cold and starving, were rescued by the defiant acts of the staff of UNHCR, who stood at the border demanding that the checkpoint be opened in front of the international media.[9] The popular Ingush president, Ruslan Aushev, also insisted that the border be opened.[10] In a characteristically angry outburst, Aushev posited, "OK, so we don't have a humanitarian catastrophe," he insisted, "but I would call it a human tragedy. When 200,000 people are displaced from one place to another, isn't this a catastrophe? Unfortunately, the Russian Federation has become the true successor to the Soviet Union, where a person's life is worth nothing."[11]

Soon thereafter President Aushev was vilified in the pages of the Moscow daily *Nezavisimaia Gazeta* for his efforts to help the Chechens. Led by Dmitrii Rogozin of the Rodina (Motherland) political party and the future Russian spokesman at the Council of Europe, the attack was later titled the "anti-Ingush syndrome."[12] Using the standard nationalist rhetoric, the young politician led a campaign accusing the Ingush president of taking "an anti-Russian position" and denounced him for insisting that the Russian government negotiate with the elected Chechen president, Aslan Maskhadov, and for falsifying the number of IDPs, allegedly for financial gain. In *Vremia MN*, Stepan Dvornikov and Anna Feofilaktova followed Rogozin's lead, arguing that Aushev was using the situation to "acquire money and humanitarian perks from the federal center."[13] Aushev had certainly sought to assert his independence against the power of the federal center in the past, but it was his humane actions with regard to the civilian population of Chechnya that served as the conscience of the Northern Caucasus that winter. But Rogozin's words merely foreshadowed later developments in PACE when the young nationalist, in the spirit of Vladimir Zhirinovskii, would use the European forum for his crude oratorical musings.

The failure to evacuate the capital, Grozny, however, became the most symbolic event. This was the decisive moment when the Russian government unashamedly revealed that it was prepared to subject the civilian population of Chechnya to a massive bombing campaign in order to take back the capital. While many civilians from the countryside had either stayed or fled the republic, the fate of an estimated fifteen to forty thousand civilians still trapped in Grozny by land mines laid by separatist forces to fortress the city and by bombardment by the Russian armed forces was unclear. The answer soon came in the form of the infamous leaflets dropped on the city on December 6, 1999, demanding that civilians remaining in Grozny leave within five days or face destruction.[14] The crude logic was that fifteen to forty thousand civilians, if unable to move out of fear for their personal safety, or because of age, physical illness, or lack of financial means, might well be sacrificed for the defeat of several thousand separatist fighters. But as the pressure from the international community increased, Françoise Bouchet-Saulnier of Médecins Sans Frontières (MSF) stood outside the Russian Embassy in Oslo, as MSF received its Nobel Peace Prize, in protest against the leaflet.[15]

The outrage worked. Two evacuation routes were organized. The first was from Chernorech'e to Alkhan-Iurt. Russia's minister for emergencies, Sergei Shoigu, waited with buses and trucks for civilians stuck in Grozny on December 12 in what appeared to be an act staged as much for the international press as for the Chechen civilian population. Shoigu gave out his cell phone number for those who wanted to leave and the gesture appeared a little strained after two months of disregarding the problem. The second evacuation route was situated northwest, heading from the Staropromyslovskii district to the village of Pervomaiskoe. According to witness testimony, both routes organized by EMERCOM worked very efficiently once in operation, transporting many to the safety of the tent camps in Znamenskoe and Sernovodsk in northern Chechnya.[16] But, ultimately, there was still no *cease-fire* to ease the process. Daily bombings of Grozny and the surrounding regions continued in the midst of the evacuation.[17]

The reasons for the Russian government's failure to establish evacuation routes at the very beginning of this campaign appear numerous. But two fundamental themes emerge from this environment, suggesting that this was more than mere negligence. The first rested with the question of ensuring that the crisis in Chechnya remained contained, that it continued to take on the *appearance* of a precision operation with minimum material damage and human collateral. Organizing safe transport would have amounted to an admission of the scale of the violence in Chechnya, and readily available safe transport might have encouraged more civilians to leave, creating a larger humanitarian crisis across the border. Moreover, being able to contain information about what was taking place inside Chechnya was also contingent on keeping the IDPs inside the republic. Indeed, the displaced did become the most important source of information for journalists and human rights monitors. In addition, opening evacuation routes would have contradicted the Russian government's central argument that it was international terrorists, and *not* the Russian bombing campaign, that were ultimately responsible for the mass exodus of the civilian population over the winter of 1999–2000.[18]

The failure to evacuate the civilian population constituted one of Russia's deepest failures of principle and leadership, in both the first and the second wars in Chechnya. And while the political questions at play were far from uncomplicated, safe evacuation of Chechen civilians should have been an uncompromising feature of this war. This failure merely mounted resentment toward the Russian government and reaffirmed a growing consensus among many civilians that they were being targeted as part of a larger campaign of racial destruction.[19]

The Humanitarian Response and Forced Migrant Status

When the IDPs first arrived in Ingushetia they sought shelter wherever they could—in rented apartments, with relatives and host families, in tent camps, in barns, in railway wagons, and in deserted factory buildings, or at "sites of compact living" (*kompakniki*),[20] also known as "spontaneous settlements." The Ingush landscape was soon dominated by IDP camps that grew more expansive over the years. Schools were established, as well as legal-counseling centers and teacher-training centers. Approximately twenty thousand Chechen civilians sought refuge in rusted railway carriages moved from St. Petersburg, Moscow, Astrakhan, Arkhangelsk, and the Urals, or in tent camps, first organized by EMERCOM, some 3.5 miles from the border in Sleptsovskaia.[21] The distribution of the IDP population was as follows: approximately 65 percent in private housing or with hosts, 20 percent in spontaneous settlements, and 15 percent in organized camps.[22]

For those without independent means, the conditions were especially dire. Families lived on old collective farms, in hangars, in oil or canning factories, in cellars, or in vacant warehouses as they waited for places in the tent camps as the winter months approached. There were an estimated 55 spontaneous settlements in Ingushetia, with the smallest holding around 40 people and the largest around 1,000.[23] Uchkhoz was in the village of Yandare, on a former state agricultural enterprise;[24] SMU No. 4[25] was at the site of a former construction company; MTF No. 1[26] was on a dairy farm. The Logovaz and Kamaz camps were set up on a market site in the Ingush capital, Nazran,[27] and MRO Rassvet was a huge warehouse with garages, auto and tractor repair shops, and storage facilities.[28] In Plievo, people lived on a poultry farm and in a deserted electric power plant. The first tent camp, Bart, was established in Karabulak by EMERCOM with 4,900 IDPs.[29] A month later, Severnyi emerged in Sleptsovskaia, with a capacity for 4,600 civilians in tents and 1,500 in train wagons. Sputnik, the largest of the camps, housed 9,000 displaced on a former chicken farm.[30] Zvesdnyi, along with Zh/D Tupikakh Nos. 1 and 2, was home to 4,600 IDPs and thirty wagons with 1,500 residents. The smallest of the camps was Iman in the village of Aki-Iurt, with 3,000 civilians. By 2000–2001, the first fully equipped tent camps, with floors, stoves, water, and electricity—Alina, Bella, and Satsita—had been built under the auspices of the UN Refugee Agency, the International Committee of the Red Cross, and the Red Crescent Society.

Essential to the effectiveness of humanitarian action is free access to victims and thorough evaluation of their needs. And the Russian authorities did not obstruct the work of the international or local aid agencies in the early part of the second war.[31] There is no doubt that this approach helped avert a major humanitarian crisis. Adopting a collaborative approach, the agencies worked together with EMERCOM, the Ingush authorities, and the UN Office for the Coordination of Humanitarian Affairs (OCHA) to coordinate aid distribution.[32] Delivering rations was the first and primary role of major agencies like the UN Refugee Agency, the UN World Food Programme (WFP), the Danish Refugee Council, Hilfswerk, and Islamic Relief. The International Rescue Committee (IRC) focused on the spontaneous settlements, distributing blankets, mattresses, and material to raise bedding off the floor; providing electricity and gas, water, and sanitation;[33] and setting up tent schools, teacher-training workshops, and accredited school courses for children. Médecins Sans Frontières and the International Committee of the Red Cross zeroed in on mobile clinics, emergency evacuation facilities, the distribution of medical supplies and equipment, and the provision of medical consultation and psychosocial counseling. For the estimated 125,000 displaced *inside* Chechnya, People in Need (PIN) first reached the capital in January 2000. Distributing food for the World Food Programme, PIN was also responsible for taking in water filters, sanitary materials, washing powder, soap, and basic building materials for roofing—nails, tiles, and plastic sheeting.

The Russian and international aid organizations managed to carve out a delicate but vital role in Ingushetia and later in the northern regions of Chechnya.[34] Unlike the bitter attitude they held toward human rights organizations, the Russian government largely accepted humanitarian agencies. No doubt seen as nonpolitical bodies whose sole responsibility was to alleviate the immediate problems of shelter, food, and medical aid, their presence was accepted as constructive and imperative to avert a full-blown crisis. Shaped to respond to individual needs, any humanitarian operation has its political limitations, and the operations in Russia were no different. Whether the international aid agencies could have leveraged more political influence from their position will always be open to question. Yet it was exactly the essentialist decisions that shape humanitarian work that were integral to saving lives in the winter of 1999–2000. Moreover, the very presence of international organizations, and NGOs, provided a much-needed safe haven for civilians away from the war. This long-term protection was vital.

The life of the IDPs was one of considerable deprivation and fear, however. They relied heavily on aid—food, clothing, and medical care—for close to five years. They were uncertain about the future, how long the war would last. And the long-term repercussions of camp life had already emerged by the winter of 2000–2001. While food supplies appeared relatively stable, immune systems were compromised by the lack of vitamins and variety in food; acute respiratory infections and tuberculosis spread as a result of the dampness and cold on the ground and the slow winterization of leaking tents. There was serious overcrowding in the tents and an insufficient number of latrines. Access to specialized medicine, oncologists, tuberculosis treatments, and gynecologists was a growing problem. The hospitals in Ingushetia were not equipped to handle so many extra patients. Ongoing problems existed with access to the simple necessities of everyday life—mattresses, bedding, winter clothing, and cooking utensils.[35]

The protection offered by international humanitarian agencies and by Ingush and Russian representatives of EMERCOM served another, less auspicious, purpose. The tented life kept civilians trapped inside a cycle of dependence. And this predicament was by no means the fault of the humanitarian agencies but was linked directly to the refusal of the Russian government to grant Chechen civilians appropriate legal status as internally displaced persons under Russian national law. Not recognized legally, displaced Chechen civilians were categorically denied the range of rights open to ethnic Russians. On arrival in Ingushetia, they were registered through Form No. 7—"Registration of a Family Arriving under Emergency Conditions"—from the Federal Migration Service (FMS) or with a G-4 stamp in their documents. Without these forms or stamps, Chechen IDPs were unable to apply for tent accommodation or obtain humanitarian aid from EMERCOM.[36] The immediate needs of tens of thousands of IDPs crossing over the border—access to food and shelter—were undoubtedly addressed with Form No. 7 and it served a distinctly

FIGURE 4.1. Internally displaced leaving Chechnya, 2000. Photograph by Natal'ia Medvedeva. © 2008, IPV News, USA.

FIGURE 4.2. IDP camp, Ingushetia. Undated. Photograph by Musa Sadulaev. © Musa Sadulaev.

FIGURE 4.3. The "Sputnik" IDP camp, Ingushetia, March 2000. Photograph by Iva Zimova. © Iva Zimova.

pragmatic purpose at the outset of the war. It was abolished by the Russian government on February 25, 2000, by Order No. 15, only to be reinstated three weeks later as civilians kept moving over the border.[37] By April 2001, however, Form No. 7 had been permanently abolished and IDPs coming across the border in the wake of the sweep operations in the villages of Assinovskaia and Sernovodsk in the summer of 2001 were unable to register with EMERCOM.

Coping with the effects of large internally displaced populations was a problem that Russia no doubt shared with Angola, Myanmar, Sri Lanka, and the Sudan. In 1998, Francis Deng, the former Sudanese ambassador to the United States, and Walter Kalin, a Swiss professor of constitutional and international public law, drafted the United Nations Guiding Principles on Internal Displacement. The principles were drafted in response to an estimated twenty-five million IDPs worldwide living without legal status as a result of "armed conflict," "generalized violence," "violations of human rights," or "natural or human-made disasters" within their own domestic borders.[38] The legal vacuum suffered by IDP populations across the world applied equally to Chechen civilians. Not having crossed an international border, the status of refugee as defined by the United Nations Convention

FIGURE 4.4. IDP camp, Ingushetia. Undated. Photograph by Musa Sadulaev. © Musa Sadulaev.

Relating to the Status of Refugees (1951) was not applicable to the Chechens in Ingushetia. And the UN Guiding Principles were no more than aspirational words—necessary, but not legally binding. The best the international community could do was to advocate that the Russian government adhere to Article 20 of the Guiding Principles—"Every human being has the right to recognition everywhere as a person before the law"—and encourage the Russian authorities to grant Chechen civilians a status that adequately addressed the scale of their personal tragedy.[39]

However, the Russian government was unwilling to provide formal legal status to Chechen IDPs through the Federal Law on Forced Migrants, the one concrete option that would have ensured dignity and long-term protection. Drafted in 1993 under the guidance of Mikhail Arutunov, of the Presidential Human Rights Commission, the law was initially framed to deal with the return of Russian citizens from former republics of the Soviet Union after its collapse in 1991. The aim of the law was to ease the integration of vulnerable groups into their new places of residence, to grant special allowances, and to assist with housing, job placement, loans, and access to health and education facilities. It provided the option of settling elsewhere in the Russian Federation and alleviated many of the problems that vulnerable groups in Russia experienced with registration of residence (*propiska*).

Article 1.1 of the law defined a "forced migrant" as follows:

> A forced migrant shall be a citizen of the Russian Federation, who was forced to leave his/her place of permanent residence due to violence committed against him/her or members of his/her family or persecution in other forms, or due to a real danger of being subject to persecution for reasons of race, nationality, religion, language or membership of some particular social group or political opinion following hostile campaigns with regard to individual persons or groups of persons, mass violations of public order.[40]

Chechen IDPs did apply for forced migrant status. The purported issue, however, rested with the official interpretation of "mass violations of public order." The Federal Migration Service simply *refused* to acknowledge that the actions of the Russian armed forces, in terms of both the scale of the bombing and the punitive sweep operations, had contributed to a "mass violation of public order" in the region. The government continued to insist that what had taken place was not a war but an "antiterrorist operation."[41] Valentin Diakov, head of the FMS, concluded, "The conducting of counterterrorist operations cannot be viewed as a mass violation of public order because it is aimed to restore it."[42] Between September 30, 1999, and June 30, 2001, eighty-nine Chechen civilians received forced migrant status. The majority of those had based their claims on fear of persecution from Islamic fundamentalist groups.[43] The Chechen applicants who based their claims on personal mistreatment by the Russian armed forces, on lost property, and on mass violation of public order were simply told in the official replies that the "antiterrorist operation" did not constitute a "mass violation of public order." They were not eligible for forced migrant status.[44]

It must be recognized that the IDPs were officially granted two important benefits linked to the Law on Forced Migrants. The first was a free journey to any region of the Russian Federation. The second was access to one of the fifteen temporary accommodation centers (TACs) across Russia.[45] The problem with these benefits, however, was the *discrimination* faced by Chechens when they traveled to large cities, notably Moscow, and attempted to register their place of residence. Although long ago abolished for violating freedom of movement and residence, Russia's antiquated *propiska* system was still in full force, controlled by local internal regulations spearheaded by Moscow's mayor, Yuri Luzhkov. The scale of this discrimination and mistreatment has been well documented. International organizations were therefore correct in their repeated claims to western migration authorities seeking to reject Chechen asylum cases that the *internal protection alternative* for Chechen civilians, faced with rising xenophobia and racism, was not a viable option. The other problem was that vacancies in the fifteen TACs across Russia were virtually nonexistent. There were already 48,000 applicants on the waiting list across Russia, with the FMS capable of providing housing to only 1,500 to 2,500 families per year.[46] Chechens who arrived at the TAC Serebryanki in the Tver region discovered that only those granted official forced migrant status were officially permitted to reside there and their food allowance could be discontinued at any time, dependent as it was on the goodwill of the center's administration.[47] The Russian government clearly did not want to provide alternative settlement to the majority of Chechen IDPs. This grew even clearer in the official response to the UNHCR, which conscientiously and repeatedly appealed to the FMS to grant IDPs the appropriate legal status. Their appeals were rejected outright.[48] The denial of forced migrant status was certainly shaped by a racial prejudice that sought to keep the Chechens inside Chechnya or tied inextricably to IDP camps with the ultimate goal of returning them to their place of origin. There was a clear consensus that the Russian government did not want Chechens traveling and settling in others parts of the Russian Federation. If the authorities had granted them the appropriate status, it would have been difficult to lodge the claim of discrimination or wanton negligence. But it is here, in the failure to address their needs as citizens of the Russian Federation, that we see very clearly an administrative prejudice based on ethnicity. It is not yet possible to determine whether the FMS issued an instruction not to grant forced migrant status, but the repeated refusal to expand eligibility to include displaced Chechens cannot be disputed.

Forced Evictions and the Politics of Normalization

The humanitarian agencies were soon confronted with a problem other than the logistical challenges of food distribution, leaking tents, and attempts to pressure the authorities to grant forced migrant status. The very presence of the IDP camps in Ingushetia became one of the fundamental obstacles to the Russian policy of "normalization" in the region. The tent camps had grown into visible symbols of the ongoing war inside Chechnya. And as long as thousands of Chechen civilians were prepared to live in leaking tents, often with no flooring, and at times in critical poverty for the sake of their personal safety, it was impossible for the Russian government to legitimate its claims that the situation inside the republic was stabilizing and that the military stage of the operations was over.[49] The IDP population was soon subject to a series of punitive measures to force them back across the border to TACs or IDP camps inside Chechnya. They were subject to physical threats, psychological manipulation, and forced eviction, leaving thousands with little choice other than to return to a landscape still inflicted with sweep operations, disappearances, land mines, and ambushes. The most striking aspect of this ongoing pressure—which reached its height from the summer of 2002 to the final closure of the Satsita tent camp on June 7, 2004—was the extent to which the security of the IDP population and their humanitarian concerns were crudely marginalized in support of the twin political goals of "normalization" and "Chechenization."

The word "normalization" was ubiquitous in the Moscow press beginning in early 2000. The Russian government and the pro-Moscow Chechen administration nurtured its use to instill an atmosphere within Russia, and globally, of gradual stabilization within Chechnya. Human rights organizations and liberal journalists scoffed at its blatant disregard for the reality on the ground. The origins of normalization lay in Order No. 1320 of the Government of the Russian Federation—"On Measures to Normalize the Social-Political Situation in the Territory of the Chechen Republic"—signed by Prime Minister Putin on December 1, 1999. Essentially, the order outlined the transfer of power of the civilian and executive authorities in Chechnya back to representatives of the Russian government and sounded the death knell of Maskhadov's administration. The policy resulted in the formation of numerous parliamentary initiatives, notably the committee headed by Nikolai Koshman, deputy prime minister in the newly established pro-Moscow Chechen administration, to plan the reconstruction of water and gas facilities and the restoration of the economic sphere. The logic of reconstruction was not in question. What was disturbing was the suggestion that the situation on the ground was ready for social and economic redevelopment at the same moment that the Russian armed forces were preparing to flatten Grozny for a second time. This *disjunction* was an insult to those suffering on the ground during the winter of 1999–2000, and most of the displaced ended up, in some form or another, victims of this semantic effort to veil the truth.

Already in November 1999 there were efforts to force the IDP population back with the establishment of "safe zones" inside Chechnya. Safe zones were allocated in the districts of Shelkovskoi, Naurskii, Nadterechnyi, Grozny (Tolstoi-Iurt, Vinogradnoe, Ken'-Iurt, Goryachii Istochnik), Gudermeskii (Gudermes, Engel-Iurt, Suvorov-Iurt), and Shalinskii (Argun, Shali). An order signed by Lieutenant General Viktor Kazantsev confirmed the existence of the military safe zones and the purported safe return of the civilian Chechen population. Those who had lived in and then fled the assigned zones were strongly encouraged to return and refused access to Form No. 7, effectively denying them humanitarian aid and housing in Ingushetia.[50] The concept of safe zones was in itself not a controversial idea. Sergei Shoigu, Russia's minister for emergencies, promised: "The government will guarantee full security to people who return to liberated Chechen villages."[51] Yet the evidence suggests that these enclaves were far from safe. The zones were not under the full control of the Russian armed forces, nor had agreements been reached between the Russian and Chechen forces that the areas were to be sealed and fighting prohibited. Serious fighting continued in Argun and Shali, with skirmishes in Gudermes,[52] and bombing was still taking place all across the region, making normal living conditions impossible.

In the first of many such official instructions, however, a notice was hung up in the Iman camp in Aki-Iurt, notifying the civilians that they were to return home.

> All refugees from the Chechen Republic in Aki Iurt! We inform all refugees from these districts in Chechnya: Nadterechnyi, Shelkovskoi, Naurskii, Achkhoi-Martan and the town of Sernovodsk, that they are to return to the population centers in those areas. In accordance with a decision of the Ministry of Emergency Situations and the Federal Migration Service of the republic of Ingushetia they will not henceforth be given humanitarian aid. 12.12. 1999.[53]

One week later, thirty-six railway carriages with refugees from the Severnyi camp in Sleptsovskaia were attached to a locomotive and pushed back over the border.[54] In January 2000, another eleven carriages were forcibly removed and pushed 3.5 miles into the village of Sernovodsk inside Chechnya.[55]

These efforts, however, were sporadic and disorganized. Fundamentally, President Aushev managed to stave off any major problems from 2000 to the end of 2001. Yet as soon as the political leadership changed in Ingushetia, the situation for the Chechen IDP population rapidly declined. Aushev unexpectedly stepped down on December 28, 2001, in somewhat unclear circumstances. Whether it was a result of pressure from Moscow over his criticism of the Chechen war, a threat to incriminate him on corruption charges, or personal exhaustion, as explained in his public statement, remains ambiguous. He was replaced by Akhmed Malsagov, as interim president, for several months until Moscow's protégé, the KGB general Murat Ziazikov, gained a victory in what were widely recognized as rigged presidential elections in March 2002.[56] In the absence of one of the sole voices of dissent, the IDPs suffered a severe loss of support. Unlike Aushev, President Ziazikov openly supported Moscow's policy of normalization, and troops entered Ingushetia one week after the elections.[57] Murat Oziev's opposition paper, *Angusht*, was banned shortly afterward. Vladimir Yelagin, federal minister for the socioeconomic development of Chechnya, Lieutenant General Kazantsev, Akhmat Kadyrov, and Murat Ziazikov gathered in May to approve a twenty-point plan titled "Plan of Activities of the Federal Bodies of Executive Power, Government of the Republic of Chechnya, Government of the Republic of Ingushetia, on the Final Measures for Return of IDPs from Ingushetia to Chechnya." In September, Igor Yunash, first deputy head of the FMS, arrived at the Iman tent camp to inform the 1,500 residents that they would have to move to alternative accommodation in Malgobek (which was unfit for habitation) within forty-eight hours or face "federal troops or OMON units."[58] The move was avoided when the camp population came out to demonstrate against the decision; the protests culminated in petitions to European ambassadors, the UN, the Organization for Security and Co-operation in Europe (OSCE), PACE, and President Ziazikov. Three of the petitioners were taken to the Ingush Ministry of the Interior for questioning and released several hours later.

Strategic decisions of the *radical* wing of the separatist fighters worsened the predicament of the displaced. The hostage crisis at the Dubrovka theater complex in Moscow in October 2002 resulted in the permanent deployment of Russian troops to the camps. As of October 31, a document check was put in place at four camps; soldiers began checking cars and persons entering or leaving; and weapons checks became more frequent and more strict. Only IDPs with official registration in the camps could move about freely.[59] The events at Dubrovka by no means helped the displaced. The Russian authorities merely came down on them harder, enabling Vladimir Gorianinov of the Ingush branch of the Federal Security Service

(FSB) to pose as a protector of the IDPs: "We can protect the refugees from a possible attack by 'terrorists.'"[60] To what extent the Russian armed forces had cause to worry that the IDP camps were housing potential terrorists is debatable. The IDP population had already been there for two years without major incident. It is also debatable whether a unit of sixty to eighty soldiers was necessary at each camp. Yet cynical strategies such as low-flying helicopters scattering leaflets with caricatures of the radical separatist fighter Shamil Basaev were unequivocally efforts to escalate fear and foreboding.[61] The IDPs understandably saw the stationing of troops as a new form of intimidation to force them out, especially after the threats at Iman in September. For approximately two hundred civilians in Aki-Iurt, the presence of Russian troops was unacceptable.[62] In a protest on November 3, the placards read: "A refugee camp is no garrison. Leave!" "Liberate the refugee camp," and "We run away from the war and the soldiers in Chechnya, and now they have sent them here!"[63]

The protests, however, did not defuse the imminent crisis. Within three months, the IDPs at Iman were again subject to pressure.[64] This time, they were too weak politically to sustain an effective campaign. And here in the village of Aki-Iurt we witness one of the first expressions of sustained psychological and physically coercive practices, a "forced eviction" as it was later termed in Ingushetia. Yet already in July, two IDP camps in Znamenskoe, inside Chechnya, had been closed[65] and the civilians forced into waiting trucks by Chechen law enforcement officers wielding truncheons.[66] The pressure on the 5,700 IDPs in Znamenskoe had been ongoing since 2000. Out of sight of the international community, human rights activists had been unable to cause an outcry about Znamenskoe, and unlike the closure of Iman, which was to take place just five months later, there were no journalists, national or international, inside Chechnya to create the required public storm. Elaine Duthoit of UNHCR and a representative of the OSCE Assistance Group met up with Magomed Gidizov, head of the State Committee on IDPs of the Chechen government, to discuss their concerns. They were told that IDPs would no longer be registered in Znamenskoe. On July 1, the local Nadterechnyi district militia, under Colonel Yunus Tungusbiev, visited both camps and announced that as of July 2 the water, gas, and electricity supplies would be shut down and the tents dismantled. Trucks would arrive to transport property and IDPs to Grozny. The instructions were to take the civilians to TACs in Grozny, which were still under construction. Two of the TACs viewed by OSCE at 11 Ponyatkova Street and 4 Vyborgskaia Street had no running water, gas stoves, or electricity, and the sewage systems were not functioning.[67]

When the FMS came under the control of the Ministry of the Interior, special task forces were assigned to deal with the situation in the camps.[68] Over the course of the week from November 26 to the closure of Iman on December 3, the gas and electricity were shut off and the exits and entrances closely monitored. UNHCR staff were told that they could not enter for fear of giving the IDP population "false hope."[69] As one IDP from Iman recounted "They told me that if I don't go they will burn down my tent, turn off power and gas in the camp and that all those who stay will be regarded as guerrillas."[70] In the words of another resident: "They were pointing at the soldiers all the time, saying if the Russians came here they would be a lot less gentle and it was better for us to leave before anything bad happened."[71] By December 3 the majority of residents had left, except for a few who remained in clay-built huts. The news agency Interfax reported starkly: "Grounds at the tent town have been reversed to arable land."[72]

According to the UN Guiding Principles on Internal Displacement, the Russian authorities were bound to provide alternative accommodation to the displaced population of Iman. UNHCR concluded that the alternative housing suggested by the authorities—an abandoned bottle factory and a dairy farm—were simply not adequate.[73] In response, MSF agreed to accelerate the construction of 180 single-room shelters to accommodate the Chechen civilians and planned to construct another 1,200. Yet at the end of January 2003, after the civilians had already been pushed out of Aki-Iurt, the MSF shelters stood empty and were eventually destroyed by the Ingush authorities under the pretext that they were not up to safety standards.[74] The other 1,200 were stalled. Soon thereafter, MSF received a letter from the Procurator's Office, ordering the demolition of the remaining shelters by March 26.[75] The provision of official alternative shelter in Ingushetia was simply *blocked*. For IDPs without independent means, there were two alternatives: return to Chechnya or move their tents to nearby settlements or *kompakniki*, to sheds, private yards, or abandoned farms. About 150 people stayed in the clay houses at Iman.[76] For those who returned to Grozny, the TACs were overcrowded and the fate of those who returned to their homes remains essentially unknown.[77]

There were two central issues at work here. The first was the forced eviction. According to the UNHCR definition, voluntary repatriation is characterized by "the absence of any psychological or material pressure."[78] The acrobatics around the word "voluntary" began in 2002, and these semantic games made catastrophic differences in people's lives. The second rested with the question of personal safety. What level of safety could both the Russian and the Chechen governments offer the civilians returning to Chechnya in accordance with universally accepted standards? By the end of January 2002, raids had begun on private homes at night, and abductions were taking place on roads, in cafés, or in markets; ambushes by separatist fighters were also ongoing.[79] The IDPs were most concerned about the security situation, both for themselves and for their young adult sons, who were the most vulnerable to the random violence. Neither the Chechen nor the Russian government was able to guarantee their safety in accordance with the UN Guiding Principles. The hypocrisy was eloquently pointed out by an open letter from MSF, stating that *if* international aid workers were prohibited from entering the region because they could be subject to kidnapping and general violence, why should Chechen civilians be subject to the same risk?[80] To counter the claims that the civilians wanted to return to Chechnya, MSF monitors surveyed 16,499 IDPs in Ingushetia in February 2003, soon after the closure of Iman: 93 percent did not want to return to Chechnya, fearing for the safety of their families; and 52 percent lived in tents that were leaking, not insulated against the cold, or had no wooden or concrete floor.[81]

One could not fault Médecins Sans Frontières and the UN Refugee Agency for their efforts to stop the closure of Iman. The pleas of Kris Janowski, the UNHCR spokesman, as well as Sergio Vieira de Mello, the UN high commissioner for human rights, were simply ignored. The policy of OCHA under Toby Lanzer was that "aid must follow the people," meaning that aid in itself was not to be used as leverage to persuade IDPs to return.[82] Pressure from Svetlana Gannushkina, Ludmilla Alekseeva, and the UNHCR when they met with President Putin on Human Rights Day on December 10, 2002, did, however, work. The UN and the Russian human rights activists became slightly more successful in their attempts to get the authorities to show more sensitivity to the situation of Chechen civilians. The previous threats to close Alina, Bart, Satsita, and Sputnik on December 20 were lifted, and the advocacy campaigns managed to stave off the winter closure of the camps.[83]

But the face of the strategy had shifted. The authorities deliberately continued to create difficult living conditions. In the first instance, hundreds of IDPs were taken off the camp registration lists for humanitarian aid. The second consistent tactic was to make official statements regarding the imminent closure of the camps. The tactic was clearly orchestrated to encourage civilians to leave *sooner* rather than be forcibly evicted later, and what happened to those at Iman was a constant reminder. Over the course of four years, the imminent closure of the camps was announced at least nine times—November 1999, December 1999, October 2000, February 2002, October 2002, December 2002, March 2003, August 2003, and October 2003. Third, IDPs were openly threatened with searches for narcotics and weapons. And, finally, after the closure of Iman, the names of IDPs were removed from the lists for government-sponsored housing in Ingushetia. By the end of September 2003, the displaced were promised 350,000 rubles (US$10,000) compensation for destroyed housing and property—but only to IDPs residing inside Chechnya.[84]

The new pro-Moscow Chechen administration also had strong incentives to force civilians back. The Chechen administration wanted the IDPs back to engage in Moscow's political solution to the problem in Chechnya. In the months preceding the constitutional referendum of March 2003, in which the Chechen population voted to stay within the Russian Federation, and the presidential elections of October, which resulted in the rise of Akhmat Kadyrov, pressure on the IDP population to move back into Chechnya to participate in the political process only increased—as part of the broader strategy of Chechenization. The pro-Moscow administration planned a referendum for March 2003 to vote on Chechnya's new constitution. At first, Kadyrov was not going to allow the IDPs in Ingushetia to vote at all, denying them political participation until he was convinced otherwise by Alvaro Gil-Robles of the Council of Europe.[85] The constitutional referendum would determine the status of Chechnya as part of the Russian Federation, as well as legislation that would set the stage for future presidential and parliamentary elections. Chechen IDPs at three food distribution centers in Ingushetia reported that the Russian authorities were threatening to cut off their food aid unless they registered to vote in the referendum. Ruslan Zhadaev recounts how he visited the humanitarian aid station as usual on March 10: "While giving me the usual ration of bread, a female employee of the station asked me to fill out a form: a statement to the territorial election commission, by which I was to confirm my intention to take part in the voting. . . . When I refused to do this, the young lady warned me that next time I would not be able to come and get bread."[86]

Just prior to the presidential elections on October 5, the Bella tent camp was closed.[87] The intrepid Chechen journalist Timur Aliev poignantly called this period the "war of the tents,"[88] and there is no doubt that the end of displacement in Ingushetia was manipulated to suit the political goals of the pro-Moscow Chechen administration. Over the next six months, Alina, Bart, and Sputnik were closed, and Satsita was finally taken down in June 2004. It is true that ceasing to be an IDP probably never occurs at the right time. But the question remains: was the IDP population of Chechnya given freedom of choice and legitimate alternatives? Were the conditions for resettlement adequate? And were the basic poverty risks averted in the government's overall policy? Chechen IDPs were not offered alternatives that could be considered adequate, neither for those who chose to stay in Ingushetia or for those who returned to Chechnya.[89] If they moved outside the region, they were subject to the discrimination of registration of residence (*propiska*) and general discrimination on ethnic grounds; if they stayed in Ingushetia without financial means, they were destined for a settlement life of unpredictability based on the frequently false promises of the FMS to substitute rental payments or provide alternative accommodation; if they returned to TACs in Chechnya or to their homes, they were faced with poor conditions in the accommodation centers and to homes, often destroyed, as they waited for compensation payments—largely abandoned to struggle on their own.

Asylum in Europe

For many, the burden of life in a tent camp or the continued impunity inside Chechnya proved too great. By 2003 thousands of Chechens were heading for Western Europe, traveling overland through Belarus to the Polish town of Terespol or through the Carpathian mountain range in Ukraine to Slovakia. The majority headed further west, to the Czech Republic, Austria, Germany, France, Sweden, and Belgium. The reasons for this sudden wave were numerous. The rise of President Ziazikov had only reinforced the perilous fate of the IDPs in Ingushetia. Not only had the closure of Iman in late 2002 set a frightening precedent, but the repeated pronouncements on the imminent closure of the rest of the tent camps generated an environment of uncertainty. In addition, the growing dominance of Kadyrov's forces inside Chechnya coincided with the rise in targeted disappearances. The obvious improvement in intelligence witnessed an upsurge in intra-Chechen rivalries—men who had fought in the first war, those placed hors de combat from the second war, and those who may have aided separatist fighters as drivers, smugglers, or couriers were targeted through internal networks and their families harassed.[90] And finally, the Dubrovka hostage crisis in Moscow in October 2002 caused a critical backlash, both in Moscow and with the stationing of troops near tent camps in Ingushetia.

The number of asylum applications from Russia to EU countries during the first nine months of 2003 was 23,465, an increase of 66 percent over 2002.[91] Although the UN Refugee Agency did not keep statistics on ethnicity, NGOs and individual governments working with refugees claimed that the majority of those in search of international protection were Chechens.[92] The granting of refugee status to Chechen civilians ranged from nearly 0 percent in Slovakia to 95 percent in Austria, and this dramatic discord in the percentage of Chechens granted refugee status or alternative protection was alarming. Slovakia had sent refugees back to Ukraine, which in turn had deported them to Russia in a "chain deportation." Ukraine refused to recognize refugees fleeing indiscriminate violence or war in its domestic legislation, despite its international obligations.[93] Nor did it abide by its commitments on the extradition of those at risk of torture. As Victoria Schmidt, deputy head of the Federal Migration Service, admitted, "Chechens do not get refugee status in Ukraine because they are citizens of Russia and are not qualified according to Ukrainian policy. There are other problems, too, that influence the situation, like Ukrainian-Russian relations and terrorism."[94] Once through Ukraine, however, the refugees were relatively safe in Poland and the Czech Republic. By 2007 there were approximately forty thousand Chechen refugees in Western Europe.

By far the most receptive country was Austria. Over the winter of 2003–4, busloads of Chechen refugees arrived in Traiskirchen, a village situated eighteen miles south of Vienna. With refugees coming from the Czech Republic, Poland, and Slovakia, the reception center, a former military barracks with room for eight hundred, was unprepared for the wave. Many of the refugees were encouraged to return to the Czech Republic by border guards, or they were simply left out on the streets.[95] Only about 30 percent of asylum seekers were granted federal assistance during the asylum procedure in Austria.[96] While the Chechen refugees waited for their first meeting with the Asylum Office, they were cared for by the Austrian branch of Caritas.[97] Yet despite the difficult beginning, the Chechen cases were fast-tracked in Austria, and as of 2007 there were sixteen thousand refugees, with some eight thousand already granted positive status. The recognition rate, the highest in Europe, was about 95 percent.[98]

In Poland the situation was dramatically different. Poland was struggling with its own domestic poverty and a high unemployment rate of 19 percent, and granted refugee status to some 10 percent of those seeking asylum. The government also offered a status called "tolerated stay"[99] and was generous and accepting overall in the first instance. "Tolerated" individuals did not receive adequate assistance in terms of medical aid and integration programs. The majority of the refugee population was spread among sixteen reception camps, about half of which were close to Warsaw, with the remainder in the eastern part of the country. But Poland lacked the crucial financial means, as many of the EU's internal border countries did, to integrate Chechen civilians and provide for the estimated 15,000 said to have passed through the country in transit further west. As of 2007, there were still an estimated 3,400 Chechen refugees in Poland, and about 50 to 60 percent of them were children.

It was on the accession of Poland and the Czech Republic to the European Union in May 2004 that further problems emerged. The chaos that the Dublin II Regulation imposed was palpable. Suddenly refugees were forced to return to the countries of first entry to process asylum requests.[100] For many, this meant the return to Poland or the Czech Republic, where support for long-term protection was severely lacking and the EU had failed to support the extra burden its legislation carried. It is difficult to ascertain how many refugees were sent back, but the estimate stands at around 10 percent. The Bielefeld Refugee Council's report concludes that the Dublin system is unfair, inefficient, resource-intensive, and an obstacle to genuine sharing of responsibility between member states.[101]

It has no doubt been difficult to mobilize a people traumatized by war. One of the main problems was not merely the integration of Chechen civilians into an uncertain life and assisting them in learning a new language and finding employment, but dealing with the resonant trauma of the war. The Austrian government was able to find Austrian psychologists and counselors with Russian-language skills, but the waiting list for counselors remained long. For those in Poland, the services were almost nonexistent, and many parents sought specialized and expensive care for their children. The challenges of a refugee existence remained vast and many.

PART TWO

THE RESPONSE

5

CHECHEN RETALIATION

> If the soldiers don't know where Basaev, Khattab, Baraev are—we'll show them. We damn them and we pray for those people that they kill. The Wahhabis hate everyone. . . . We reared these bandits ourselves and are prepared to answer for them. But it's impossible to destroy an entire nation. Women and children have nothing to do with this.
> —*Chechen civilian*

> Independence is not a whim or an ambition. It is the necessary condition of our survival as an ethnic group.
> —*President Aslan Maskhadov*

> If it pains you to see your victims in Moscow, then remember ours in Chechnya.
> —*Osama bin Laden, November 2002*

RETALIATION FOR THE AGGRESSION imposed on Chechnya by the Russian armed forces took various forms and the Chechen separatist movement was far from innocent in its response. Its acts of revenge were at once provocative, desperate, dramatic, and cruel. Such acts evoke little sympathy and can only be condemned as part of a broader landscape of violence bereft of the crucial principle of distinction. By 2002, *currents* within the movement had abandoned the self-image of a national separatist movement and began to adopt an increasingly strong Islamist discourse couched in the language of *jihads, caliphates, jamaats*, and *amirs*.[1] Whether this ideological shift was a result of a desperate search for moral support and a stronger political identity under the growing influence of radical actors like the quixotic and unstable Shamil Basaev, Zelimkhan Yandarbiev, and Abu Ibn Al-Khattab, or for pure political capital and its promise of power, the logic of resentment remained at the core of the resistance.

The Chechen separatist movement engaged approximately 2,000 to 4,000 fighters, backed by a considerable number of civilian supporters working as couriers, drivers, or cooks, or providing protection. The Russian armed forces had, at different periods, 80,000 to 120,000 troops in Chechnya. The index of violence was completely asymmetrical. Yet the crimes committed by the separatist movement need also to be categorized by the laws of war beyond the politicized and reductionist frame of terrorism. How we interpret the acts of the movement depends in the first instance on how we define the nature of the conflict in Chechnya. To what degree was the second war in Chechnya an internal armed conflict? And how did the war change in shape from 1999 to 2005? How then do we understand and define the acts of war committed by Chechen forces?

The Russian government chose to bracket the second war in Chechnya as an "antiterrorist operation" to counter the application of the 1949 Geneva Conventions and Russia's international obligations regarding internal armed conflict. Contrary to how we understand counterterrorist operations as precise, targeted operations conducted by law enforcement agencies, the first and second wars in Chechnya were large-scale campaigns with a high intensity of violence that involved fuel-air munitions, iron bombs, surface-to-surface missiles with high-explosive warheads, massed artillery, and tank fire,[2] all of which clearly allowed for the application of Article 3 common to all four 1949 Geneva Conventions on "armed conflict not of an international character." The current trend of dismissing the Geneva Conventions for their purported lack of utility with respect to contemporary forms of warfare merely appeases governments like the Russian Federation and the United States, which operate in legal vacuums when fighting certain forms of violence. It also completely eliminates responsibility for the actions of the *opposition,* whose legitimacy is effaced by attempts to cast nationalist movements as no more than criminalized bands or terrorist organizations. Undoubtedly, the Geneva Conventions need modification to deal more adequately with asymmetrical wars. With 2,000–4,000 troops, the Chechen forces had a clear, hierarchical command structure and were sufficiently organized and motivated to constitute a belligerent force whose declared aim was territorial independence. Between 1999 and 2001, there were at least 1,000 battle-related deaths a year; from 2002 to 2004, there were 25 to 999 battle deaths a year.[3] The Russian side may not have *declared* war in September 1999, but the methods deployed and the consequences evoked fell well within the formal international definitions of warfare.[4]

The practices of hostage taking and suicide bombings were no doubt strategies of war deployed by the Chechen forces. And they, too, were serious war crimes according to international law. Currents within the separatist movement pinpointed nonmilitary targets and launched deliberate, premeditated acts of aggression against Russian civilians, consciously moving the conflict outside the borders of Chechnya to inflict their own form of collective punishment on the Russian population. It was a strategy deployed in response to the inequity of power, and it had three fundamental objectives, which shifted in emphasis over the course of the latter part of the conflict. The first objective was the cessation of military activity and the withdrawal of Russian troops from Chechnya. The second was to target the Russian civilian—a symbol of innocence revenged for the deaths of thousands of Chechen civilians. And the third was to attract publicity, to provoke extreme fear and public alarm in Russian society.

The early seizures of hostages by Chechen separatists in Budennovsk in 1995 and Kizliar in 1996, during the first Chechen war, were seen as dramatic and brutal, but effective, means of bringing the Russian government to the negotiation table. By 2002 this interpretation had shifted. The change was not merely a response to the heightened language of terrorism that defined the post–September 11 agenda, however. Doubt emerged about the *motivation* and intent of the radical Chechen wing. Was the sole aim of the violence to terrorize Russian civilians in revenge? What material gain could the separatists have hoped to achieve when President Putin had already starkly refused to negotiate? There was no withdrawal of Russian troops, cease-fire, or end to sweep operations. Were the movement's decisions still strategically viable? To what degree were the radical separatists working to protect their own people with their actions, with genuine conviction, or were they working in the interests of Islamic fundamentalism, the influence of which had grown notably stronger?

Understanding the motives of the radical strain of the separatist movement does not justify the acts, but it does allow a glimpse into a pattern of warfare that must be placed in historical context. The retaliation by Chechen separatists was a cumulative process that grew in response to acts of aggression by the Russian armed forces and the pro-Moscow Chechen

FIGURE 5.1. Shamil Basaev and Aslan Maskhadov, region of Urus-Martan, 2000. Photograph by Natal'ia Medvedeva. © 2008, IPV News, USA.

administration. The aggression imposed by the Russian armed forces was disproportionate and catastrophic for the civilian population of Chechnya. The methods deployed to quash the separatist movement were barbaric and cruel. The issue concerns the tactics that were available to the separatists, and whether they were deployed strategically to benefit the material and political aims of the movement itself. By 2002 a number of contingent factors began to cast doubt on the integrity of the radical separatists. The ultimate aim—the removal of Russian forces—remained the same, and although the intensity of the conflict had waned, sweep operations like those at Assinovskaia and Sernovodsk, filtration points, torture, and enforced disappearances were still part of everyday life in Chechnya. The problem was: *who* was conducting the acts of retaliation and what motivations were guiding their actions?

One can only condemn the acts of the radical separatists on two grounds: morality and political incompetence. And clearly these grounds intersected. The political incompetence was rendered most clearly in the call for a Confederation of the Mountain Peoples of the Caucasus. Those who conducted the incursion into Dagestan in August 1999 and the raid into Ingushetia in 2004 sought to spread strife among neighboring republics for ends that did not genuinely reflect the ultimate goal of independence, or the immediate needs and desires of the Chechen population. While many may have sympathized with the cause of Chechen independence, few agreed that the entire Northern Caucasus deserved to be drawn into the conflict. This incompetence was matched by the growing dissonance in the movement between Aslan Maskhadov and the military commander Shamil Basaev, which cast doubt on the cohesion and shared vision of the separatists. Was Basaev working for his own political power, or did he truly believe in the force of his strategy? Regardless of Basaev's motives, he engaged with radical ideologues like Zelimkhan Yandarbiev, Movladi Udugov, and Ruslan Elmurzaev to adopt an Islamist framework with the support of foreigners Al-Khattab and Amir Abu Al-Walid Al-Ghamdi to organize attacks that were not merely morally corrupt but achieved little strategically for the cause and did not ameliorate the suffering of Chechen civilians.

The most radical acts of the second Chechen war were taken after the strengthening of foreign influence in the ousted Chechen government of Ickheria. This coincided with the moment when the separatist movement was growing tired and weakened by years of war. The pro-Moscow administration was in control in Grozny. The Chechen fighters were becoming bored and frustrated in the mountains. Many had openly expressed their increasing sense of impotence, unprepared to wait it out as the military arm of Fretilin in East Timor had done for over twenty-five years. And with the Islamist frame crudely sewn onto a nationalist agenda, the separatist movement collapsed under the weight of the radicals' strategic and brutal disasters.

Budennovsk and Kizliar

Hostage taking as a strategy of war deployed by Chechen separatists began in earnest during the first war in June 1995. Having lost the last Chechen stronghold, the mountain village of Shatoi, then president Dzhokhar Dudaev threatened new strategies to counter the separatist movement's dwindling military options: "The struggle is not over, it assumes new forms."[6] Shamil Basaev, along with 150 fighters, crossed the northern border into Russia in the early hours of Wednesday, June 14, 1995. The fighters attacked the small town of Budennovsk with the purported intent of destroying the military airfield holding the Su-24 "Fencer" planes that were bombing Chechnya. Whether the separatists ever reached the Russian base is a contentious issue,[7] but they did attack the local police station and town hall, hoisting a red, green, and white Chechen flag on the front of the building in a bold display of nerve. They rounded up hostages from the streets, the market, and administrative buildings to spread a paralyzing terror throughout the city. As one observer from the local market recalled: "The Chechens blocked both exits and drove the crowd into the center of the square. The other fighters moved along Kalinin Prospekt. People were moving in all directions, running from the bullets and from being taken hostage."[8]

The hostages were herded along the streets as human shields. At around 1:00 P.M., they were forced onto the first floor of the local hospital. For Basaev's deputy, Aslambek Abdulkhadzhiev, the motive was clear: "Why was the world silent when Shali was bombed, when some 400 people were killed or wounded? In fact, the evil we did in Budennovsk was not even 30 percent of what they did in Shali. And what was the world community's reaction when they wiped out Samashki and Serzhen-Iurt?"[9] Approximately 1,600 hostages were held in the Budennovsk hospital. The demand of the separatists was clear—the cessation of military activity, the withdrawal of Russian troops from the southern regions of Chechnya, and negotiations with President Dudaev.[10]

On the fourth day of the crisis, the Russian Special Forces unsuccessfully stormed the hospital on two separate occasions. An estimated thirty civilians were killed, either by Russian gunfire or by Chechen fighters.[11] Women were forced to stand at the windows and shout to the Russian Special Forces: "Don't shoot!"[12] In between the two attacks, Basaev released 150 pregnant women, and children, from the maternity wing. He then shot six hostages, followed by five more when the press conference he demanded did not take place on time.[13] The surviving hostages continued to suffer from severe cramping and dehydration. After five days of intolerable fear, the crisis was finally mitigated by Sergei Kovalev, Russia's human rights commissioner, when he gained access to the hospital and set up the infamous telephone conversation between Prime Minister Viktor Chernomyrdin and Basaev.[14] It was agreed that in return for the release of the hostages, Basaev and his forces would be guaranteed safe passage to Chechnya. The fighters would be accompanied by one hundred volunteers from the hospital until they arrived at their point of safety. The agreement stated that urgent negotiations—on the withdrawal of Russian troops from Chechnya and the disarmament of the Chechen forces—would resume immediately. Once the cease-fire was under way, all political questions would be settled by peaceful means.[15] The immediate demands were met. All the hostages were released after crossing the border into Chechnya. The total number of reported dead was 105.

Basaev's actions were driven in part by grief over the death of eleven members of his family in an air raid on Vedeno in May 1995. In his own defense, he claimed, "I am not a terrorist or gangster. I am an ordinary Chechen who rose up in arms to defend his people."[16] For Basaev, Budennovsk was a forced step in response to the indiscriminate bombing of Grozny from 1994 to 1995 by the Russian armed forces and to the growing failure of the separatists to cope with the inequity of manpower and weapons between themselves and the Russian military. But the subsequent negotiations on ceasing military activity, which were meant to arise from Budennovsk, broke down.

Salman Raduev, the twenty-eight-year-old son-in-law of President Dudaev, and his combat group, the "Lone Wolves," launched a copycat raid in Kizliar, a small steppe town in Dagestan, seven months later. On January 9, 1996, on Dudaev's orders, Raduev's group conducted a military raid and later seized a civilian hospital.[17] Situated four miles from the border with Chechnya, Kizliar had one of the largest Russian populations in Dagestan and the raid was essentially an exact reenactment of the events in Budennovsk. The decision to invade Kizliar had allegedly been ordered by Dudaev, against the advice of Aslan Maskhadov, commander of the Chechen forces, and his deputy, Shamil Basaev. Between 2:00 A.M. and 3:00 A.M., Raduev's group destroyed three helicopters at a Russian air base. Around 5:00 A.M. they began breaking into nearby apartment buildings, detaining civilians, and taking them to the town hospital and maternity clinic, eventually capturing an estimated 1,500 hostages. The young Raduev echoed Basaev's words from June: "We will die here, but we will stop the war in Chechnya." Raduev threatened to kill ten hostages for every dead Chechen, should Russian troops attempt to storm the hospital.[18]

"We can turn this city to hell and ashes," he declared, sporting a green headband, the symbolic color of Islam. "Budennovsk and Kizliar will be repeated again until Russia recognizes Dudaev and the Chechen republic."[19] Raduev's attack led to the death of an estimated twenty-five Dagestanis and two Russian soldiers. All the hostages were released, except for 160 forced to accompany the Chechen fighters as a human shield across the border. This time, the Russian government reneged on its promise of safe passage and launched a full-scale attack on the village of Pervomaiskoe as the convoy approached the Chechen border. After a three-day battle, about half of the Chechen fighters escaped back to Chechnya. Twelve hostages died in the attack. The promise of safe passage that had defined Budennovsk was never repeated.

Budennovsk was the mark of events to come. And the strategic success of that hostage crisis for the Chechen fighters was no doubt a motivating and deciding factor in subsequent decisions, many years later, to stage acts of equal proportion in the Russian capital. From the Chechen side, it signaled the beginning of the separatist movement's capacity for extreme violence and its disregard for civilian life, in violation of the Geneva Conventions, in particular Common Article 3 and Additional Protocol II. Under Common Article 3, the radical separatists violated 1(a) "violence to life and person," 1(b) "taking of hostages," and 1(d) "the passing of sentences and the carrying out of executions without previous judgment." Under Article 4 of Additional Protocol II, their actions violated 2(a) "violence to the life, health and physical or mental well-being of persons," 2(b) "collective punishments," 2(c) "taking of hostages," and 2(h) "threats to commit any of the foregoing acts."[20]

It was not the hostage raids that ultimately won the first war for the Chechen separatists, however. It was the death of President Dudaev in April 1996, coupled with the strategic success of the final Chechen offensive in Grozny in August. The hostage sieges undoubtedly carried a psychological resonance that contributed to the final negotiations and to the cessation of military activity. The mere *threat* of future seizures and military raids on Russian territory must have played a role in the signing of the Khasaviurt Peace Treaty of August 31, 1996. Yet this tiny republic was set on a road of temporary and unstable peace, with the treaty postponing the question of independence for five years.

Dubrovka and Operation Boomerang

The unstable peace in the interim period of 1996 to 1999 witnessed a burgeoning alliance between radical forces inside Chechnya and Islamists from abroad. The radical forces under the command of Shamil Basaev and Arbi Baraev began to make strategic military decisions, independent of the Maskhadov government. There was a logical continuation in the acts, but the dissonance bred serious consequences when Basaev and his supporters, under the auspices of the Islamic International Peacekeeping Brigade (IIPB), led an incursion into Dagestan in August 1999, provoking the second Chechen war. Having secured support for his Confederation of the

Mountain Peoples of the Caucasus from village combat units (*jamaats*) in Dagestan, Basaev sought to spread his agenda with the help of Ingush, Chechen, Circassians-Cherkess, and Circassians-Kabardins across the region. Blame for unwarranted aggression could no longer be placed squarely on the shoulders of the Russian government. The idea of a Confederation of the Mountain Peoples was a provocative play for power that served little purpose for the Chechen people and promoted unnecessary strife in the surrounding republics who had long since decided to stay out of Chechen politics. Moreover, people grew alarmed and upset by the apparent involvement of broader terrorist networks that clearly sought to use the nationalist cause in Chechnya for their own ideological ends.

The popular idea that the radical Chechen wing under Basaev sought a confederation across the Northern Caucasus only under the influence of Al-Khattab's jihad is incorrect. The proposal to consolidate access to the Black and Caspian seas had been discussed as early as 1991 among the Chechen political and intellectual elites.[21] The idea had been lingering long before the adoption of a radical Islamic framework, although the latter provided the language and resources for its execution. Moreover, supporters of the Wahhabi creed in Dagestan under the leadership of Baguaddin Mogomedov had sought refuge in Chechnya in 1998 after being forced out of the neighboring republic, and in turn openly encouraged Chechnya's intervention in Dagestan.[22] The incursions into Dagestan by the IIPB sounded the death knell for the separatist movement's international legitimacy. And most would agree that the Russian government had legitimate cause to respond. Basaev and the local shura declared Dagestan an independent Islamic republic before his forces were pushed back. Yet the response of the Russian armed forces set the tone for the coming years: no dialogue, no moderation, and no negotiations. At the beginning of the second Chechen war, President Putin quickly vowed, "There will be no new Khasaviurt, no new Budennovsk."[23]

The most hostile acts of the radicals in the second Chechen war did indeed coincide with the adoption of a new consultative assembly, or shura, in June 2002.[24] Within the government of the Chechen Republic of Ichkeria, a Shariah-based order was imposed on the government in 1999, and the shura became the highest organ of power. By 2002, several radical Islamists from Arab states had taken on top military and political offices. And the Chechen extremist Abdul-Khalim Sudalaev was appointed head of the Shariah Court.[25] Al-Khattab had been killed by a poisoned letter in March

2002 and was replaced by Amir Abu Al-Walid Al-Ghamdi, a veteran of the Afghan, Tajik, and Bosnian wars, from Saudi Arabia.[26]

The hostage crisis in Moscow's Dubrovka Theater from October 23 to October 26, 2002, was testimony to the new resolve of the radical strain and the influence of foreign jihadists in the newly appointed shura. Just after 9:00 P.M. on October 23, 2002, forty-one Chechen fighters arrived in three minivans at a theater complex on Melnikov Street in Moscow. Twenty-two men in camouflage and civilian clothes, the majority of whom were wearing black balaclavas, entered the foyer of the theater, firing shots during the second act of the musical *Nord-Ost*. The men were accompanied by nineteen women in Saudi-style dress—black veils and jilbabs—with inscriptions in Arabic printed across the tops of the veils. Each woman had eleven pounds of explosives strapped to her waist, and each held a pistol in one hand and detonators, linked to short wires attached to the explosives, in the other. The men entered the auditorium, going directly to the stage, and the women took positions down the two side aisles. Two black banners with white inscriptions were immediately positioned, one at the back of the stage, another on the front of the balcony. Written in Arabic, the slogans read: "There is no god on earth other than Allah, and Mohammed is his Prophet. Freedom or Paradise!"[27]

Movsar Baraev, the twenty-five-year-old nephew of Arbi Baraev, was the titular leader of the group and made his demands quickly. The hostages were instructed to call whom they could and report that they had been taken hostage. The demands were the same as they had been in Budennovsk in June 1995—the withdrawal of Russian troops from Chechnya, and Chechen independence.[28] "This approach is for the freedom of the Chechen people and there is no difference in where we die, and therefore we have decided to die here, in Moscow," declared Movsar Baraev. "If we die, others will come and follow us—our brothers and sisters who are willing to sacrifice their lives, in Allah's way, to liberate their nation."[29] Sitting next to Baraev was Ruslan Elmurzaev, code-named "Yasir" or "Abubakar," who later turned out to be in control of the operation. He had very little to say about the nationalist cause but proclaimed, "I want to say to our enemies, we desire death in the path of Allah more than they desire life."[30] Despite the nationalist origins and goals of the attack on Dubrovka, it had all the trappings of an Al Qaeda–style operation. And here we note the union of Islamism and nationalism—a call for the cessation of the war in Chechnya packaged in Islamist discourse. A prerecorded tape, with the hostage takers outlining their demands, was released by Al Jazeera television in Doha, Qatar, on October 24. The banners hanging in the theater were written in Arabic, not in Chechen or Russian, as part of this newly constructed image. The fighters were reading the Koran and listening to Arabic music.[31]

The emergence of the black widows underscored the new tone. The martyr belts fitted to their waists, along with their black veils and jilbabs, were emblematic of their own dramatic theater. An atmosphere of hopelessness and a desperate search for social justice outside the normal legal parameters were tragically mixed with the pathologies that shaped their final resort to violence. Trauma experts Anne Speckhard and Khapta Akhmedova have revealed through their interviews with the relatives of the black widows similar stories of personal trauma, lost family members, bombings, and the destruction of homes. We learn that after the death of relatives, black widows experienced isolation and alienation from friends and families and depression. They took up prayer and other religious rituals, began wearing head scarves, and encouraged others to join them in their newfound beliefs.[32] And the Wahhabi mission promised renewed power, purpose, and social justice. At the very least, the black widows could choose death on their own terms. As one black widow said, "We have chosen to die here, in Moscow, and we will take with us the souls of the unfaithful."[33] Among the black widows, who ranged in age from nineteen to forty-four, was Arbi Baraev's widow, Zura Baraeva. She had lost her husband in June 2000 but Zura Baraev was also part of a notorious criminal family.[34] Two sisters, Raisa and Fatima Minaeva, were more typical of the black widows. Both sisters had lost their husbands, their father, uncle, and several cousins in the war.[35] When the BBC interviewed Kirya, a twenty-four-year-old university student inside the theater, who had lost her husband, her brother, and her cousin, she echoed a familiar protest: "Our women, children, and old folk are dying. No one pities us. Even if we all die here, this will not end. Many more will take our place."[36]

The conditions in the theater were stifling. There were 979 hostages; 100 of these were school-age children.[37] Within the first fifteen minutes, nationals from the Northern Caucasus and Georgia were permitted to leave the hall. Fifteen children under the age of twelve, along with two pregnant women, were then released. All the male hostages were instructed to move to the left and women to the right. Over the course of the next four days, the hostages were given chocolate, candy, ice cream, water, and juice from the snack bar. They were nevertheless subject to dehydrating thirst. They were forced by the humiliation of their confinement to use a collective toilet in the orchestra pit and to sit or lie for four days in small theater seats that severely restricted their blood circulation. Every hostage experienced the events differently, depending greatly on who was guarding them. Two individuals were shot dead, neither of whom was a hostage. The first, Olga Romanova, slipped past the barricades and entered the theater, apparently intoxicated. It is widely believed that she may have been a Federal Security Bureau (FSB) operative sent in to provoke the hostage takers. The second, Gennady Vlakh, also entered the theater, allegedly in search of his sixteen-year-old son.

The hostages later testified that despite the claims by the hostage takers that they were ready to die, their actions spoke otherwise.[38] Radios and a small television were set up in the theater to follow events in the Russian media. By the evening of October 26, Baraev told the hostages that preliminary talks were going well. Lieutenant General Viktor Kazantsev, the Presidential Envoy to the Southern Federal District, called one of Baraev's deputies to say he was coming to negotiate face-to-face and to wait until 11:00 A.M. the following day. "Look, all I ask is that you don't lose your cool," said Kazantsev in a cell phone conversation. "Don't take any unnecessary steps, OK?"[39] According to one witness: "Baraev's mood changed, we all felt it. He said, 'At last Kazantsev is coming for talks. You can relax until 10:30 A.M.' "[40] Yet the phone call had been a ruse to buy more time. The FSB released fentanyl through the ventilation system, drugging the fighters and hostages. The gassing was a strategic success and the Russian Special Forces units Vympel and Alpha entered the theater. The rescue process, however, was a disaster. The evacuation team had not been warned about the gas. They did not have the appropriate equipment, respirators, or enough ambulances. One hundred and twenty-nine hostages died. Pulled from the theater on their backs, with their heads lolling backward, they died from choking on their own vomit or from swallowing their own tongues.[41]

The hostages had spent fifty-seven hours in the theater. And many of those who survived Dubrovka were well aware of the mixed motives for the violence. Tamara Starkova confessed later:

> I hate the Chechens so much, I even hate their children. I don't know if that'll ever go away. They murdered my daughter and husband. But those women had families, children. They told us their husbands and brothers had been killed. What would I have done in their shoes? I think I'd have done the same as them. Now I carry on

> for my little boy's sake. But if he'd died too and I was left with no one. . . . I think I, too, would have strapped on a bomb-belt and gone to blow myself up.[42]

Alexander Stahl said of one of the gunmen: "In general, it seemed to me that he was all mixed up. He jumbled together revenge for his loved ones, a war of liberation, and jihad . . . they were all very stubborn and kept parroting phrases someone had rammed into them, about paradise and sabers. I did not hate the terrorists, and, in general, I felt pity that someone had forced them onto the path of evil and war, and had stolen from them a normal life."[43]

When one looks at the video footage of Dubrovka, one immediately sees the dissonance between the Islamic veneer and the nationalist discourse. The *performance* of the act was greatly refined with modern technology, televised broadcasts, and the support of Arab mercenaries. The motives, however, that defined the hostage takers were mixed. Those seized in the theater spoke of the black widows as seeking revenge for their grief. Movsar Baraev was not fighting against the American infidels, or calling for a global Salafi jihad, hoping to destroy Western domination and create a worldwide Ummah. The root of the resentment was still the indiscriminate violence inflicted by the Russian armed forces on Chechen civilians. It was a way to restore power to those who felt profoundly traumatized and humiliated by years of fear. The median age of the fighters was twenty-four. Hostages speak of the younger ones playing with the cell phones, chatting openly with the hostages. If the median age was twenty-four, these men and women had been around fourteen years old, adolescents, when the first Chechen war began in 1994.[44]

Dubrovka made public the tensions in the separatist movement. One cannot deny that Aslan Maskhadov was a complex figure with a consistent goal, and it is impossible to ascertain just what the Chechen president knew about the proposed attack. Yet he removed Basaev from the post of deputy commander in chief of the Chechen armed forces after the theater crisis and declared publicly, "Shamil thinks, I'm sure, he's absolutely sincere, that in the conflict with Russia, all methods are permitted for the Chechens," said Maskhadov. "In the view of the specific circumstances, I can't agree with this. Today Shamil Basaev isn't part of the armed forces of the Chechen Republic."[45] But a senior U.S. official in Moscow called Maskhadov "damaged goods" with links to terrorism. The senior official went on to assert in a nonsensical and completely predictable post–September 11 response that "the Chechen leader should be excluded from peace talks."[46] Grigorii Yavlinskii of Yabloko confided that "his view of Maskhadov has changed. If Maskhadov commanded the rebels in the theater, he said, he could never participate in a political settlement."[47] The issue of Maskhadov's role is still controversial. Many have cast doubt on the Chechen president's claims of innocence. But if one traces the history of Maskhadov as a military commander up to 2002, it is difficult to believe that these public statements were in any way disingenuous. The Russian government alleged it had phone conversations linking Maskhadov to the hostage takers. But the evidence is spurious, at best.[48]

According to the rhetoric of the Russian government, the Chechen president was no longer a viable option for negotiations. Dubrovka had completely discredited him. But this response seemed more than a convenient excuse to continue tackling the rise of radical Islam in Chechnya through the use of extreme force. To what extent Maskhadov had control over other aspects of the separatist movement is unknown. There were twenty-two male hostage takers in Moscow out of a force of 2,000–4,000 Chechen fighters. Exactly what Maskhadov was willing to do or capable of doing, what compromises he would have been prepared to make, was also unknown. But simply because he did not control Basaev does not mean that he did not exert influence over other aspects of the separatist movement. It is impossible to know what the dynamics and sensitivities were among each of the fighting units. Simply no effort was made by the Russian government to even begin an exploration of what options were available to cease the military activity. There were other forces in Chechnya. There was a civilian population that largely despised the radical Wahhabis. There were moderates in the ousted Chechen government who were consistently open to negotiations. There was an international community capable of assistance and open to broad-based discussions across the political divides. But options for mediation were blocked at every front. As far as the Russian government was concerned, the pro-Moscow Chechen administration under Akhmat Kadyrov was in place and preparations were under way for the referendum and presidential elections of 2003.

There was something deeply unsettling about the expectations of the radical Chechens. If Chechnya was to be liberated of the Russian armed forces, would the troops be replaced with another authoritarian, this time fundamentalist rule that would only institutionalize Shariah law and spread its caliphate across the Caucasus? Had the Chechens become a pawn in the Islamic fundamentalists' ultimate goal—to sow discord and violence across the region? In this sense, the co-opting of the nationalist cause was an ingenious strategy of the Wahhabis. And Dubrovka marked a new tone. Valid questions began to emerge about the legitimacy of those conducting the campaign in the name of the Chechen people and the degree to which Russian civilians would suffer. Osama bin Laden made several noteworthy speeches that mentioned the Northern Caucasus. Chechnya was but one of several nationalist battlefronts across the world that were contributing in highly disputed degrees to Al Qaeda's international jihad. "Every day, from east to west," bin Laden stated in a characteristic speech, "our umma of 1200 million Muslims is being slaughtered in Palestine, in Iraq, Somalia, Western Sudan, Kashmir, the Philippines, Bosnia, Chechnya and Assam."[49] Frequently deriding Russia as an imperial power that mirrored U.S. expansionist ideas, he wrote: "This Muslim nation has been attacked by the Russian predator which believes in the orthodox Christian creed. The Russians have exterminated an entire people and forced them into the mountains, where they have been devoured by disease and freezing winter, and yet no one has done anything about it."[50]

The attacks only accelerated after Dubrovka. In the spring of 2003, Basaev launched Operation Boomerang in retaliation for the violence directed at Chechen civilians and the families of Chechen fighters by the Russian armed forces. His new rhetoric embodied a philosophy of open revenge and collective punishment.[51] Russian civilians, according to his logic, were not only financing the war but had elected the government responsible, in his view, for a genocidal war on the Chechen nation.[52] No Russian individual, in Basaev's mind, was "innocent."[53] Amir Abu Al-Walid similarly declared that the Russian people bore responsibility for electing the Putin government and must now pay "with their blood and their sons."[54] Suicide terrorism replaced hostage taking, peaking in 2003. In the days before the presidential elections in Chechnya in October, a suicide bomber, suspected to be a Chechen, blew herself up outside the Rizhskaia subway station in Moscow. This was followed a week later by the downing of a Tu-134 jet en route to Volgograd and a Tu-154 to Sochi. On leaving Moscow's Domodedovo Airport, two Chechen female suicide bombers detonated within three to four minutes of each other in what was clearly a planned attack, reminiscent of September 11. The explosions killed ninety passengers. Basaev claimed responsibility: "By the Grace of Allah, the Shakhid battalion, Riyad us-Saliheen has carried out several successful operations on the territory of Rusnya. The regional Shakhid unit of Moscow was responsible for the blasts on Kashirskoe Road and the Rizhskaia metro station in Moscow. The downing of the airliners was carried out by the special operations unit."[55]

Beslan

The last act orchestrated by Shamil Basaev under Operation Boomerang was the attack on School No. 1 in the small North Ossetian town of Beslan. Students were gathering in the courtyard of the school on the morning of Wednesday, September 1, 2004, when an estimated thirty to fifty fighters surrounded the quadrangle in a semicircle, fired into the air, and ushered between 1,200 and 1,300 parents, teachers, and students into the corridors of the school and finally into the gymnasium at around 9:20 A.M.[56] "Children everywhere were screaming," recalled Larisa Tomaeva, "some for their mums, some for their dads, some for grannies. People were walking over the top of each other and anyone who ended up on the ground just got trampled on."[57] The hostages were forced to sit, with their hands above their heads, on a basketball court no more than twenty-five yards long and ten yards wide. Explosives were taped to the basketball hoops and backboards, as well as suspended from wires down the middle of the room. Trip wires ran down the center of the room. A bomb was hooked up to a foot pedal on the floor, with the detonator controlled by one of the fighters. As the former president of Ingushetia, Ruslan Aushev, later recalled after entering the school for negotiations, "When I entered the gym, I immediately realized that no fewer than a thousand people were there. The gym, as well as the adjacent changerooms and toilets, was crammed with people like herrings in a barrel."[58]

Although Beslan has been depicted as Basaev's *Nord-Ost*, there was little of the Islamic symbolism that was so striking about the hostage taking at Dubrovka.[59] Only two black widows were present. No banners with slogans written in Arabic were strategically placed, nor was any Arabic music played. None of the fighters was reading the Koran. This attack undoubtedly took on a more sinister hue. Not only because the majority of targets were children but because the treatment of the hostages with regard to food, water, medicines, and access to the bathroom was of an order far more abhorrent than that of the theater crisis. And this tone was shaped by the leaders of the attack. The hostage takers were no longer averse to killing hostages to illustrate just how resolute they had become. Ruslan Betrozov was killed with a single shot to the back of the head when he asked the fighters to cease firing into the air and for people to remain quiet and calm.

Similarly, when Vladimir Bolloev refused to kneel, he was shot and left to bleed to death on the floor. Approximately thirty male hostages were taken to move furniture to barricade the doors to the building. In what was an effort both to remove potential resistance from male hostages and to underscore the fighters' determination to create shock and alarm, the men were taken to a classroom and left with the two black widows. The explosive belts of the two women were detonated from outside, blowing up the room and killing the majority of the hostages, along with the two women, who had allegedly protested taking children as hostages.[60] The bodies of the men were unceremoniously dropped from a first-floor window where they lay for two days in the heat. When former president Aushev arrived to negotiate with Ruslan Khuchbarov ("the Colonel"), the Ingush leader of the operation, he was shown the bodies from the first-floor window as a symbol of this new decisiveness.

Beslan was not a direct retaliatory attack in the way that Hamas responded after the Hebron massacre or the massacres of 'Oyoun Qarah and the killing of Palestinians at the Al-Aqsa Mosque in Jerusalem. When Aushev entered the school on the afternoon of September 2, he was given a list: stop the war; withdraw the Russian armed forces from Chechnya; include Chechnya in the Commonwealth of Independent States (CIS); do not permit a third force in the region. The withdrawal of Russian troops had to be announced on state-run television, and hostages would be released once the declaration was made.[61] Although the withdrawal of Russian troops was one condition, so too was the release of twenty-seven Caucasian fighters who had been captured during the military raid on the Ingush Ministry of the Interior headquarters in June, which killed ninety people. Aushev negotiated the release of twenty-six hostages, mainly mothers with nursing-age children. No senior Russian figures emerged in Moscow to speak about the crisis, and the courage of the marginalized Aushev stood in stark contrast to the silence from the capital. President Putin made his definitive statement on September 7, and when asked why he would not enter into talks with the separatists, he said: "Why don't you meet Osama bin Laden, invite him to Brussels or the White House, ask him what he wants and give it to him so he leaves you in peace?"[62]

This refusal to negotiate with the fighters only aroused hostility toward the hostages. "On the second day," recalled one witness, "they became sharply more vicious, they began to see that our leaders did not care about us and did not want to negotiate with them. They asked for Dzasokhov [Alexander Dzasokhov, the president of North Ossetia] and he did not

FIGURE 5.2. Aida Sidakova, a six-year-old schoolgirl, attempts to gather herself up after the explosion in the school in Beslan. Photograph by Dmitrii Beliakov, September 3, 2004. © Dmitrii Beliakov.

come. After that they began to say that our government did not need us and that everyone had forgotten about us."[63] Fifty-two hours into the siege, the crisis in Beslan ended in the storming of the school and the deaths of 326 hostages, 181 of whom were children. What provoked the storming was an explosion inside the school. According to the report of Yurii Savel'ev, an academic specialist on the physics of combustion, titled "Beslan: The Hostages' Truth," the explosion was the result of a shot from a rocket-propelled infantry flame thrower or a RPG-7VI grenade thrower launched from the temporary Headquarters of the Federal Security Bureau.[64] The report of the Duma Committee, led by Alexander Torshin, concluded that the explosion was "the result of a blunder" whereby a bomb strung up in one of the basketball hoops fell out.[65] Savel'ev's comprehensive report ultimately provides a far more detailed narrative and convincing evidence to support his claim.[66] Moreover, his argument was subsequently supported by a videotape released by the North Ossetian Procuracy.[67] What is certain is that the successive firing of grenades by the Special Forces did result in the collapse of the roof of the school, causing the majority of the deaths inside the building.

The schoolchildren, their parents, and teachers lived in intolerable and inhumane conditions for over two days. The fighters stopped giving out water. The children were subject to such excruciating thirst that many drank their own urine. Visits to the toilet were stopped and the hostages sat with their hands above their heads in unbearable heat. The hostage takers were essentially prepared to starve the hostages. "The second day was really terrible," recalled Lidiia Tsalieva, the principal of Beslan School No. 1. "They argued all the time. . . . The children were going crazy. The heat was unbearable. I pleaded with them, 'Please let them drink, please.' "[68] One hostage recalls of Ruslan Khuchbarov: "He behaved himself in the hall aggressively. . . . And when the children asked him 'May I go to the toilet?' he answered, 'I'm not your uncle, I'm a terrorist. I cannot let you do whatever you want.' "[69] Other observers recall that Vladimir Khodov, the deputy leader of the group, a convicted murderer and rapist of Ukrainian origin, was the cruelest and most unpredictable. His mother had married an Ossetian and moved to North Ossetia where Khodov also resided.

The response from Maskhadov was resolute: "Those Chechens who take part in these acts put themselves on a par with Russian soldiers guilty of mass and systematic atrocities against the Chechen civilian population."[70] Maskhadov and Akhmed Zakaev, the foreign minister of the Chechen Republic of Ichkeria, had agreed in principle to go to Beslan and negotiate with the fighters if they could be assured safe passage. But Maskhadov admitted what everyone knew—these brutal acts merely weakened the cause of national independence. "If we want to preserve our national identity and to maintain the moral righteousness of our struggle," he concluded, "we must decisively disassociate ourselves from those few whose reason has been clouded by revenge."[71]

All agree that the taking of hostages, especially children, is a deplorable act. Blame of ignorance, nonaction, can be lodged against adults, not children. The logic was that the fighters wanted to take from the adults that which was most precious to them—their children—to show how serious and committed they were. And the cruelty of their retaliation may have had just as much to do with several confluent factors: the ongoing presence of the Russian armed forces in Chechnya, the growing influence of the pro-Moscow administration under Kadyrov, and the recruitment of fighters for the establishment of a Caucasian front. The sense of waning effectiveness may also explain the background of the fighters involved. The leader of the group was Ruslan Khuchbarov, an Ingushetian. Among them were

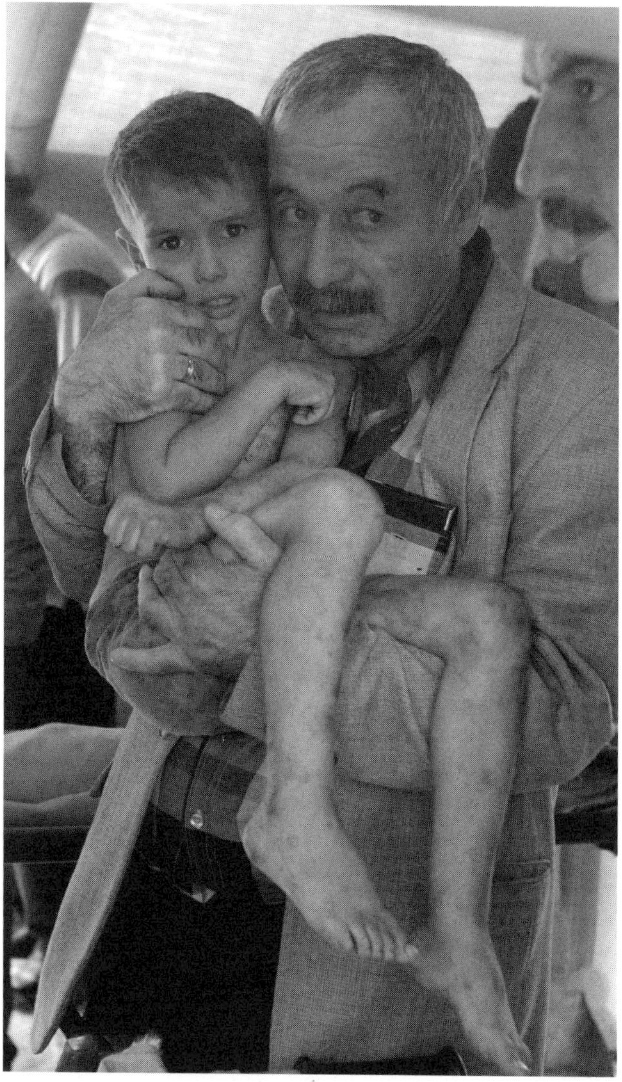

FIGURE 5.3. A man with a child rescued from the school in Beslan after the explosion. Photograph by Musa Sudalaev, September 3, 2004. © Musa Sudalaev.

Ossetians, Ingush, Ukrainians, Chechens, two British-Algerians, and a Georgian—the nationalities of these hostage takers cannot be dismissed.[72] It indicates something about the campaign—the growing influence of the *jamaats* across the region and a real diffusion in the aims of the Chechen separatist movement. This certainly gives weight to the idea that Basaev's goal was to extend his influence across the Caucasus with interethnic combat units, notably the Ingush and Ossetians under the United Islamic Combat Unit "Yarmuk."[73]

This argument is also sustained by the choice of location for the attack—North Ossetia, a region still tense from the war of 1992 over the Prigorodnoe territory. The fighters clearly hoped to spark a conflict between Christian Ossetians and Muslim Ingush. It is for these reasons that the intent of the fighters became tainted with goals that may have stemmed from, but no longer exclusively reflected, the crisis in Chechnya. The caliphate was a goal to be attained by force against smaller republics not interested in being drawn into this decade-long war. The change in the tone of the radicals was illustrated, yet again, on Maskhadov's death in early 2005 and in the appointment of Abdul-Khalim Sadulaev of the Shariah Court as the new president of the Chechen Republic of Ichkeria. The first thing the extremist did was prohibit negotiations with the Russians, a tactic Maskhadov never deployed.[74] Moreover, a United Caucasus Front was announced, combining the Ossetian, Ingush, Kabardino-Balkarian, Stavropolian, Karachaevo-Cherkessian, Adigean, and Krasnodar sectors of the western front.[75]

There is no doubt that after Dubrovka the Western media's portrayal of the Chechen separatist movement became one-sided and often completely decontextualized. The Western press produced a litany of articles, most of them sinking into the ideology of the day, bereft of historical context with ad nauseam claims of an Al Qaeda connection. This was Russia's September 11—the means of the Beslan terrorists were equal to those of the Nazis, and so on and so on.[76] These were a series of acts that led to the unnecessary trauma and deaths of many hundreds of largely Russian civilians. The point here is that the horror experienced by a targeted group remains the same, no matter which word we use. Capturing the fear that hostage seizures provoke is almost an impossible task. In the same way that the Russian armed forces punished Chechen civilians, the Chechen separatists blamed Russian civilians for the policies of their government. Russian civilians, too, became the recipients of a philosophy of revenge that deeply penetrated the radical separatists. They sought to instill fear in the same way that the aim of state violence was to instill fear. Perhaps the separatists were hopeful that Russia's civilian population would react and force a resolution to the crisis; the result, however, was a brutal acceleration of violence that only deepened an already fragile atmosphere of prejudice and xenophobia against Chechens both in Russia and by Russian forces inside Chechnya.

6

CIVIL SOCIETY REACTS

All of our human rights NGOs—Memorial, Helsinki Watch, Amnesty International, Common Cause, Civic Dignity, and many others—are shouting at the top of our lungs, trying to be heard by something that has lost its right to be called a society, even less a civil society.
—Elena Bonner, human rights activist, May 2000

It's just the dog barking at the passing caravan. That is the principle here.
—Vitali Yaroshevskii, deputy editor of Novaia Gazeta, *October 2006*

CIVIL SOCIETY IN MOSCOW and Chechnya faced a challenge of a different order when the second Chechen war broke out in September 1999. Without the mass public support that had defined their protests during the first war, Russia's burgeoning civil society encountered the dark side of the growing authoritarian regime. The first war had been shaped by protests on the street in Moscow and a civil society that sought to defend its nascent freedoms from the dominance of the state. The reasons for this desperate response were clear. Three years after the fall of the Soviet Union, the Russian public was still in the throes of the excitement that had defined the years after the 1991 coup. The decision by President Yeltsin to send troops into Chechnya in November 1994 was viewed not only as a threat to the establishment of democracy in Russia but as a mark on what had been a relatively peaceful breakup of the Soviet Union.

Yeltsin also had at his side some remarkable individuals. They included men like the former Soviet dissident Sergei Kovalev, who at the outbreak of the first war was Russia's first human rights commissioner and head of the Presidential Human Rights Commission. It was his pleas from Grozny, his vocal horror at what was taking place on the ground, that defined the response to the war in Moscow. Moreover, he was supported by a liberal press, in the form of *Obshchaia Gazeta, Novoe Vremia, Izvestiia, Moskovskie Novosti,* and the extensive coverage of events by Yevgeni Kiselev and his team at the independent television station NTV. The shock and surprise at Yeltsin's decision to bomb Grozny resonated in Moscow, and the images of destruction broadcast over the independent stations inspired mass demonstrations against the war, including a peace march from Moscow to Chechnya.[1]

The second war witnessed a different Russia and a different public response. In a country tired of the turbulent aftermath of Gaidar's shock therapy and the financial crash of 1998, the apartment bombings in Moscow and the incursion into Dagestan were merely additional threats to a Russia already reeling from a decade of instability. The response by the general public appeared to be one of exhaustion and frustration, and these legitimate emotions led to a response quite unlike that in the winter of 1994. The point was that the radical wing of the Chechen separatist movement under Shamil Basaev and Abu Ibn Al-Khattab had also given the Russian public and the government legitimate reason to be concerned. The apartment bombings in Moscow in September 1999 were never proved to be the acts of the separatist fighters, but the incursion into Dagestan by the radical wing was an act that few could support. The later hostage crises at Dubrovka and Beslan were similarly seen as acts that did little to defuse the conflict. The radical fighters were ultimately responsible for providing the *pretext* for the Russian armed forces to resume a war in Chechnya. And this provocation contributed greatly to the suffering and destitution of the separatists' own people.

For the intellectual elite in both Russia and Chechnya, their quest for information and their attempts to maintain their own personal safety and intellectual integrity were thwarted by an extraordinary rise in state-sponsored propaganda. The reorientation was striking. The Russian government was well aware that the failure of its counterpropaganda strategies in the first war had enlisted greater support for the Chechen separatists. Shifting the charge against Chechen fighters from separatist violence to terrorism backed by international networks was an ingenious and cleverly orchestrated strategy. And the way the Russian authorities achieved this was to ensure that the media came under the control of the state, channeling information and creating an atmosphere of fear for those who sought independent information and for human rights activists who were seeking to understand the reality on the ground. This tactic was startlingly consistent and was sustained by world events, especially in the aftermath of the September 11 attacks.

It is testimony to the durability of the liberal strain of civil society in Russia that it managed to maintain a level of questioning and doubt around the government's claims. Despite its complicated position, civil society in Russia managed to keep the question of Chechnya on the international agenda. And the actions of certain sectors countered the deep failure of the liberal and democratic parties in the Duma and in public life. Yabloko and the Union of Right Forces (SPS) managed to garner only 5 percent of the seats in the Duma election of 2003. Undoubtedly, greater pressure fell on the intellectual elite, the liberal journalists, and human rights activists with the failure of the democrats. Although badly in need of political power to back their response, the NGOs and liberal journalists nevertheless fought alone, finding in the intense new nationalism espoused by the Putin government a clear attempt to fuse patriotism with unconditional loyalty to its policies in Chechnya. And the cost for dissent was high. Victims of a new set of state policies, the press experienced an attack on their freedom that was unambiguous with regard to Chechnya, and there was little they could do to influence events. The situation for human rights activists was equally harsh, although somewhat different. It was the Chechen human rights activists who found themselves the real victims of physical threats, harassment, and murder from all sides of the conflict. Moscow's activists found themselves caught in the president's fluctuating attempts to appease the West, to remain within the orbit of high-power politics, but to witness the government's ultimate rejection of the criticisms of the EU and the Council of Europe with regard to human rights violations in Chechnya.

The Journalists: Babitskii, Politkovskaia, Abdulaeva, and Aliev

One of the first victims of the second Chechen war was press freedom. Wanting uncritical support for its actions in the region, the Russian government quickly placed prohibitive regulations on journalists seeking to work in the Northern Caucasus. Information flows out of Chechnya were channeled and controlled by the only television satellite relay dish situated at the Russian military base in Khankala on the eastern outskirts of Grozny, along with the Press Center of the Joint Command of Federal Forces. The independent Russian television stations NTV and TV-6 were soon put under increasing pressure, especially after the sale of 30 percent of NTV to the state-controlled Gazprom monopoly, along with a hundred regional newspapers. Journalists, both foreign and Russian, were confined to the territory of the Khankala military base and only permitted to enter the republic when accompanied by a Press Center official. Access to Chechnya was limited to press tours by the military itself and a constant barrage of press releases published by the Ministry of Defense broadsheet *Krasnaia Zvezda* or Rosinformcentre, a government public relations firm set up in Moscow sought to shape the public image of the war. Journalists were prohibited from meeting with civilians and from traveling independently to towns and villages.

In the treatment of journalists by the Russian armed forces, we witness the lengths to which the Russian government was prepared to go to control the information coming out of Chechnya. And this is a dimension that needs to be highlighted. The modus operandi was to make the other side *nonexistent,* as well as to counter the narratives of civilian suffering that would inevitably emerge as the bombing campaign began. Despite the severe restrictions, however, it was still difficult for the Russian government to completely orchestrate the picture of Chechnya. There were several journalists who shaped a constant opposition to the government's version of events. Among them were the Russian journalists Andrei Babitskii of Radio Free Europe/Radio Liberty, the late Anna Politkovskaia of *Novaia Gazeta,* and the Chechen journalists Mainat Abdulaeva of *Novaia Gazeta,* Timur Aliev of *Chechenskoe Obshchestvo,* and the freelance writer Ruslan Isaev. *Novaia Gazeta, Novye Izvestiia, Nezavisimaia Gazeta,* and *Kommersant* in Moscow formed the backbone of the most independent and analytical coverage of Chechnya in the capital, with *Chechenskoe Obshchestvo, Groznenskii Rabochii,* and *Golos Chechenskoi Respubliki* providing news as close to the ground as possible in Chechnya and Ingushetia. On the Internet, Grani.ru, Primanews.ru, newsru.com, and Gazeta.ru formed the soul of the liberal opposition via cyberspace, and Ekho Moskvy voiced opposition across the airways.

Andrei Babitskii, the thirty-six-year-old journalist from Radio Free Europe, was the first to challenge the obstacles to press freedom. Familiar with the territory from the first war, he entered Chechnya illegally in the fall of 1999 and wandered by foot with the separatist forces into Grozny and surrounding regions, violating Articles 13 and 15 of the 1998 federal law No. 130-FZ On the Fight against Terrorism, which prohibited journalists from making contact with "terrorists" in Chechnya.[2] The first aim of the Russian Press Center at Khankala was to cut off any alternative sources of information about the separatist movement. The Russian government sought to eradicate any possible public sympathy for or sensitivity to the position of the Chechen fighters. No insight into their internal workings, no historical links or arguments, no alternative view other than that they were "terrorists" was to emerge in the public arena. Babitskii threatened this strategy on a fundamental level. First and above all, he reinforced the crucial distinctions between the moderate and radical separatists. He traveled with the fighters. He did exactly what the Russian government did not want. He attempted to keep the aims of the separatists in the public mind, to ensure that the public remember that Aslan Maskhadov had been elected president in 1997 and had been recognized by both Russia and the international community.

It seemed inevitable that Babitskii would become a victim of his own news coverage. And the retaliation against him set the tone for the rest of the journalistic community. He was picked up by the Russian Federal Security Service (FSB) on January 16, 2000, and taken directly to Chernokozovo. Although it was not until February 4 that news reached the international press about the detention facility, Babitskii's experience only confirmed the barbaric conditions and cruelty of Chernokozovo when he was interned there until February 3. Although Babitskii was subject to multiple beatings, the authorities were careful not to torture him. In a bizarre and illegal act, Babitskii, a *civilian*, was given the option of being exchanged for two Russian POWs with the Chechen side. He agreed to the exchange, which turned out to be a hoax. He was merely put in the hands of pro-Moscow Chechen forces, a spectacle that was filmed and then used for propaganda. Babitskii was held for an additional three weeks, from February 3 to February 23. In March, he was charged with aiding paramilitaries in Chechnya, under Section 24, Article 208, of the Russian Criminal Code, for the "organization of an illegal armed formation or participation in it."[3] Though that charge was soon dropped, he was then charged with violating Russian passport regulations after being given false documents in Dagestan. He was fined US$300 and amnestied.

Babitskii's detainment signaled disaster for the rest of the journalistic community. President Putin's view on press freedom was crystal clear in the wake of Babitskii's detainment. "He is clearly in the services of the enemy," the president concluded. "What he does is far more dangerous than firing rounds from automatic weapons."[4] And this charge was to be repeated by those who interpreted press freedom as unpatriotic. As Erik Batuev, a Russian journalist, recalled of an interview with the FSB in 2000: "When you go and do your professional duty," they said, "never lose sight of the fact that you are a Russian citizen. Always remember that."[5] Outside of attempts to implicate Babitskii under Article 208 of the Criminal Code, other legal maneuverings later emerged that sought to establish legal conditions for criminal proceedings against unpopular journalists and reconstruct a landscape of self-censorship among journalists and editors. Most notably it was the charge of "public calls to extremism," an evolving and expanding term in Russian law, as well as the measure to prohibit "public slander directed toward figures fulfilling the state duties of the Russian Federation," that exemplified more than a subtle shift in the government's approach to press freedom.[6]

Restrictions on press freedom also resonated in the public sphere. Public surveys illuminated for Babitskii and his peers the enormity of their task. How were they to penetrate a strongly reemerging racial prejudice with regard to Chechens and open the public mind to the complex and brutal dimensions of the war? Some polls illustrated that Russians felt that the information they were receiving about the war was indeed limited.[7] Yet the focus on the plight of Russian soldiers via the main government television channels and press outlets, at the expense of the daily consequences of the war for the civilian population, no doubt influenced public perceptions of the war. Polls and surveys illustrated that public concern rested with two pervading trends: the number of Russian troop casualties and the economic cost of the war. In one survey, fewer than 5 percent of the respondents reported concern for human rights abuses perpetrated by Russian troops against Chechen civilians.[8] And in some instances, the surveys exposed a vitriolic hatred rooted in the alleged genetic disposition of Chechens for bestiality and violence. Characteristic examples included: "Just annihilate them as a nation. Just annihilate them as a republic, wipe them from the face of the earth."[9] When Swedish journalist Asne Seierstad was interviewing Russian civilians, another respondent concluded: "Civilians! What are civilians? Inside every Chechen is a fighter. There are no peaceful people in that place. . . . The Chechens are evil from the inside. They are evil in their souls. They're like wolves, and live according to the rules of that beast. . . . With Chechens it's best to kill them immediately, otherwise they shoot you in the back."[10] In popular culture, in novels like *Okhota Beshenogo* by Viktor Dotsenko, Chechens were regularly portrayed as rapists, savages, criminals, or "mountain wolves."[11] Similarly, films like *Voina* (War) and *Grozovye Vorota* (Thundering Gates) managed to entrench these stereotypes further in the public psyche.

Andrei Babitskii sought respite in Eastern Europe in the aftermath of his detainment. He faded from the scene to settle in Prague, and reappeared in 2002 with his book *Nezhelatel'nyi Svidetel'* (Undesirable Witness). He returned to Chechnya in 2003 and 2005 without incident. Natal'ia Kononova, the pseudonym of a *Novye Izvestiia* correspondent, went into hiding in Russia after her apartment in the Ingush capital, Nazran, was raided. The formerly independent television stations NTV and TV-6 soon fell under the Kremlin's long shadow, leaving the forty-six-year-old Russian journalist Anna Politkovskaia, who had started her career with the daily newspaper *Izvestiia* during the heady days of perestroika. She moved to the liberal paper *Obshchaia Gazeta* and flew to Grozny in 1998 to interview President Maskhadov.[12] In 1999 she joined *Novaia Gazeta*, well-known for its lucid critiques of the Kremlin. She began reporting on the region soon thereafter.

Anna Politkovskaia's most staggering achievement was her ability to bring new urgency, again and again, to the question of Chechnya. Her primary motive was to keep the war *personal*. Her second motive was to counter the defeatism of Russian civil society as the war dragged on. As a journalist, she faced the unenviable challenge of recounting stories of woe and extreme personal pain for over seven years. She also faced the editorial challenge of keeping those stories on the front pages of *Novaia Gazeta*. In her articles for the biweekly and in her two main books, *A Dirty War* (2001) and *A Small Corner of Hell* (2003), Politkovskaia managed, through a series of poignant individual sketches, to force the tragic reality of Chechnya into Russian life. Her writing often lacked nuance and it was almost always angry or urgent, and frequently didactic. Politkovskaia was far from a dispassionate analyst. She called on her readership to extend help, to "call the author on her pager (232 0000, #49883)."[13] Yet it was precisely that rhetorical style, backed with some astounding investigative journalism, that kept the tempo of her writing alive over so many years of covering the war. It grew into a defining characteristic of her persona, a style she seemed to adopt as much for herself as for others—to keep her *own* indignation alive. "There are people who can analyze this," she wrote, "but few who can sympathize. And since feelings are so rare now, they are the most important thing in my calendar."[14]

What Politkovskaia did with particular effectiveness was capture the appalling conditions within the Russian armed forces serving in the region. She devoted more than half of her articles to the Russian soldiers disenchanted and confused by their own role in Chechnya, those "exhausted men with unbalanced minds," as she depicted them.[15] What emerges from her dispatches are the sorry stories of the bureaucratic fate of the corpses of Russian soldiers once deemed missing in action; the putrid tinned meat from the Semikarakorsk meat-processing plant in Rostov, dished up to hungry soldiers; the rotting feet stuck in worn-out army boots; the drunkenness, the drug abuse; the desertion and the often brutal relations between senior officers and foot soldiers; the absence of benefits and insurance for the wounded returning home; the soldiers' mothers determined to remove their sons from the region.[16] What emerges from Politkovskaia's writing is more than an attack on the Russian government for failing to address the deterioration of the Russian army. It is an attempt to understand from where *exactly* the massive human rights violations in Chechnya stemmed and what environment gave rise to them.

In her search for answers, Politkovskaia was rarely forgiving. Yet she sought to illustrate that there were indeed some in the Russian armed forces who felt they were powerless victims of the government's policy in the Northern Caucasus, and that the fate of Russian soldiers, or the elderly Russian civilians caught in a retirement home in Grozny, was just as inconsequential to the Russian government as the fate of Chechen civilians. But this picture was eclipsed in her work by an army she also knew to be riddled with profiteering and deep racism, massive looting, corruption in the higher ranks over oil, trade in human bodies, dead and alive, and the selling of ammunition to the separatist forces. For Politkovskaia, "the bedlam here is commercially profitable." Chechnya was, she argued, a "cash cow."[17] And with her unrelenting investigations she traced that corruption back to the Ministry of Defense and the United Command of Federal Forces in Chechnya.

No less important was the degree to which Politkovskaia kept the voices of Chechen civilians alive. While pontificating on international relations, she moved effortlessly to the local, drawing, yet again, on a story of a wretched civilian as she struggled to understand the *strategic* sense of targeting Chechen civilians who probably hated the radical strain of the separatist movement more than the Russians themselves.[18] She firmly believed that there were Russian generals who were "implementing a policy of mass liquidation of the civilian population."[19] She was instrumental in exposing the conditions of IDPs inside Chechnya, especially those in the village of Chiri-Iurt, located at the base of the mountains, close to the "Wolves Gate." The courage that took her inside the region exposed a village with woefully inadequate humanitarian aid, with villagers suffering from dystrophy, blocked by Russian troops, and a local administration left to care for up to eleven thousand IDPs in five makeshift camps seeking refuge from the bombing and sweeps in Duba-Iurt.[20] "As soon as you enter the former dormitory of the old cement factory, which had turned into a refugee settlement, you hear wailing," Politkovskaia wrote. "A protracted half animal monotone evoking the farthest reaches of despair. When these people find out you are a journalist, they cling to your clothing, your hands and feet . . . as if something essential depended on you."[21] She continued to draw attention to the fate of IDPs in villages such as Chechnya-Makhety, Tovzeni, and Sel'mentauzen in the Vedeno district.

By the time she wrote her second book, Politkovskaia had started to make the crucial distinctions she had largely avoided up until 2001. She began to disentangle the strains within the Chechen separatist movement and, although she had little sympathy for any of them, she avoided placing the entire blame on president Aslan Maskhadov's shoulders. Whether this was a result of her friendship with Akhmed Zakaev, Maskhadov's special envoy to Europe, is difficult to determine, but she begins to insist on the importance of negotiating with Maskhadov. She breaks down the separatist movement into three distinct categories: the "westernizers," like Maskhadov, who oppose Wahhabism; the "easternizers," like Shamil Basaev; and the "blood avengers" seeking revenge for the deaths of their relatives who acted outside the politics of the movement. She begins to insist that by categorically refusing to negotiate with Maskhadov the Russian government "support the Basaev-Khattab group."[22]

By the third year of the war, Politkovskaia's writing begins to exhibit a tone of deep sadness. And, in her frustration, she often had few good words left for anyone. Her despair was so deeply felt and her statements were often apocalyptic, connecting the situation in Chechnya with the fall of Russia. Her desire for an international protectorate fell on deaf ears. Her criticisms of human rights activists and the Organization for Security and Co-operation in Europe (OSCE) mission in Chechnya were harsh and unwarranted, marginalizing both the efforts and the restrictions on those working in the region.[23] The tragedy was that Politkovskaia longed for a moral clarity that her government was unable to give her. "Everything depends on the man who 'carries out the order,'" she reported.

"Everything depends on his intellectual level and moral qualities."[24] "Nobody yet knows," she posited later, "what the authorities actually want from the Chechens. Do they want them to live in the Russian Federation or not?"[25]

Politkovskaia's coverage of the war elicited numerous responses. On February 20, 2001, she was arrested by the FSB, kept in a field and then a bunker, and threatened with rape and a mock execution. She was released two days later. In October 2001, she received e-mail threats from Sergei Lapin, or "Kadet," an officer from a Ministry of the Interior (MVD) unit from Khanti-Mansiiskii, serving in Grozny.[26] The month before she had published an article titled "People Disappearing," alleging that the troops from Khanti-Mansiiskii were responsible for disappearances.[27] Following the threats, she was ordered by her chief editor to leave Russia for her own safety. She traveled to Austria where she remained for one month. When flying down to cover the hostage taking of the schoolchildren in Beslan in 2004, Politkovskaia was drugged en route and ended up in hospital in Rostov, until she was returned to Moscow for treatment.[28] As the pro-Moscow Chechen administration under Akhmat Kadyrov, and then his son Ramzan, took greater control, Kadyrov junior summoned her several times, accusing her of supporting "the bandits." She was murdered outside her apartment door on October 7, 2006, President Putin's birthday, as she was preparing what would be her final article, "Karatel'nyi Sgovor" (Punitive Arrangement), which was devoted to Ramzan Kadyrov's units that were conducting torture and disappearances. It is suspected that the story may have been the reason for the contract-style killing.

While Babitskii and Politkovskaia displayed the best of a mature perestroika generation, the Chechen journalists Timur Aliev, Musa Muradov, Umalt Dudaev, Ruslan Isaev, and Mainat Abdulaeva[29] managed to report on what was taking place in their own society. Most were freelance writers for Radio Liberty/Radio Free Europe, the Caucasus Reporting Service (CRS) that was part of the Institute for War and Peace Reporting (IWPR), or Prague Watchdog. They consciously and consistently distanced themselves from the propaganda wing of Movladi Udugov, who was instrumental in pursuing the language of Islamic fundamentalism and inflaming hatred on the Kavkazcenter.com Web site that contributed very little to the reputation of the separatists.

Soon after Politkovskaia published her famous article, "The Concentration Camp Village," on Chiri-Iurt in January 2000, Chechen journalist Mainat Abdulaeva was working and living in the gutted capital. Born in

1974 and a native of Grozny, Abdulaeva started her career with the Chechen newspaper geared toward teenagers, "Respublika," at the age of sixteen and stayed on in Grozny for most of the first and second wars. She collaborated with the children's journal *Raduga* and the literary journal *Orga*, and beginning in the spring of 1995 she worked as a freelance journalist for, among others, *Novaia Gazeta*, Radio Free Europe, and Echo Moskvy. At the age of twenty-six, she published her first article for *Novaia Gazeta* titled "Here People Want to Live."[30] The title was a direct allusion to the frequent signs visible around Grozny painted on doors and buildings, such as "People Live Here!" or "Don't Shoot! Women and Children Live Here!" The article's depiction of life in Grozny over the winter of 1999–2000 was reminiscent in tone of Evgeny Zamyatin's *The Cave*, a heartfelt and tragic article on surviving in Grozny. "It is surprising how war affects people differently," she writes. "In some it awakens a profound instinct of self-preservation, in others, the instinct is completely dulled. In a dank, dirty cellar, where the newspaper refuses to burn because of the dampness, it is impossible to count the people from the rats. The lean, wet rats are finished by the famine. They no longer jump aside in fright when you approach them. Instead they wander about slowly and wearily, emitting a disgusting squeal at the first sight of food."[31]

When asked in an interview about her views on the war, she responded,

> To this day, for me, the most tragic consequence of these two cruel wars is that Chechen society, having lived for many years in such difficult conditions in a moral and physical sense, has lost something that for many centuries was the most typical, defining quality of this nation, namely its solidarity, a feeling of responsibility for others, trust and feeling of pride. All these years of war and mass terror, this conscious policy of intimidation have gradually been superseded by an atmosphere of mutual distrust which is only warmed by the authorities' thirst for profit and enrichment at any cost.[32]

The threats against Abdulaeva persisted for many years from both sides of the conflict. She was lucky to survive for as long as she did inside Chechnya, traveling to sites of bombings and of alleged disappearances, or depicting civilian life, working alone and taking advantage of her local knowledge and resident documents. The threats against her and the house searches intensified after she published an article in Western Europe on Ramzan Kadyrov and his forces. As soon as the threats began to affect her family and friends, she was forced to leave for Germany in 2004 where she now lives in exile.

It was the thin, four-page weekly broadsheet *Groznenskii Rabochii*, under Musa Muradov, however, that managed to reach civilians inside Chechnya. In the spring of 1995, Muradov returned to Grozny from Moscow, where he had escaped with his family in the early stages of the first Chechen war after President Dudaev had attempted to co-opt the paper as the government's official broadsheet. He resurrected the paper in the spring of 1999 and published it until his staff was forced to flee their offices when the Russian armed forces invaded in September. They moved across the border into Ingushetia, along with thousands of IDPs, and set up an office in a three-room apartment in Nazran.[33] Remaining in circulation with a small print run of three thousand copies, *Groznenskii Rabochii* was the last remnant of the prewar Chechen media. Every week, a vehicle packed with hidden copies of the paper crossed over the border. The staff took turns doing one-week reporting rotations in Grozny, and relied on a handful of freelance correspondents. Traveling as civilians with local registration stamps in their passports, the staff and the stringers of *Groznenskii Rabochii* could move relatively freely, without the military escorts demanded of other journalists, and with some ease through checkpoints.

Muradov's refusal to write panegyrics for either side of the conflict generated predictable enemies for the broadsheet. The Russian armed forces grew increasingly irritated with his staff's relative freedom of movement throughout the region. Searches by the local FSB and MVD began on their office in Nazran, and the security forces accused Muradov of supporting President Maskhadov after the paper's extensive coverage of the living conditions of the IDPs. In 2001, a summons was posted in the office, declaring that the Shariah Court had convicted all the newspaper's employees and sentenced them to the death penalty.[34] Muradov later received a letter from Maskhadov stating that although he did not always agree with the materials published by the paper, he was not responsible for the summons, nor would he take the lives of the journalists who worked for the paper. Muradov and his staff then began receiving threatening phone calls from Wahhabi extremists. In the fall of 2001, the office was forced to move, yet again, this time to Moscow, and the staff scattered across the country to avoid ongoing threats.

While *Groznenskii Rabochii* was forced out of the region, Timur Aliev, a young Chechen journalist, founded the weekly newspaper *Chechenskoe*

Obshchestvo. The paper began running without official registration in early 2002, and in the main it published bulletins on the basis of information coming from other local publications, or news from close friends. With a print run of five thousand, *Chechenskoe Obshchestvo* began in earnest in August 2003 and Aliev's distanced prose was a necessity. Like *Groznenskii Rabochii*, it countered the battle of images and ideas perpetuated by the propaganda wing of the Chechen separatist movement via Chechenpress.com and Kavkazcenter.com, and by the Russian press agency ITAR-TASS. Aliev, like Politkovskaia, explored the human cost. He did so in a style quite different—observed, distant, combining the opinions of political analysts and historians from Moscow and Grozny—drawing the local intellectual community into the conversation of his reports. Like *Oslobodenje*, the Sarajevo daily that was published throughout the war in Bosnia, the newspaper had the central aim of providing reliable news from a local perspective.

The nature of the Russian campaign in Chechnya was shifting when Aliev began *Chechenskoe Obshchestvo*. Pressure on the Chechen journalist came internally from all directions: the pro-Moscow Chechen administration, the separatists, and the Russian armed forces. Six months after the launch of the newspaper, he received a list of the names of 170 supposed "traitors" to the Chechen Republic of Ichkeria, in which his own name was included. The named, according to the list, which was signed "Sword of Ichkeria," were to be eliminated.[35] By August 2003, retaliation was coming from a different direction. Aliev's publisher, Souleiman Kostoev, of the Ingush publishing house Poligrafkombinat, was summoned to the Ministry of the Interior and advised to cease the publication of the newspaper. Aliev himself was summoned to the Ingush Ministry of the Interior to meet Bashir Gandarov on July 28 and questioned specifically about the newspaper's reporting on human rights violations. He was told that the ministry considered his paper "anti-government" and strongly advised him to suspend publication.[36] Given the threats, *Chechenskoe Obshchestvo* soon appeared in the pages of *Novaia Gazeta* after Politkovskaia arranged to have the main features of the weekly printed in her own paper. Aliev managed to resurrect the paper's circulation in the aftermath of the presidential elections in December.

The attack on press freedom was the first blow to civil society in Russia. The restrictions on the press exposed the vast government campaign to mute the reality of Chechnya. It is indeed questionable whether the press could have mobilized antiwar opinion nationally, even with unfettered access to the region. There was little sense of national unity in Russia. As long as terrorism served as the key word of pro-war mobilization, it was hard to find a strategy to help rekindle a national opposition to the conflict or an uncensored space in which to pursue it. The independent press did succeed, as far as it could, in arousing and sustaining debate, but it was undermined by parallel forces that sought to openly and violently link its coverage to the language of patriotism, or by radical forces seeking loyalty to Islamic jihads and caliphates. The bulk of the intimidation was no doubt generated from the Russian side and from the pro-Moscow Chechen administration. And this combination of intrusive politics and misinformation campaigns forced a cruel fate on a handful of journalists, the select few prepared to marginalize their personal safety to export news from a changing, but consistently violent, landscape.

The Moscow Human Rights Community

If the second Chechen war proved anything, it was that human rights activists would remain largely in isolated opposition to the policies of the Russian government. While journalists struggled to export news from the region, human rights activists sought to chronicle and expose the minutiae of everyday life in Chechnya. For many advocates, the Russian government's first reaction to the separatist incursion into Dagestan was an appropriate response to unprovoked aggression.[37] Oleg Orlov, one of the most respected activists in Russia, was still supporting air strikes as late as November 1999.[38] However justified the Russian armed forces' stand against aggression was, the issue quickly turned into a matter of proportion, and the slide into an appalling and horrendously costly war soon provoked feelings of dread among a human rights community well versed in the 1994–96 war. There is no doubt that the activists in Moscow felt that stepping over the border into Chechnya could have been achieved with a force of far fewer than 120,000 Russian troops and that President Putin's refusal to negotiate only signaled disaster for the region. What they did not anticipate was the extent to which they would be deliberately isolated from the region. And unlike the leverage they exerted during the first war, in the Russian parliament and among the population at large, their voices found little political support from the 5 percent democratic representation in the Duma or from their tired compatriots.

The Russian government's approach to the war in Chechnya was fundamentally schizophrenic. At times, the government was quite able to control the movement of human rights activists. At other times, it was unable to control the defiance and anonymity of the local fixers on the ground, who were monitoring and collating information to bring back to human rights organizations based in Ingushetia. Such channels, courageously opened by Chechen civilians, were the backbone of monitoring in the region. Formally, human rights groups were banned. Human Rights Watch, the famed U.S.-based human rights organization, could not enter the republic and was denied permission to enter on ten occasions.[39] The Russian human rights organization Memorial had limited access to 25–30 percent of the territory. Oleg Orlov and Alexander Cherkasov of Memorial had official IDs as aides (*pomoshnik deputata*) to parliamentary deputy Sergei Kovalev. In a testament to the power of government papers in Russia, regardless of who had them, the staff of Memorial were guaranteed significantly freer movement through checkpoints.

The human rights community launched its monitoring campaign in Chechnya against a rather ambiguous historical background with the post-Communist state. A culture of cooperation between human rights activists and the state had been established when Sergei Kovalev was appointed head of the Human Rights Committee of the Supreme Soviet under President Boris Yeltsin. This culture was spearheaded by the liberal human rights activists Ludmilla Alekseeva, Oleg Orlov, Father Gleb Yakunin, Valerii Abramkin, and Kovalev in the wake of Andrei Sakharov's death in 1989. These were new encounters for the dissident community, and Kovalev and his ilk struggled hard to create a presence in the parliament and to influence legislation on prison reform and states of emergency. But this changed when the first Chechen war broke out in November 1994. Kovalev was so marginalized by Yeltsin that he stepped down in disgust in January 1996 with a poignant resignation letter published in *Izvestiia*. His colleagues still sought cooperation, most notably in the Expert Council established by Yeltsin in June that year. But this too fell apart when the government newspaper *Rossiskaia Gazeta* led a clearly orchestrated attack on human rights activists, under the pen of Aleksei Kiva. "Our human rights activists," he argued, "have been preoccupied with God knows what, except the defense of the elemental rights of the common man." The most important component in the building of a human rights culture in Russia was patriotism, he argued. "It's impossible to ignore the fact that, for many dissidents, the West has become their second home."[40]

The government human rights institutions formed in the early Yeltsin years were gradually absorbed by the presidential administration and by nationalist forces in the Duma. They soon shaped what Elena Bonner shrewdly called "a parallel human rights movement,"[41] which rarely spoke the critical language of human rights and was severely compromised in its approach to the pressing problems in Chechnya. Kovalev was replaced by Oleg Mironov of the Russian Communist Party, appointed in a secret Duma vote in 1998. Mironov did publicly critique human rights issues, but he was by no means strident on the topic of Chechnya and at times encouraged a strong-arm approach in the region. Vladimir Kartashkin, the well-known apologist for the Soviet Union and its persecution of dissidents in the 1970s, was appointed head of the Presidential Human Rights Commission, which advised the president on human rights concerns. Similarly, President Putin organized events such as the Civic Forum in 2002 and established the Public Chamber in 2005 to encourage the formation of GONGOs—government-organized nongovernment organizations.

There were several fundamental issues at work in the Russian government's response to the human rights community in Moscow. The most pronounced was that President Putin clearly wanted to dominate civil society, and the Russian armed forces wanted to control journalists and activists in Chechnya to avoid the inconvenience of having to abide by international humanitarian law and to prevent the exposure of human rights violations. The press campaign against the human rights community during 2004 was not dissimilar to Kiva's campaign after the first Chechen war, but it was decidedly more virulent and widespread. Month after month articles accused the human rights movement of being "unconstructive."[42] Later attacks included references to the "fifth column" of left- and right-wing radicals receiving foreign funding. And the idea that the role of civil society was to serve Russia's national interests was repeatedly iterated by Sergei Lavrov, the Russian foreign minister.[43]

Against this background, many of the most notable actors returned to classic dissidence. The generation of activists that had led the response to the first war was much older by 1999. Sergei Kovalev was sixty-nine, Elena Bonner was seventy-six, and Father Gleb Yakunin was sixty-five. They were joined, however, by a strong human rights community that had burgeoned over the eight years since the collapse of the Soviet Union and who in general shared concern about the direction of Putin's leadership. This resonated in the All-Russia Emergency Congress in Defense of Human Rights, held in Moscow in January 2001, the largest conference in the history of the Russian human rights community, attended by over one thousand human rights activists from across the country. Although there was debate over the word "emergency" in the title of the conference, all agreed that there were grounds for concern.[44] This was the first semblance of a serious public debate on the new Putin government. A General Resolution was issued by the participants, concluding that "the democratic foundations of the Constitution have eroded, leading to what can be described as a creeping constitutional crisis. . . . The restrictions and violations of human and civil rights and freedoms in various areas of life have borne unmistakable signs of a slide towards authoritarianism."[45]

A resolution on the question of Chechnya was quickly passed. Its central thesis was that the war had "taken on the character of a punitive expedition. . . . Federal forces are at war not so much with the armed formations resisting the federal authority of the Russian Federation, as much as carrying out terror against the civilian population."[46] All the most pressing issues were addressed: a call for an immediate resumption of negotiations with Maskhadov, with the assistance of the OSCE; for Russia's ratification of the International Criminal Court (ICC); for a referendum, governed by international organizations, to decide Chechnya's status; for the legal status of IDPs to be agreed upon; and for open hearings on the disappeared to be convened in the Duma. The participants took the resolution to the Parliamentary Assembly of the Council of Europe (PACE) and decried the weakening of Western resolve and pressure on Russia in regard to the war, accusing the West of complacency and inconsistency in dealing with the Russian government.[47]

Ultimately, the task for Moscow's human rights community was to exert its power through collating empirical material and to exert moral pressure on national and international actors. The Moscow office of Memorial remained the most cohesive and powerful of the human rights organizations. It possessed sufficient, although by no means adequate, material support—but it was the closest thing to an institutionalized NGO in Russia. Those who worked for the main office in Moscow remained largely untouched. They were too well respected abroad—with a longstanding reputation with PACE, the UN, and other international human rights organizations, they worked closely with activists and governments abroad. But Memorial's standing also allowed them to leverage a position inside Russia and to open cooperative talks with state institutions. Along with the Moscow Helsinki Group (MHG), they helped initiate a seven-month experiment in dialogue that began in January 2002 between human rights groups—Echo of War, the Russian-Chechen Friendship Society (RCFS), the Union of Chechen Social Organizations, and the Union of Progressive

Youths and Students of Chechnya—and the FSB, the Unified Group of the Armed Forces (OGV), the Chechen Ministry of the Interior, and officials of the Special Representative of the President of the Russian Federation on Human Rights and Freedoms in the Chechen Republic.

The main objective was to discuss the ongoing human rights concerns. At the first and second meetings, on January 12 and February 28, the human rights organizations pushed for an order that demanded fundamental rules of procedure for "cleansing" operations in Chechnya. Enacted to compel the Russian armed forces to provide lists of those detained, to identify themselves with ID cards, and to promote wide acquaintance with the content of the order among the inhabitants of Chechnya, Order No. 80, signed by Lieutenant General Vladimir Moltenskoi, acting commander of the OGV, on March 27, 2002, was a concrete decree (*prikaz*). This was a decree that the human rights forces could coalesce around and it looked like a positive springboard for action and regulation. Yet it quickly grew clear that Order No. 80 was being openly flouted on the ground.[48] This brief interlude of dialogue ended in failure when government officials failed to appear at a meeting in Znamenskoe in July.[49] The consensus among the NGOs was that there was no genuine official interest in alleviating torture or disappearances.[50] For some, like the Memorial activist Alexander Cherkasov, the human rights community had become a screen for ongoing abuses and violence.

Local Chechen Resistance

While the staff of the Moscow office of Memorial suffered intermittent harassment, those inside Chechnya suffered the worst fate. The dangers they faced while investigating cases and living alongside the Russian armed forces were a challenge of a different order. When Shamil Tangiev and Lidiia Iusupova opened Memorial's Grozny office in 2000, they exposed themselves to enormous risk. Tangiev traveled to towns and villages alone in his private car, or with colleagues, to conduct interviews and to document and photograph reported human rights violations. Achieving this as a young man of thirty-two when Chechnya was covered by a tight network of military checkpoints was exceptional. After losing his parents, an uncle, and an ethnic Russian neighbor when they were shot by Russian soldiers and their bodies later burned during a *zachistka* in Grozny in January 2000, Tangiev took his law degree from the Institute of Economics and Law in Nazran and began to work for Memorial in April 2000.

The truth was that human rights activism was precisely where Chechen civilians could exert personal power. It proved to be one of the only ways to recover the *dignity* Chechen society had been so crudely deprived of. Growing to become one of the most important methods of expressing discontent, it reanimated the idea of justice for Chechen civilians. Documenting human rights violations became an organizing principle around which fears, anger, and disillusionment could coalesce and find new direction in a search for authenticity and truth. Individuals converged with a common goal: to fundamentally reject the violence that animated all sides of the conflict. The new generation of activists learned that everyday life in Chechnya was a *political* arena, despite their apparent powerlessness and the absence of human rights training in monitoring, activism, or advocacy. They had to learn their lessons quickly. This repressed, but empowered, local sector gave face to a reality, however despairing, with a sustained attempt at impartiality and focus.

On one level, the intent of the Russian government was unequivocal with regard to human rights activists. From 1999 to 2005, thirteen human rights defenders were murdered and six disappeared, and the evidence against the Russian armed forces was substantial.[51] While Memorial suffered harassment and death threats in Chechnya, it was the indigenous Russian-Chechen Friendship Society (RCFS) that was targeted most cruelly by the shifting violence. On the evening of October 2000, Ruslan Akhmatov, an RCFS employee, was struck fatally in the back of the head while walking home from the office. Just over a year later, Luisa Betergirieva, another RCFS employee, was killed at a checkpoint in Argun while trying to enter the town to interview civilians at the local hospital. She was turned away. Once her vehicle had turned around, Russian soldiers opened fire and Betergirieva was killed instantly. Five days later, the RCFS director's brother, Akhmad Ezhiev, was shot in his home at 3:00 A.M. by masked men who arrived in an APC. In early 2004, the body of Aslan Davletukaev was discovered near Gudermes; his body showed evidence of a gunshot wound and torture. He had been kidnaped on January 10 at 10:00 P.M., when around fifty armed men entered his home in the village of Avtury and took him away.

Other methods of intimidation centered on detainment, torture, beatings, and harassment of RCFS members.[52] Similar acts were perpetrated against members of the Sintar organization and the Chechen Committee of National Salvation. The central aim here was to establish the same landscape of fear and self-censorship that defined the Russian government's attitude toward journalists. Between 1999 and 2005, Imran Ezhiev, RCFS's leader, was detained seventeen times and often beaten and tortured. It was not long before legal harassment emerged as a mode of intimidation against the RCFS human rights paper *Pravozashchita,* which was based in Nizhni-Novgorod and Chechnya. The harassment began with threats directed at Oksana Chelysheva, the coeditor of *Pravozashchita,* and Stanislav Dmitrievskii, the executive director of RCFS, when flyers were posted on their doors carrying warnings such as: "We say no to the pro-Chechen vermin that live among us at our expense. Death to the enemy! We are waiting for you."[53] In 2005 the Ministry of Justice ordered RCFS to halt the publication of *Pravozashchita.* Dmitrievskii was arrested and charged with "inciting ethnic hatred" under Article 282 (2)(b) of the Russian Criminal Code. He was given four years of probation, with a two-year suspended sentence, and intimidated into silence.[54]

While individuals and organizations were relatively easy targets, the public demonstrations and the pickets initiated by the local population in Chechnya grew increasingly difficult to control. By 2001 Chechen civilians were tired of the indiscriminate violence, and local resistance began to form an integral aspect of civilian defense for those brave enough to pursue it. The protesters usually made concrete demands—the release of unlawfully detained prisoners, an end to the shelling of populated areas, the punishment of those guilty of crimes against the civilian population. Reaching their height during the spring and summer of 2001, protest rallies by Chechen civilians took place in response to the escalation of sweep operations that year. In Chiri-Iurt, women lay on the ground in front of an APC, demanding the release of the detained. Other women formed a circle around a group of men detained in a field on the outskirts of Tsotsin-Iurt, which led to their eventual release. After being constantly harassed during 2001, several hundred women in the town of Argun dragged crushed and abandoned car chassis onto the road, blocked the bridge crossing the Argun River, and demanded the release of a local schoolteacher detained on May 3 that year. Several hundred men and women gathered near the village of Novogroznenskoe, blocking the traffic on the main road passing through Chechnya. Remaining there for three days, they constantly chanted, "No to murders, sweeps, robbery and camps!" "Where are you, leaders of Chechnya? Where are the muftis? Where are the judges? They are killing us with your agreement!"[55]

FIGURE 6.1. A meeting in the village of Starye Atagi, March 12, 2002. © Memorial Archive, Moscow.

The women and elderly men who made up the local resistance were sometimes threatened with verbal abuse or shots were fired into the air to disperse them.[56] For the most part, it depended on who was in charge in the village, but their actions in some instances were successful and led to the release of many of the detained. This engagement reinforced again a modicum of civilian power against the overwhelming state power exerted in the region. On all sides it was evident that the response had to come from *within,* since no international efforts were going to significantly alter the reality on the ground in Chechnya. The long agony of the Chechens had already been marginalized by the international community. It would not be marshaled with the coming of the second Chechen war.

7

INTERNATIONAL FAILURE

The Russians barked and everyone lay down and gave up.
—*Anonymous*

Sometimes I ask myself, why doesn't the whole world stand up! The whole world should be weeping for us.
—*Chechen IDP, IDP camp, Ingushetia, 2002*

The call to establish a tribunal for Chechnya similar to the tribunal at The Hague is absurd. . . . Russia has its own judiciary system and no one can take away its sovereign right to administer justice on its territory.
—*Yevgenii Voronin, deputy official spokesman for the Russian Foreign Ministry, March 2003*

RELATIONS BETWEEN WESTERN EUROPE, the United States, and Russia did not fundamentally change over the course of the second Chechen war. There were many platitudes and forthright condemnations regarding the indiscriminate violence being used by the Russian armed forces and the retaliation by the Chechen separatist movement. Yet no dramatic measures were ever taken. There were several developments that require elucidation here, however. Not only for the sake of amplifying the integrity of the actors behind them but for what they exemplify about the Russian government's engagement with international human rights bodies, and about its return to and perpetration of an entirely *defensive* posturing that undermined the minimal achievements of the period from 1991 to 1994. The Russian government allowed both the Organization for Security and Co-operation in Europe (OSCE) and the Council of Europe to send missions to Znamenskoe in Northern Chechnya, ostensibly to observe political developments and the human rights situation. The question that concerns us here is to what extent did these missions manage to accomplish anything of significance for the civilians of Chechnya. Moreover, were they ever meant to succeed, given the constraints, both physical and structural, that were imposed on the experts by both the Russian government and their institutional sponsors?

The UN Commission on Human Rights

The international governmental struggle against the impunity in Chechnya was ultimately led by a group of concerned parliamentarians from the Council of Europe and a disparate group of diplomats and recruited political officers who made up the missions to the region. Yet the role of the UN Commission on Human Rights, as the purported leading governmental forum on human rights, is worth mentioning here for what it displays about the changing alliances between countries over the conflict in Chechnya. Mary Robinson, the UN high commissioner for human rights, proved to be an admirable spokeswoman on the region. As consciously as any human rights activist, she set about launching the reality of Chechnya onto the world stage in early 2000, urgently calling for an international commission of inquiry into the humanitarian conditions and human rights violations in the region. "My mandate requires that I be a voice for those who don't have a voice," she concluded in relation to Chechnya, "desperate people with no sense that the world cares enough."[1] But her defiant criticism was quickly struck down. And the vitriolic language she encountered was the first sign of what would later become the standard Russian response to any criticism—constructive or otherwise—on the situation on the ground in the republic. Robinson was crudely denounced by the Russian Foreign Ministry in a series of press releases that maligned her criticisms as a personal "crusade."[2] She was attacked for clinging to notions of "torture, filtration camps and the need for a so-called independent international presence in the region."[3]

Robinson was clearly affected by her visit to Chechnya in early 2000. Her report notes with distress her conversations with IDPs at the Sleptsovskaia camp, which she visited for several hours. In response to her report, the UN Commission on Human Rights initiated its first formal reproach of a permanent member of the Security Council in its criticism of Russia.[4] The 2000 and 2001 UN resolutions initiated by the EU expressed alarm at the indiscriminate and disproportionate violence of the Russian armed forces and called for a national-based and independent commission of inquiry. They also called for immediate invitations to visit the region to be sent to the UN Special Rapporteurs on extrajudicial, summary, or arbitrary executions, on torture and other cruel, inhuman, or degrading treatment or punishment, and on violence against women (as well as its causes and consequences), and to the UN Special Representatives on displaced persons and on children and armed conflict. The resolutions also urged the Russian government to begin immediately a political dialogue and negotiations with the Chechen side. While the 2000 resolution was a compromise on the initial draft that had called for an international commission of inquiry,[5] it was passed with 27 votes for, 7 against and 19 abstentions; and the 2001 resolution was passed with 22 votes for, 12 against and 19 abstentions. In the words of the Russian Foreign Ministry, the first resolution was emblematic of "the best Cold War traditions."[6] The ministry refused to accept the terms of the resolution.

It was not Robinson but the member states that ultimately controlled the votes in the UN Commission on Human Rights, however. The resolutions on Chechnya drew to a sudden halt in the aftermath of the September 11 attacks on the United States and a change in one-third of the seats on the commission. The commission's deliberations grew chaotic and highly volatile, and little constructive conversation on human rights issues took place after 2002. Country resolutions on Iran, Equatorial Guinea, and Zimbabwe were all voted down. The EU's third resolution on Chechnya was rejected by a vote of 15–16–22. Exploiting the anxiety that emerged after September 11, the Russian Federation networked heavily before the final vote, urging "all those who were against terrorism in all its forms, those who were against armed separatism, those who did not accept politicization and double standards of the Commission, to vote against this resolution."[7]

By 2003 the war in Iraq consumed most of the debates in the commission. Libya, one of the world's most flagrant violators of human rights, was appointed to the chairmanship. The body was dominated by countries with less than admirable human rights records—Malaysia, Syria, the Democratic Republic of Congo, Algeria, Vietnam, Cuba, Pakistan, Sudan, and Zimbabwe—that repeatedly underwrote each other's abysmal conduct in an effort to promote their own economic interests. Russia openly began to exploit the North-South divide and the ties forged in the fight against terrorism. The EU resolution on Chechnya was dropped for a second time. By 2004, Chechnya had for all intents and purposes been forced off the commission's radar by the politicking of the Russian representatives. The uncontested election of Sudan to the commission as it was pursuing a campaign of ethnic cleansing in the region signaled the death knell of the world's most important annual forum for discussing human rights issues.[8] Russia had finally ensured the absence of Chechens as a political and human presence in the international human rights equation.

The Council of Europe

While the UN Commission on Human Rights was constrained by its institutional framework, others were given more latitude. Independent members of the Parliamentary Assembly of the Council of Europe (PACE) soon formed the central core of opposition to the obstructionist policies of the Russian government and acted as a consistent counterweight to the disinformation campaign that accompanied the conflict in Chechnya for over six years. The site of this campaign was largely played out in the PACE auditorium in Strasbourg, and its leaders were Rudolf Bindig, a German from the Socialist bloc, and Lord Frank Judd, the British MP and former head of Oxfam.

Rudolf Bindig was to prove the ablest, most politically active advocate for human rights in Chechnya, reporting on human rights violations in the republic for a decade. As head of the PACE Committee on Legal Affairs and Human Rights, he sought to protect the reputation of the European Convention on Human Rights (1950), ratified by Russia in 1998, with a persistence only compromised by the council's executive arm, the Committee of Ministers. Bindig successfully advocated for the suspension of Russia's voting rights in April 2000 in protest over the campaign in Chechnya, but failed to convince the committee to completely suspend Russia's membership. He was given the same treatment as Mary Robinson, this time by Dmitrii Rogozin, the former leader of the fascist organization Congress of Russian Communities and author of *We Will Reclaim Russia for Ourselves*. Appointed as Russia's representative to the Council of Europe in 1999, Rogozin led the semantic war in the Parliamentary Assembly. Typical statements following the dissolution of Russia's voting rights included: "The session showed that Russia is losing the information war regarding the events in Chechnya. We have not yet managed to change the biased attitude of Europe to Russia's actions in Chechnya."[9] As the seats in Strasbourg stood empty until Russia's voting rights were restored in January

2001, Rogozin argued from Moscow: "We do not practice political tourism. PACE has executed itself."[10]

While the UN Commission on Human Rights failed to negotiate an international commission of inquiry, the Council of Europe did manage to leverage an unusual agreement with Russia. Alvaro Gil-Robles, the council's commissioner for human rights, called on the Russian government to establish a permanent human rights office in Chechnya. President Putin responded by appointing Vladimir Kalamanov as Russia's special representative for human rights in Chechnya. Kalamanov, then forty-nine, a professional diplomat and a graduate of Moscow State Institute of International Relations, headed a department in the Ministry of Nationalities and Federal Relations, and had run the Federal Migration Service between April 1999 and February 2000. Three Council of Europe experts were also granted permission to assist Kalamanov on the ground in the region. Established in May 2000, Kalamanov's office was a dubious institution[11] and was part of a broader strategy by the Russian government to create a "parallel human rights movement"[12] to counter the influence of nongovernment human rights organizations. The office was mandated to strengthen the judicial system in Chechnya, organize legal assistance to persons in detention, and assist in identifying human rights violations committed by Russian servicemen.[13] A corresponding office housed in an abandoned winery was set up to receive complaints from civilians throughout the region, to process them, and to dispatch them to either the civilian or the military prosecutors. The office had no power to investigate complaints or initiate criminal proceedings.[14]

The Council of Europe mission was the first international presence on the ground during the second Chechen war. The team arrived in Znamenskoe, thirty-seven miles northwest of Grozny, on June 21, 2000. The mission lasted for thirty months. The team's raison d'être was to assist Kalamanov with the administration of the office; to set up a registration system for complaints from Chechen citizens of alleged human rights violations by Russian servicemen; to train local staff; and to install an operative archiving system.[15] Edo Korljan, a Croatian on the Council of Europe's Anti-Torture Committee, Eva Hubalkova of the Czech Republic, a former legal aide in the European Court of Human Rights, and Peter Liskova of Finland, a former special representative on the Council of Bosnia-Herzegovina (1997–2000), were the first three individuals on a rotating mission. Joining a local staff of fifteen Chechens in the central office, the experts arrived in Znamenskoe to discover that the main office had no bank account, the staff had yet to be paid, and there was no functioning postal service to receive the complaints.[16] Volunteers in the districts had been commissioned to distribute pamphlets on the services offered by the office and to collect complaints, eventually forming twelve branches across the republic. Some of the branches, dependent on the individuals behind them, were credible; others were not.[17] The cost of securing the safety of the Council of Europe team, and their salaries, was estimated at EUR 60,000 to 70,000 a month.[18]

The complaints nevertheless poured in. With no civil or criminal court system working in Chechnya during 2000, civilians lodged their complaints regardless, traveling to the central office to hand them over personally or lodging them with the local branches.[19] By September, the main office had received 4,167 complaints and had registered 3,500 of them.[20] Within four months, the office staff had consulted 8,129 people.[21] The majority of the complaints contained allegations about illegally detained or missing relatives, illegal restrictions on freedom of movement, noncompensation for property damaged or confiscated during either the first or the second war, lack of administrative or judicial remedies, failure to provide assistance to obtain places in IDP camps, or conditions within IDP camps. Complaints also covered refusal to pay salaries or salaries in arrears, car re-registration, problems with caring for the elderly and sick, and bribes at checkpoints.[22] At that time, there were still no procedures in place for civilians to process claims on property damages incurred during the second war.[23]

The mission had no mandate to monitor human rights or initiate political negotiations. It was, for all intents and purposes, a *technical* mission, sent to train the local Chechen staff to register and archive the complaints and to build a corresponding database to filter and redirect them to the civilian or military prosecutors. Within nine months, it had grown abundantly clear that the prosecutors were not going to respond competently to the complaints lodged by Kalamanov's office. In 2001, the Council of Europe experts concluded that the major problem they encountered in their work was either the completely unsatisfactory nature of the replies from the Russian prosecutor or the absence of any replies.[24] Of the 429 applications sent to the civilian prosecutor by spring of 2001, they had received 169 replies. The military prosecutor was notably worse. The office had received only 3 responses to 82 applications.[25]

Chechen civilians traveled regularly to the office in Znamenskoe to lodge their complaints. At times they requested to speak with the experts in confidence, independent of the Chechen staff, who were still thought to represent the federal structures. And some came merely to talk, to describe conditions in their villages or elaborate on certain events they had witnessed. Many civilians were well aware of the restrictions on the mission, that it too was a victim of the circumstances in which it found itself. But the motive to explain, as it was with other human rights organizations, was driven by the fundamental human desire for others to know, to acknowledge, and perhaps even to understand what was taking place on the ground.

Formally, the mission was not supposed to negotiate with the prosecutorial bodies. By 2002 it had begun to filter out cases with sufficiently strong evidence and to set up meetings with local prosecutors to determine progress in an effort to apply consistent pressure for results. The mission discovered, however, that some local prosecutors were subject to their own burdens. When and if they attempted to penetrate cases, to investigate, their own lives were threatened by military personnel who cautioned them against proceeding further. Although it is next to impossible to understand how deeply this atmosphere of fear penetrated the prosecutorial bodies, similar situations existed elsewhere.[26]

The Council of Europe mission managed to gather impressions by talking to locals and officials. They traveled to Grozny regularly and, less frequently, to the Gudermes, Argun, Naurskii, and Nadterechnyi districts. The experts' interlocutors were varied—from local prosecutors, military commanders, and Federal Security Bureau (FSB) representatives to the imams and the councils of elders with whom they consulted on local concerns. Moreover, they provided a direct and constant insight into *everyday* life in Grozny and surrounding districts from 2000 to 2003. Their interim reports grew notably bolder and more comprehensive.[27] They exposed the complete lack of public transport in the capital, which made it difficult for the elderly to travel; the lack of foodstuffs, humanitarian aid, electricity, and gas; and the inadequate and humiliating living conditions. Schools lacked books and, overall, were in poor condition.[28] The hospitals lacked antibiotics, analgesics, thermometers, and other instruments. In the hospital in the Oktyabr'skii district in Grozny, there was no equipment to administer blood transfusions, no X-ray machines, and no sophisticated medicines.[29] Moreover, the mission concluded that the ecological situation in Chechnya was "alarming," as burning oil wells and homemade refineries continued to contaminate the soil, the air, and the water.[30]

Kalamanov was an astute diplomat, well aware of the ambiguous position his office occupied. He admitted in 2001: "I'm like the clown in the circus—I have no formal powers, but everyone can see me and hear me."[31]

This was an honest confession. Kalamanov did manage to organize the release of over two hundred detainees from Chernokozovo soon after the conditions in the prison were exposed in early 2000. Moreover, he managed to facilitate regular private or public forums where human rights advocates could speak openly and truthfully about the human rights landscape. Kalamanov was succeeded by Abdul-Khakim Sultygov as Russia's human rights representative to Chechnya in July 2002. A native of Grozny and a trained economist, Sultygov implemented several changes. During his first four weeks he prohibited the Council of Europe mission from traveling anywhere.[32] The complaints archive was moved from Znamenskoe to the ground floor of a bombed-out building in Grozny, and he fundamentally shifted the mandate of the office itself. A well-known careerist, Sultygov began to stress that the role of the office was now one of development, with an emphasis on the socioeconomic revitalization of Chechnya as the 2003 referendum grew closer. It was difficult for the mission to take the new representative seriously. By 2003, he was denying publicly that torture was taking place in Chechnya. There were "no bad feelings from among the prisoners," he claimed.[33]

The Council of Europe experts had conflicting emotions about their role. Some felt like honored guests, others like largely ignored nuisances or not-so-welcome witnesses in Chechnya. The moral pressure applied by the mission was significant. Even as indirect witnesses, the mission managed to counter the official rhetoric of the Russian government with firsthand evidence and to force the Committee of Ministers in Strasbourg to discuss its interim reports. Chechnya remained on the agenda in Europe as long as the mission continued.

The Committee of Ministers, however, had rejected Bindig's proposal to suspend Russia's membership in the Council of Europe. The committee issued a weak communiqué at its 106th session, on May 10–11, 2000. To most, the obliqueness of the communiqué was unfathomable. There was no outright condemnation of the violence in Chechnya, and no mention of the impunity and ongoing human rights violations. What was clear was that Europe's foreign ministers were prepared to allow Russia to override international law, UN resolutions, and the European Convention on Human Rights to keep Russia within its orbit of influence. The logic, aside from business and resource interests, appeared to be that it was better to have Russia inside under nominal European control than outside. If Russia was included in Europe's leading institutions, it would perhaps change its behavior. The logic is legitimate, but constructive engagement seemed to be the only idea on the strategic table. And the ultimate failure of the committee was not to condemn, consistently, repeatedly, and harshly, the actions of the Russian armed forces. This timorousness marked Europe's public defeat by the Russian public relations machine. And the offense was a serious one.

The assembly together with Human Rights Watch was unable to convince a single one of the council's member states to lodge an interstate complaint against Russia. Filing a multimember lawsuit against Russia before the European Court of Human Rights would have sent a strong signal of objection, even if the judicial ramifications had been minimal. Yet the only official response to this proposal came from Portugal. Discussions took place with other European countries, including Germany, Switzerland, the United Kingdom, and the Netherlands. But all were reluctant to pursue the course alone. "The message was pretty much the same everywhere," recalled Diederik Lohman, then a senior researcher for Human Rights Watch. "No one wanted to take the initiative. No one wanted to be the bad guy."[34]

For Rudolf Bindig, Lord Judd, and those left in the assembly, the final hope for engagement with the Russian government rested with the establishment of a Joint Working Group (JWG). With its voting rights restored in January 2001, the Russian delegation returned to PACE that winter and the Europeans sought a new lever of influence. The JWG would become one of the most controversial initiatives surrounding the war. Lord Judd was clearly a man of goodwill in a less than enviable position. His leading objective was to find a political solution to the conflict in Chechnya. By forming a working group of Russian Duma deputies and members of the assembly, he had hoped that they could work on issues together to barter solutions. But the Russian position was already fixed. Not only would the government not negotiate with Aslan Maskhadov, but it would force a political solution on Chechnya, which was the March 2003 referendum, followed by presidential elections in October.

During 2000, well before the hostage tragedies of Dubrovka and Beslan, Judd started to make some of the most damaging public statements on the war in Chechnya in an effort to build Russian confidence in the JWG. Creating a picture of parity between the crimes of the Chechen separatists and those of the Russian armed forces, he concluded, "There has been no monopoly of unacceptable behavior in this tragic saga."[35] Later, in September, he restated: "We must be clear, as I have said before, that there is no monopoly of wrongdoing in this war."[36] In doing so, Judd began to strip the conflict in Chechnya of its historical context and failed to insist that the facts of the war always be kept in the foreground of discussion. Judd's political motivations were clear, as were his moral motives—assist the people on the ground in Chechnya by ending the fighting. Few could criticize his motivations; what mattered was that the fighting stop. Yet in his focus on the political outcome, he defused the historical facts. Sitting in Moscow, Sergei Kovalev, Russia's former human rights commissioner, lamented, "Lord Judd and his counterparts became entangled in maneuvering between the truth and political expediency. . . . The Council of Europe puts zero pressure on countries violating its rules. Violators get accustomed to this and eventually realize that this chattering in PACE means nothing."[37]

The motorcade of the expert mission on the ground in Chechnya was bombed in April 2003, and the mission was taken out of Chechnya permanently. By the end of that period, Kalamanov's office had received 45,985 visitors and lodged 9,952 complaints. Of those complaints, 2,056 related to disappearances.[38] The office had followed up on 767 of them. Two hundred and twenty-one persons had been released, 49 of whom were dead on release. The remaining 546 were unaccounted for. The office was closed down after the removal of Abdul-Khakim Sultygov in January 2004, and the post of special representative for human rights in Chechnya was abolished.[39] In 2006, Nurdi Nukhadjiyev was appointed Chechnya's first human rights commissioner. While the exact fate of the archive is unknown, it is thought to be housed in Nukhadjiyev's office in Grozny.[40]

The Organization for Security and Co-operation in Europe (OSCE)

The relationship between the OSCE and Russia was shaped during the first Chechen war. President Yeltsin permitted Tim Guldimann, the Swiss diplomat, to guide the political negotiations that resulted in the Khasavi-urt Peace Treaty in 1996. Guldimann's role had been to build confidence and contacts between the opposing sides in an effort to establish a consensus for peace.[41] The mission was ultimately successful. By 1999, however, this openness and willingness to include the OSCE as a political negotiator had been essentially reversed. It took Mircea Geoana, the OSCE chairman-in-office and Romanian foreign minister, to negotiate a return presence for a six-person OSCE Assistance Group to Chechnya, whose mandate differed considerably from that established in 1995. A rotating mission arrived in Znamenskoe in June 2001, one year after the Council of

Europe mission. Living next door to the council's compound, the Assistance Group remained in Chechnya for eighteen months.

The precise mandate of the OSCE Assistance Group was in perpetual flux. Unlike the Council of Europe, which was able to negotiate its role as a technical mission, the OSCE Assistance Group attempted to maneuver a space for the organization's fundamental priorities: dialogue and negotiations, promoting human rights, establishing facts concerning their violation, and peaceful resolution of the crisis.[42] Yet the Russian government was adamant that no political negotiations would ever take place with the Chechen separatist movement. The OSCE group could not meet with the opposing side, despite the fact that President Maskhadov repeatedly dispatched emissaries, documents, and appeals to Jorma Inki, the head of the Assistance Group.[43]

The tension around the mandate was mirrored inside the mission. Some members of the team sought to stretch the mandate of the group, to create a proactive culture in the investigation and follow-up of human rights abuses during sweep operations and disappearances. Others felt that observing political developments, assisting with the drafting of the Chechen Constitution, and humanitarian work were all the group could expect to achieve without risking the closure of the mission. Getting the mandate reinstated in the first instance had been a delicate task that took a great deal of diplomatic skill. Agreeing on what to do, how much to say, and what action to take were perhaps the group's most difficult moral dilemmas.

Like the Council of Europe mission, the Assistance Group could not travel further south than Argun. Yet coming as an outsider to Chechnya was a difficult task. Protected by special forces from the Ministry of Justice (GUIN) with restrictions on their movements, the group found the monitoring of human rights difficult given the security obstacles. The first thing civilians saw was a group of men surrounded by federal GUIN troops. Traveling in military jeeps, visiting Grozny and villages, some members did manage, however, to conduct their own investigations into sweep operations and disappearances. Despite a great deal of traveling and waiting, the group had several hundred files on disappearances by the end of its mission. Over eighteen months, the OSCE team had made countless inquiries in Grozny and held numerous discussions with Nikolai Kostuchenko, the chief prosecutor of the Chechen Republic, and the Bar Association of the Chechen Republic, which resided in a small room in downtown Grozny, in an attempt to place pressure on the prosecutorial bodies.

The reports sent to OSCE's secretariat office in Vienna were a combination of important local information and standard news reports, taken occasionally from dubious sources like Interfax. The official "activity" and "spot" reports did provide a picture of various regions when accessible, yet they differed substantially in detail and analysis, as they depended on access and the personal standards of the individual responsible for the drafting.

By the end of 2002, the Russian government was insisting that the Assistance Group concentrate *solely* on humanitarian relief. With over forty local people employed on small projects all over Chechnya, the group had grown more preoccupied with humanitarian and development work. It had established a printing press in Znamenskoe, set up programs for preschool children, co-funded the rehabilitation of School No. 28 in Grozny, and instituted qualification courses for adults in accounting and computing. Extended day classes for IDP children, new playgrounds and restrooms, and general monitoring of the conditions of IDPs in the temporary housing in Gudermes, Grozny, Argun, Assinovskaia, and Sernovodsk occupied large amounts of time.

Humanitarian work, however, threatened the very core of the OSCE's guiding principles. The compromise was unacceptable to the secretariat, and the mission closed in December 2002.[44] The closure of the mission coincided with the OSCE's decision to end its monitoring activities in Estonia and Latvia, a step Moscow viewed as being detrimental to ethnic Russians in those countries.[45] The final decision to close the OSCE office in the Baltics may have influenced the Russian government's decision to close the office in Znamenskoe, but the efforts to curb the mandate of the Assistance Group had been there from the outset. By mid-2003, the international human rights presence had for all intents and purposes been closed down in Chechnya.

The tragic reality was that whatever news came out of Chechnya was not going to fundamentally change the international landscape. To a large extent, the experts on the ground were caught in a situation in which the onus of responsibility must have felt like a terrible burden, coupled with natural feelings of guilt and powerlessness. Whether the international actors succeeded in placing pressure on the prosecuting bodies is difficult to determine. While these bodies were clearly under pressure from the Russian military itself, the extent of outside influence was probably minimal. The presence of the missions did contribute to a field of "witnesses," however, and this was important. Yet Chechnya was full of local witnesses, and one did not need international experts to substantiate what was going on in the region. What their presence did do was to expose the depths of the complexities inside Chechnya. There were many local civilian administrators committed to affecting the situation, processing the raw data on people's lives and pushing it through the system—however corrupted by fear or incompetence.

One has to ultimately question what the value of these missions actually was. Were they merely used to foil criticism from Western Europe and to counter Mary Robinson's initial alarm? The answer is certainly affirmative. Yet they also suggest something more deeply alarming about the Russian government's response to the West over Chechnya. Not only were human rights concerns not essentially important in Chechnya, but Russia would not accept the international assistance it so sorely needed on questions so central to its democratic credentials. Moreover, by marginalizing the OSCE and consciously excluding it from political negotiations and human rights monitoring, and pushing it toward humanitarian relief, the Russian government was attempting to refashion the nature of the relations between these two bodies. Humanitarian relief was permissible, but human rights investigations were not. It was emblematic of the approach the Russian government had adopted from the very beginning of the second war.

As an aspiring world power, the Russian government did care how the world perceived it. It maintained a diplomatic veneer with the OSCE and the Council of Europe, and this was instrumental to its broader aspirations of keeping its foot inside Europe. This gave the OSCE and the Council of Europe some degree of leverage, however powerless the missions ultimately felt themselves to be. Yet the defensive posturing of the Russian government marked a serious step back from the early years under the Yeltsin administration.

The United States and the War on Terror

The war on terror perhaps had less effect on the relationship between the United States and Russia than it appears at first glance. The U.S. stance on Chechnya had already been firmly established under the Clinton administration in November 1994, at the outbreak of the first Chechen war, and did not fundamentally shift after the September 11, 2001, attacks. The question of Chechnya had always been secondary to a host of other issues, from missile defense and the ABM Treaty to NATO expansion. The war on terror was simply another alliance in a range of geostrategic interests.

Russia, however, won the propaganda war in Europe and the United States over Chechnya after the September 11 attacks, and, whether or not European and U.S. diplomats, politicians, or the political elite were fully convinced that Russia was fighting international terrorism in Chechnya on a magnitude similar to that which the United States was engaged in, this rationale proved a convenient escape route to sublimate the disturbing stories that continued to come out of the region.

The post–September 11 alliance that emerged between the United States and Russia did, however, mark a sudden, if temporary, decline in the number of open critiques of the situation in Chechnya. This decline was accompanied by the new and very public friendship President George W. Bush sought with President Putin, marked famously by the lines: "You're the kind of guy I like to have in a foxhole with me," and, even more flattering, "I looked the man in the eye. . . . I was able to get a sense of his soul; a man deeply committed to his country."[46] For Bush, relations with Russia had been "transformed" in the wake of September 11.[47] In the lead-up to the war against the Taliban and Osama bin Laden that began in Afghanistan in October 2001, the United States lobbied hard and successfully to ensure a strategic and military presence in Central Asia. Given that this was Russia's sphere of influence, the United States needed Russia's assistance to exert pressure in the region. Moreover, Russia offered to share intelligence, to provide airspace for humanitarian assistance, to participate in international search and rescue efforts, and to increase assistance to the Burhanuddin Rabbani government in Afghanistan.

Other alliances also emerged for Russia after September 11. The German chancellor, Gerhard Schroeder, was concerned with maintaining the flow of natural gas to Western Europe and he used the 9/11 attacks to garner favor with President Putin as well as with Gazprom, the Russian oil company of which he would later become an employee. In the aftermath of the attacks, he noted, "Regarding Chechnya, there will be and must be a more differentiated evaluation in world opinion."[48] "Differentiated evaluation" was no more than a perverse linguistic attempt to circumvent the chilling reality of Chechnya and marked a crude betrayal of those suffering on the ground. A senior member of Schroeder's Social Democratic Party was less oblique in his assessment of the changing relations with Russia after the attacks on the United States: "Silence on Chechnya is the price for this new solidarity. . . . And I don't think Germany will be the only country to pay it."[49]

Putin took strategic advantage of the new alliances. He sought to achieve two ends: to counter criticism on Chechnya and to form a new alliance with the United States. "Terrorism . . . is a truly global threat of the new century," he declared. "Without any exaggeration, I think there is every reason to compare what has now happened, in its magnitude and cruelty, with what the Nazis got up to."[50] On Chechnya he was famously resolute, and this type of hyperbole sought not only to dilute the nationalist origins of the Chechen crisis but to enhance the discourse of exaggeration already prevalent after September 11. The return to immediate national security challenges for the United States matched the strategy that had been preoccupying the Russian government since late 1999.

Moral disapproval on the question of Chechnya from those with influence was neither consistent nor resounding enough. The United States did not cave in *entirely*. While it certainly failed to take appropriate action in bodies such as the UN Commission on Human Rights, where it had supported EU resolutions on Chechnya prior to September 11, it could not in good conscience dismiss the ongoing violations as news continued to leak out, especially after the attacks on Argun in the winter of 2001–2. The evidence was too damning. Moreover, representatives of the U.S. State Department met with Ilyas Akhmadov, the Chechen foreign minister, in a hotel in Washington, D.C., for discussions in January, a move vehemently opposed by the Russian government.[51] The remarks, however, remained tepid. And when the radical strain of the Chechen separatist movement responded with Dubrovka and Beslan, the climate of antiterrorist rhetoric only escalated. Beslan was, according to some commentators, Russia's September 11.[52]

A War Crimes Tribunal for Chechnya

The 1990s limped to a close, defined by a final decade of ethnic conflict in the former Yugoslavia, the genocide in Rwanda in 1994, the ethnic cleansing of Kosovo Albanians in 1999, and Indonesia's eventual relinquishment of East Timor in the same year. This was the decade that flirted most famously with humanitarian intervention, culminating in the NATO bombing of Serb military targets in March 1999. Most argued that Western powers had little leverage over events in Chechnya. Humanitarian intervention was not an option, and the most frequently employed arguments were those having to do with Russia's still considerable nuclear threat, its resources of natural gas and oil, and the importance of protecting the fragility of its burgeoning transition to democracy.

All the arguments concerning the international community's options in Russia were legitimate ones. The highly charged reaction of the Russian government to NATO's intervention in Kosovo in 1999 no doubt served as a caution to Western Europe and its alliance countries regarding Russia's unpredictability. Rumblings from government ministries in Moscow in the first weeks of NATO's attack on Serb military targets included possible use of force, arming Belgrade in defiance of an international embargo, pulling out of weapons and security agreements.[53] Russia's NATO representatives were pulled out of Brussels and Moscow. The government dispatched a part of its Black Sea fleet through the Bosporus to the Mediterranean, under the pretext of surveying the situation.[54] The comments by the presidential administration were certainly startling—illustrating that the Russian government would in no way countenance any threat to its sphere of influence in Serbia. "I have already told NATO, the Americans, the Germans," cautioned President Yeltsin, "don't push us towards military action since that will certainly lead to a European war or even a world war which is inadmissible."[55]

This hostility was largely countered by the new alliance that Russia and the United States formed over the war on terror. Yet a proposal to PACE to install a UN peacekeeping force, first initiated by Tomasz Wojcik, a Pole of the European People's Party, was quickly shelved. This was later reshaped by Ilyas Akhmadov, the Chechen foreign minister, into a proposal for a UN interim administration in Chechnya. Backed by an enormous advocacy campaign undertaken by Olivier Dupuis and the European Radical Party, this proposal secured the support of 145 members of the European Parliament and 38,000 signatures from journalists, academics, and other concerned individuals. But the option was never given any real attention.[56] Multilateral approval for such an intervention would never have been secured by the UN Security Council.

No serious steps were ever taken to administer criminal punishment or preventive justice in Chechnya. No international war crimes tribunal, on the model of those for the former Yugoslavia, Rwanda, or Sierra Leone, was ever seriously considered. The only such attempt to genuinely acknowledge the depth of violence in Chechnya and its consequences was the self-styled initiative of the Glasnost Defense Foundation in Moscow, which quickly organized its own tribunal—"The War in Chechnya: An International Tribunal"—summoning expert witnesses to testify about events during the first war.[57] Taking place at the end of the first war, the founders of the tribunal did not seek the status of an international or domestic governmental tribunal. As well as attempting to impose legal responsibility on certain individuals, and to promote "the public moral condemnation of top officials responsible for committing war crimes and crimes against humanity," the aim of the tribunal was to ensure that the evidence surrounding the crimes would not be forgotten. In this sense it served the same role as Truth and Reconciliation Commissions.[58]

Human rights activists discussed the possibility of a public hearing in Europe over the course of the second war. But operational restrictions and rejection by European funding bodies prevented them from undertaking it.[59] It was not until Rudolf Bindig took a provocative and controversial step in March 2003 that the idea was again publicly debated. In a move that marked the apogee of his frustration, he called for the establishment of a war crimes tribunal on Chechnya on the model of the international tribunals for Rwanda and the former Yugoslavia. This was more than a rhetorical shift. Russia's lack of accountability and cooperation had evinced such frustration in Bindig that he felt it was time to respond in a manner that might truly convey his understanding of the enormity of the impunity in Chechnya. And since neither a national nor an international commission of inquiry had ever emerged, Bindig's move was a direct reaction to the absence of a comprehensive and systematic response to these crimes, by both Russia and the international community.

Bindig's announcement came two weeks before the planned referendum in Chechnya on March 23, 2003. His Russian critics interpreted his gesture as a strategy to "torpedo" the political referendum. The Parliamentary Assembly nevertheless supported Bindig's suggestion, in a vote of 92 to 27, approving Resolution 1600: "[We] consider proposing to the international community the setting up of an ad hoc tribunal to try war crimes and crimes against humanity committed in the Chechen Republic."[60] In the final draft, Bindig decided to remove his earlier comparison with the international tribunals for Rwanda and the former Yugoslavia.[61] This also left open the option for a nongovernment war crimes tribunal.

In reaction to Bindig's proposal, Viliam Smirnov, deputy head of Russia's Presidential Human Rights Commission, told the news agency Ria Novosti: "Chechnya is an inalienable part of Russia. And Russia has a judicial system of its own. It can handle domestic affairs independently. . . . An important political process is under way in Chechnya, and there is nothing like what the authors of the resolution called 'an atmosphere of impunity' in the republic."[62] "There won't be a tribunal on Chechnya, and there won't be PACE in Chechnya as well. None of their representatives will travel to the republic," Dmitrii Rogozin threatened in televised remarks from Strasbourg. "We will use today's vote to close the issue of Chechnya in PACE once and for all."[63]

The net result of the failure of international actors to organize either a government or nongovernment war crimes tribunal is that the conflict in Chechnya remains largely undefined. No *judicial* lines were or have been drawn according to international law with the guidance of qualified lawyers and judges. One arena, however, that has sought to counter this malaise is the European Court of Human Rights in Strasbourg under the auspices of the Council of Europe. It now stands as the only avenue for moral justice and financial compensation for Chechen civilians. The generation of Chechens that suffered the forced deportations of 1944 was silenced for nearly half a century. The current generation should not be subject to the same psychological repression and should be given a voice. Events in the former Yugoslavia were deconstructed and given legitimate juridical categories as a means of bringing to the surface the dimensions of the crisis itself through the war crimes tribunal. This was essential to strengthening international norms of accountability and establishing the facts. Even if we recognize that the little likelihood of a government-sponsored war crimes tribunal for Chechnya with enforceable and binding verdicts is a faint one, the establishment of a nongovernment initiative should be an urgent international priority.

8

SEEKING JUSTICE IN EUROPE: CHECHENS AT THE EUROPEAN COURT OF HUMAN RIGHTS

> The Russian government was operating what we call an administrative practice: an atmosphere of impunity in which it was very clear that no one was going to be punished for violations of human rights.
>
> —*Bill Bowring, lawyer for Chechen applicants at the European Court of Human Rights, 2005*

CHECHEN CIVILIANS HAVE FACED a distinct pattern of discrimination in the Russian legal system. The explanatory framework for *how* and *why* this is taking place is complex and must be sought on multiple levels. The picture of a systemic failure to prosecute perpetrators of massive human rights violations, however, is clear. Every case before the European Court of Human Rights bears new evidence that the Russian authorities, whether local or federal, military or civilian prosecutors, were opening criminal cases, then "playing ping-pong" with investigation files, shifting them back and forth between various officers from the Achkhoi-Martan District Prosecutor's Office to the Northern Caucasus Military Prosecutor's Office in Rostov-on-Don; opening and closing cases; or leaving investigations open indefinitely to avoid public scrutiny in the courts.[1] The recalcitrance of the authorities to punish in the period from 1999 onward was also reflected in a second important fact. Chechen civilians found themselves conducting their own investigations, gathering witness testimony at the sites of crimes, collecting evidence, speaking with human rights organizations, forcing local authorities to conduct autopsies, and doing site investigations with forensic experts. This became the fundamental condition of daily life for those interested in legal recourse. Thousands have suffered the painful reality of summarily executed, disappeared, or tortured relatives, only then to face the challenge of a legal black hole determined by a confluence of factors—political insolence, fear of criminal punishment, and bureaucratic and investigatory inexperience.

One of the overwhelming benefits of Russia's membership in the Council of Europe has been the extended jurisdiction of the European Court of Human Rights to the Russian Federation. The court's role as a partial corrective to the impunity in Chechnya has witnessed the burgeoning of one of the most important legal recourses for Chechen civilians. As of 2007, Chechens had two hundred applications pending judgment. The European Court of Human Rights is not a solution to the problem of criminal punishment or reconciliation in Chechnya, however. And herein rests the ultimate disappointment for those seeking a final vindication for the war crimes in Chechnya. With no criminal jurisdiction in Russia, the court *cannot* indict or charge individual perpetrators, it rarely summons witnesses, and it does not conduct individual investigations. The role of the court is to negotiate the arguments of both the applicant and the state authorities, on the basis of evidence provided, and then to draw a judgment on whether the Russian state has violated the European Convention on Human Rights and to award financial compensation for damages.

The role of the European Court of Human Rights in the Chechen conflict is no doubt a controversial one. What indeed is the court's ultimate purpose beyond declaratory condemnations? Is it no more than a moral arbiter acting in a Western European vacuum? And does its shadow role in Strasbourg threaten to undermine the need for genuine criminal trials? One Chechen civilian has concluded in stark terms that the role of the court is to force the Russian government to pay a fee for taking human life.[2] One cannot disagree with this conclusion. And most would probably concur that the court is by no means a sufficient response to the scale of the violence that occurred from 1999 to 2005. And it is vital that we do not forget the proper context for dealing with the war crimes and crimes against humanity that took place in Chechnya on both sides. The question bears directly upon thousands of lives. But the reality is that the European Court of Human Rights is the one consistent judicial recourse that remains dedicated to exposing the seriousness of the crimes in the Northern Caucasus and building a base of documentary evidence. As with the Kurdish cases in southeast Turkey in the 1990s, the volume and critical nature of the violations in Chechnya are forcing the Council of Europe, albeit slowly and under pressure from civil society, to intensify pressure on Russia to reform the country's domestic legislation and to open criminal trials in response to the Chechen judgments of the European Court of Human Rights. The judgments, without compliance, as Philip Leach has argued, are of little consequence.[3] Yet as of 2007, there were several determined individuals searching for more effective ways to pressure Russia to comply with the recommendations of the council. Just how successful the collective impact of the judgments and increased rigor in the Council of Europe will be is still impossible to determine.

The relationship between the European Court of Human Rights and the Russian government illustrates the ambiguous position Russia continues to hold within the Council of Europe. For despite President Putin's statements on the politicization of the court,[4] and the Duma vote rejecting Protocol 14 to fast-track applications, the Russian government is not prepared to completely alienate the court or the Council of Europe. Thus, even if the government continues to only sporadically and reluctantly punish individual perpetrators and remains embedded in an overwhelming ethos of self-protection, the process in Strasbourg is turning over. What the responses to the judgments tell us is the degree to which the Russian side is prepared to engage in a certain, if muted, degree of cooperation. The Russian Constitutional Court also sees the decisions of the European Court of Human Rights as binding, and several procedural and substantive codes have been reformed as a result of interactions with the Council of Europe.[5]

On some level, there appears to be a broader effort to reform domestic legislation. Yet with regard to Chechnya the strategy is clearer. As of 2007, the Russian government has continued to acknowledge the court judgments but manifestly avoids any follow-up through domestic criminal trials. The willingness to accept the court's mandate may well be an ongoing strategy to appease the conscience of Western Europe and to *avoid* discussion of more serious criminal trials. It is a risky game. The paradoxical truth is that every judgment risks exposing that much more about the Chechen crisis, the role of the Russian armed forces, and the recalcitrance of the prosecutorial bodies. As a consequence, much of what the court does and much of what it can achieve threatens to continue uncovering new evidence. What the wider implications of this process will be is uncertain.

NGO Justice

The shift toward the European Court of Human Rights came about because of what Chechens did constructively to change their own status and because of what was done for them by nongovernment organizations. One of the essential features of this development is that Chechens were encouraged to respond to the violations in the republic as citizens of Europe, rather than as citizens of Russia. And in this sense they defied the structural obstacles put in front of them, demonstrating the power of individual action and the transnational organizations working with them. It was Anna Kornilina, a young international relations student working for Memorial, who was responsible for initiating the first cases. She was sent to Nazran by Memorial in October 1999 to interview victims of human rights violations.[6] Gathering testimony, she met with Magomed Khashiev on the border between Chechnya and Ingushetia, and Medka Isaeva in an IDP train wagon in Nazran. Kornilina gathered the testimonies and researched the case law on the Kurdish minority in southeast Turkey. By 2002, the European Court of Human Rights had ruled in 366 cases on Turkey; 44 were applications from Kurds. The case law from Turkey and Northern Ireland would act as central precedents in forthcoming Chechen cases.

With the head of the Moscow branch of Human Rights Watch, Diederik Lohman, Kornilina gathered the Chechen testimonies and prepared the applications. The first application was filed in July 2000. At first, the Russian government argued that Kornilina had drawn up the power of attorney letters incorrectly, and cited the absence of her signature on the official memorandum as a procedural error. This attempt to dispose of the applications on technical grounds was refuted by the court and the cases were approved for hearing in December 2002.[7] While Lohman and Kornilina responded directly to the stark refusal of the Russian Prosecutor's Office to indict people for the crimes committed in Chechnya, Moscow's human rights activists and European parliamentarians battled it out with the Russian side in the Council of Europe to determine exactly how many cases the military courts had heard since the beginning of the second conflict in Chechnya. A list of Russian servicemen convicted of crimes against the Chechen civilian population was finally forwarded to Sergei Kovalev by Sergei Fridinskii, deputy prosecutor general of the Russian Federation, in April 2003.[8] In 42 criminal cases out of a total of 168 investigations, only 19 of the 51 servicemen charged were convicted. The remaining 32 servicemen were put on probation, confined to restricted military service, condemned to pay a fine, or amnestied.[9] As Rudolf Bindig concluded so emphatically when told that the case on the massacre in Staropromyslovskii had been closed for failure to identify the perpetrators,[10] "I have by now come to the conclusion that the decisive factor in the equation cannot be inability—it must be unwillingness."[11]

Human rights monitors in Russia laid the original foundation for the Chechen cases heard by the European Court of Human Rights. They set in motion a remarkable tradition, broadening the opportunities to ensure that Chechen civilians had access to legal counsel. Quickly recognizing the pressing nature of this task, Lohman established an organization independent of Human Rights Watch to provide legal assistance to those willing to apply to the court. With seed funding from the Dutch government, the Stichting Chechnya Justice Initiative was founded in Moscow, Nazran, and the Netherlands in late 2001. In London, Bill Bowring set up the European Human Rights Advocacy Centre (EHRAC), with funding from the EU, in 2003. Directed by Philip Leach, EHRAC is currently working on forty cases, with three lawyers in Moscow and five human rights liaison officers in the regions of Russia. Together, the Stichting Chechnya Justice Initiative, EHRAC, Memorial, and several independent Chechen lawyers serve as the core of the Chechen legal teams in Strasbourg.

Part of the struggle for the legal teams has been managing expectations. Potential applicants soon learn that a case may take up to five years, a perpetrator will not be indicted and punished, and applicants may or may not be granted financial compensation. More urgent is the issue of personal safety. It is clear that there are individuals or military units concerned about what the court may disclose during the examination process. Cases have been fast-tracked out of concern for the security of the applicants. More recently, names have been removed from the applications and replaced with letters of the alphabet. In May 2003, the human rights activist Zura Bitieva was murdered by the Russian armed forces, along with her husband, her son, and her brother, in their home in Kalinovskaia, northwest of Grozny, after lodging an application. Bitieva and her son, Idris Iduev, had both been detained at Chernokozovo in January 2000 and her application was linked to their ill treatment. The court was unable to directly link the murder of Bitieva to her submission in May 2003, but the evidence is highly suggestive. And a pattern has emerged. Bitieva's brother took on the case after his sister's death; he disappeared soon after.

In June 2002, Said Magomed Imakaev disappeared four months after submitting an application regarding the disappearance of his son. Sharfudin Sambiev lodged a complaint in July 2003, after his son Amir Pokaev disappeared from Starye Atagi. Some ten months later, his second son was abducted and found dead on the roadside after a search of the family's home, where it was discovered that the documents relating to the court case had been taken.[12] Said-Khusein Magomedovich Elmurzaev was murdered after filing an application with the court when the body of his son, Idris, was found on the outskirts of Serzhen-Iurt on April 9, 2004. Others have been beaten,[13] or subjected to verbal or written threats—against either the applicants or family members—or to house searches. In a total of thirteen cases, there have been twenty-nine counts of abuse.[14] Two applications have been formally withdrawn.

Human Rights Case I: *Isaeva, Iusupova and Bazaeva v. Russia*

The European Court of Human Rights ruled against the Russian government for the first time in February 2005. By June 2007, eleven judgments on Chechnya had been published by the court. And some of the cases bear rehearsal here. What is so significant about the judgments is not merely what they reveal about the Chechen conflict itself, but the ways in which they index the deep failure of principle in Chechnya, the self-censorship and the recalcitrance of the Russian government to identify individual perpetrators or military units suspected of involvement in summary executions, disappearances, or torture. The central problem for the European Court of Human Rights has been dealing with the repeated failure of the Russian authorities to hand over uncensored investigation files, thereby obstructing access to conclusive evidence to back the government's claims. One of the repeated arguments of the Russian side has been either that certain documents are not relevant to the case or that the release of documents containing sensitive military and security information would be a violation of Article 161 of the Russian Criminal Code.[15]

One of the first judgments in Strasbourg was a combined case, *Isaeva, Iusupova and Bazaeva v. Russia*, on the bombing of the Red Cross IDP convoy on October 29, 1999, near the village of Shami-Iurt on the Rostov-Baku Highway.[16] Among the thousands of civilians trying to leave Grozny on that day were Medka Isaeva (forty-six years old), Zina Iusupova (forty-four years), and Lipkhan Bazaeva (fifty-four years old). As already discussed in chapter 4, the Russian television channels RTR and ORT had announced a "humanitarian corridor" out of Grozny. Unable to cross over the border into Ingushetia, the convoy, which stretched for an estimated 4.5 to 7.5 miles, was forced to return to the capital. As the convoy turned back, it was attacked by twelve S-24 nonguided air-to-ground missile strikes, with an impact radius of over three hundred yards, from two Su-25 planes. The strikes, according to testimony, took place intermittently from approximately 2:00 P.M. to 4:00 P.M., with the planes flying as close as two hundred yards above ground level. Isaeva was wounded; her two children and daughter-in-law were killed. Iusupova was wounded and Bazaeva's car, containing the family's possessions, was destroyed. Twenty-five civilians are estimated to have been killed.[17]

The Russian government never disputed the attack. It argued instead that what took place that day in Shami-Iurt was a result of military necessity. The Russian defense argued that on October 29 there had been two Kamaz trucks full of Chechen fighters on the Rostov-Baku Highway, firing large-caliber infantry firearms at the two Su-25 planes. The highway was allegedly empty except for the two trucks. The pilots testified that they only saw the civilian convoy after the missiles had been dropped. The civilian witnesses, both the applicants and those from the Red Cross, testified that they had not seen any trucks with fighters nor witnessed any firing at the planes from the road. As Ruslan Isaev, chairman of the Chechen Committee of the Red Cross, testified,

> I and my colleagues categorically deny that the planes were allegedly shot at from the convoy. Starting from the cross-roads with the road to Urus-Martan, not only did we not see any cars with an anti-aircraft gun, but we did not see a single armed person. . . . I cannot state that the pilots deliberately aimed at the Red Cross convoy, but they could not have failed to see our trucks with the crosses on the ill-fated bridge, and afterwards they were striking at the civilian convoy for four hours.[18]

The British lawyer Bill Bowring led the Chechen legal team, along with the Russian lawyer Kiril Koroteev and Philip Leach. The team targeted three points: impunity, proportionality, and inefficient domestic remedies. Bowring first argued that a climate of impunity existed in Chechnya and there was little chance that perpetrators would be criminally punished.[19] Leach contested the Russian government's claim that the actions were taken out of military necessity. He argued that the "acts were grossly disproportionate" to the threat. Since there were no functioning courts or investigative bodies operating in the republic over the winter of 1999–2000, Koroteev argued that domestic remedies were simply unavailable to the Chechen civilians.[20]

The Russian defense, led by Pavel Laptev, was unable to provide sufficient evidence to substantiate its claim of military necessity. No plan of attack or assessment was provided to the court. The complete investigation file was not submitted, nor was the Russian government able to provide (1) convincing evidence that the Su-25 planes had been shot at; (2) evidence of the two destroyed Kamaz trucks on the highway; or (3) the identities of the Chechen fighters who had allegedly been killed. More revealing were the contradictions in the testimonies from the pilots, "Ivanov" and "Petrov" and the air traffic controller "Sidorov" (pseudonyms).[21] Ultimately, the court could not determine whether Chechen forces had been on the highway or not. It based its judgment on the *assumption* that a military response may have been warranted, given the general situation in Chechnya that fall. Indeed, the court never undermined the difficulty faced by the Russian armed forces. Given this assumption, it then based its judgment on the question of proportionality and on whether appropriate care had been taken with regard to the planning and conduct of the operation for the civilian population.[22] The court concluded that the pilots should have been informed of the planned exit corridor for October 29 and there should have been a forward air controller on the mission. It could not accept the pilots' reasoning that such a large convoy, involving thousands of people, suddenly appeared after the missiles had been fired, on two separate occasions, at 2:15 P.M. and again at 3:30 P.M. It argued that the inconsistencies in the pilots' statements, the failure to produce mission reports, plans of attack, and debriefings, and the introduction of new evidence four and a half years later evoked serious doubts about the legitimacy of the Russian government's claims.[23] Finally, the court concluded,

> No efforts were made to collect information about the declaration of the "safe passage" for civilians for October 29, 1999, or to identify someone among the military or civil authorities who would be responsible for the safety of the exit. Nothing has been done to clarify the total absence of coordination between the public announcements of a "safe exit" for civilians and the apparent lack of any considerations to this effect by the military in planning and executing their mission.[24]

The court therefore ruled that the Russian state had violated its commitment to all the applicants under Article 2 of the European Convention on Human Rights: "Everyone's right to life shall be protected by law." The Russian state had failed to provide an effective remedy under Article 13. And, finally, it had failed to honor Article 1 of Protocol 1, which states that every person is entitled to the peaceful enjoyment of his or her possessions.[25] The applicants were awarded EUR 45,000 in compensation.

What is striking about the *Isaeva, Iusupova and Bazaeva v. Russia* case is what it illustrates about the changing role of the European Court of Human Rights in what has traditionally been the domain of international humanitarian law. The court is not judging the Chechen cases according to the 1949 Geneva Conventions, Common Article 3, and Additional Protocol II on internal armed conflicts. The role of the court is to judge on individual cases. It is, however, *sub silentio* applying the principles of humanitarian law in the Chechen cases, notably the principle of proportionality.[26] Unlike humanitarian law, the European Convention on Human Rights can be applied to any conflict, from small-scale riots to full-scale insurgent wars with national armies; it does not make the distinction between "civilian" and "combatant" and in effect provides greater protection for noncivilians. Paradoxically, the standard of judgment in the Chechen cases is much higher.[27] And the European Court of Human Rights is essentially countering the poor record of applying international humanitarian law to internal armed conflicts with a new history of case law.[28]

The conflict in Chechnya should undoubtedly be judged as a Protocol II conflict, with the separatists a significant belligerent force, also subject to the rules of warfare. Yet the Russian government never acknowledged the second Chechen war as an armed conflict. The problem for the court and the applicants' legal teams concerned the Russian government's failure to define its terms under domestic law, as in the case of *Isaeva, Iusupova and Bazaeva v. Russia*. It called the Chechen conflict an "antiterrorist operation," but on repeated occasions was unable to supply the court with answers regarding how its actions in Chechnya actually fit within its domestic legal framework. Russia's Law on the Suppression of Terrorism states: "Servicemen, experts and other persons engaged in the suppression of terrorism shall be exempted from liability for such damage, in accordance with the legislation of the Russian Federation."[29] No provisions were provided for potential abuses of power or for how and when rights might be suspended for reasons of national security.[30]

Human Rights Cases II and III: *Bazorkina v. Russia* and *Luluev v. Russia*

Enforced disappearances now make up the majority of cases before the European Court of Human Rights. As of 2007, the Stichting Chechnya Justice Initiative had sixty-one cases in process. The case of Khadzhi-Murat Iandiev, brought to the court by his mother, Fatima Bazorkina, in December 2006 was the first judgment in a case of enforced disappearance.

In early February 2000, the Chechen separatist forces escaped Grozny, along the Sunzha River, and fell into an open field laden with land mines. As narrated in chapter 1, hundreds of fighters were wounded and sought medical aid from the main hospital in the southern village of Alkhan-Kala, three miles away. Soon thereafter, the village was taken by the Russian armed forces, and hundreds of fighters were later captured in buses organized for their exit.[31] Among those fighters was twenty-five-year-old Khadzhi-Murat Iandiev. On February 2, 2000, Iandiev's mother, Fatima Bazorkina, was watching NTV's coverage of the capture of Alkhan-Kala. While she was watching the broadcast, her son appeared on the screen in an exchange with a Russian colonel. "Take him away, damn it, finish him off there, shit—that's the whole order. Get him out of here, damn it," the colonel instructed the surrounding soldiers. "Come on, come on, come on, do it, take him away, finish him off, shoot him, damn it."[32] It was later established that this was Colonel General Alexander Baranov, commander of the Northern Caucasus Military District, who had given the order to execute Bazorkina's son. Two versions of what happened to Iandiev then emerged.[33] Several witnesses testified that he was made to stand against a fence for an hour and a half, under the guard of Ministry of Justice troops (GUIN). The other version was given by Ryan Chilcote, a CNN reporter traveling with the Russian armed forces who testified that Iandiev was made to stand against the fence for some ten minutes, put in an APC and taken away. He testified that a Russian general came up to him and said, "Hey, Ryan, want to shoot an execution?"[34] The other Chechen forces who were also detained that day were taken to a filtration point in Tolstoi-Iurt and then on to Chernokozovo. There was no record of Iandiev ever arriving at either of the detention points.

After seeing the NTV report, Fatima Bazorkina went immediately to Tolstoi-Iurt, Chernokozovo, and other detention points across the Northern Caucasus in search of her son. She spent three months waiting outside Chernokozovo and walking from village to village with other mothers searching for their disappeared sons.[35] She applied to prosecutors, both district and federal, the Ministry of the Interior, the Ministry of Justice, and Kalamanov's human rights office. The OSCE mission, the Stichting Chechnya Justice Initiative, and Memorial assisted her. The military prosecutor of Unit No. 20102 responded in November 2000 that for lack of evidence involving the Russian armed forces, no criminal case would be opened. Regardless, however, the Chechen Prosecutor's Office opened Criminal Investigation No. 19112 in July 2001. Later a prosecutor from the Grozny District Prosecutor's Office admitted: "No real investigation has taken place and the necessary steps have not been taken to establish and investigate the circumstances of the case."[36] Over a period of five years, the Bazorkina case was adjourned and reopened five times.

The evidence available to the court was revealing. The issue for the court was not whether Iandiev had been a fighter, which he clearly had been; the issue was his presumed summary execution by a state official. Witnesses for the Russian side testified that Colonel General Baranov's words were not a *proper* order, but rather a "figure of speech" vented in the heat of the moment. Great efforts were employed by the Russian defense to support this argument. A professor of linguistics from Moscow State Pedagogical University testified that Baranov's words could not be considered an "insult," nor were they directed at Iandiev or anyone in particular.[37] From the vantage point of the court, however, Iandiev was presumed dead. No information on his whereabouts had emerged in six years, nor had the investigation been able to supply a plausible explanation of what happened after he was captured. The court was unable to explain the delays in the investigation and the fact that key witnesses had been interviewed in 2005, five years after the event.[38] It took the court three attempts to gain access to the full investigation file. The court ruled that there had been a violation of Article 2 of the convention, on the right to life, and a failure to conduct an effective investigation. The body of evidence was conclusive enough to show that Iandiev had been detained and threatened with execution by a senior officer and that his personal safety had been placed under extreme threat. The authorities failed to provide a reasonable explanation of what happened to him, and the argument that he had escaped during an ambush was not supported by the subsequent investigation. Finally, the Russian state had violated Article 5—"Everyone has the right to liberty and security of person"—by holding Iandiev in unofficial detention. Strasbourg ruled in Iandiev's favor, awarding his mother EUR 35,000 in damages and EUR 12,241 for costs and expenses.[39]

While ruling on the fate of Iandiev, the court also judged on the rights of Fatima Bazorkina. Iandiev's mother put forward the claim that not only her son but she, too, had suffered treatment that violated Article 3 of the convention—"No one shall be subjected to torture or to inhuman or degrading treatment or punishment."[40] There was insufficient evidence from the NTV video to prove that Iandiev had been tortured. An obvious limp indicated that he had been wounded in action, but the question of torture after his disappearance was indeterminable. The judges, however, did conclude that Bazorkina had suffered inhumane treatment as a result of the prolonged and inconclusive investigation—the failure of the Russian state to adequately investigate the whereabouts of Iandiev, especially after five male bodies, dressed both in camouflage outfits and in civilian clothes, were discovered near a cemetery on the outskirts of Alkhan-Kala in mid-February 2000—and, finally, the trauma of witnessing an order to execute her son.[41] This was an extremely important development. The drafters of the 2006 UN Convention for the Protection of All Persons from Enforced Disappearances had struggled to gain recognition of disappearances as a "doubly paralyzing form of suffering"[42] for the victims as well as their families.

Likewise, the court concluded that Turko Luluev, who brought a case on the disappearance of his wife, Nura Lulueva, had been the victim of inhumane treatment under Article 3 as a result of the anguish caused by the disappearance, the manner in which the complaint was dealt with, and the adjournment and closing of the investigation at least eight times.[43] Nura Lulueva, a forty-year-old nurse, and her two cousins set out early on June 3, 2000, to sell cherries at the Severnyi market on Mozdokskaia Street in the northern part of Grozny. While at the market, sometime between 7:00 A.M. and 9:00 A.M., the three women were abducted by men in masks and camouflage uniforms. Zavala Tazurkaev, who ran out onto the street when she heard the screams of the women, was also detained.[44] Despite the protests of local civilians and members of the Leninskii Temporary Department of Internal Affairs (VOVD), sacks were placed over the women's heads and they were taken away in an APC. It was later alleged that Regiment No. 245 of the Sofrino Brigade of the Ministry of the Interior (MVD) was conducting a security check that morning on Mozdokskaia Street, and the hull number on the APC that transported the women was established to be 110.

Following the same tracks worn down by Fatima Bazorkina, Lulueva's husband began the search for his wife on the afternoon of June 3. After he made a personal request for an investigation, Criminal Investigation No.

12073 was opened on June 23. By August, the investigation had been adjourned and the Chechen Department of the Federal Security Service (FSB) informed Luluev that his wife had not been detained by law enforcement officers, the FSB, or the Ministry of Defense. Again, Luluev returned to the Chechen Prosecutor's Office to complain that he had not been granted victim status or questioned. He urged the Prosecutor's Office to locate the APC (hull no. 110) and insisted that he and his family, witnesses present at the market, and members of the Leninskii VOVD be questioned. In February 2001, the investigation was again adjourned.[45]

Nine months after her abduction, Nura Lulueva's body was discovered at the mass grave in Dachnyi, near the Khankala military base. She was one of the four women, among the fifty bodies, discovered in February 2001.[46] On hearing of the mass grave at Dachnyi, Turko Luluev traveled there to identify the body of his wife and her two cousins. A forensic report concluded that his wife had died from multiple skull fractures inflicted by a blunt solid object. Her body was transported to the village of Noiber for burial on March 5.[47]

From the vantage point of the court, there was no evidence to suggest that there were other armed paramilitaries on Mozdokskaia Street on June 3, 2000, other than Russian servicemen conducting a security operation. The court concluded, therefore, that Nura Lulueva had been abducted by state officials. The court felt that the body of evidence was sufficient to prove "beyond reasonable doubt" that the Russian state was responsible for Nura Lulueva's death and had violated Article 2 of the convention. The same complaints that stemmed from the Bazorkina case reappeared here. The court's role was also to determine whether "reasonable steps" had been taken to secure evidence with respect to the investigation, particularly with regard to promptness, evidence gathering, and forensic analysis. The problem for the court was that the effectiveness of any investigation depended in part on the files provided by the Russian side. If the entire investigation file was not handed over, the court had no other option than to assume. It could not accept, however, why it had taken twenty days for the investigation to open, and then only at the urging of Turko Luluev himself. It also concluded that the manner in which the investigation was conducted could not be described as thorough and efficient, since it was plagued by delays in taking even the most trivial steps. In particular, after a number of witnesses testified in June and July 2000 that the detained women had been taken away in an APC, this information was not followed up. No attempts to track down the APC were made, even after the witnesses had indicated its hull number, in December 2000. The first official inquiry concerning the APC dates to 2005, that is, after this information had been demanded by the court.[48]

The question that too few have asked is why more Chechen applicants have not applied to the European Court of Human Rights under Article 14 of the convention. Turko Luluev argued that the violation against his wife occurred *because* of her Chechen origin.[49] This was the first Chechen case in which Article 14 of the convention was employed. The article states that rights and freedoms shall be "secured without discrimination on any ground such as sex, race, color, language, religion, political or other opinion, national or social origin, association with a national minority, property, birth or other status."[50] The court was regrettably silent on this issue. It sidestepped the allegation by arguing that this complaint was addressed by Articles 2 and 13 of the convention and it was not considered necessary to examine the complaint separately.[51]

The issue with regard to Article 14 is no doubt a difficult one. But the racial slurs and humiliations directed at Chechens have thus far been marginalized in the judgments of the cases. The Kurds suffered a similar failure to address the issue of racial prejudice in the execution of crimes against them. The most recent precedent was the landmark case of *Nachova v. Bulgaria* of 2004, in which the court unanimously concluded that the Bulgarian state was responsible for the deaths of two Romani men. For the first time in its history, the court also found a violation of the guarantee against racial discrimination contained in Article 14, taken together with Article 2, and in doing so stressed that the Bulgarian authorities had failed in their duty "to take all possible steps to establish whether or not discriminatory attitudes may have played a role" in the events at issue.

There are numerous reasons why the court is not addressing this issue in relation to the Chechen applicants. And none is entirely adequate. The first is that any accusation of racial prejudice would have resounding political consequences for the court and would no doubt anger the Russian government. The second reason rests with the still undetermined status of Protocol 12, which deals expressly with the issue of equality. The protocol has not yet been ratified, but it was devised in response to the failure of the court to deal with questions of ethnic hatred and prejudice. Waiting for Protocol 12, however, should not in any way diminish the court's responsibility for addressing issues of racially motivated crimes, especially in cases related to Chechnya. The third difficulty for the court is one of proof. Giovanni Bonello, a Maltese judge of the European Court of Human Rights, has argued persuasively that the "beyond reasonable doubt" standard should not be the standard for proving allegations of discrimination, in particular in cases concerning the deprivation of life or inhumane treatment, and rather that the "balance of probabilities" standard of proof should be applied.[52]

Human Rights Case IV: *Chitaev and Chitaev v. Russia*

The Russian government categorically denied the use of torture in Chechnya. It was not until January 2007 that the European Court of Human Rights unequivocally refuted this claim with the first judgment on torture in *Chitaev and Chitaev v. Russia.* Two brothers, Arbi and Adam Salaudiyevich Chitaev, lived with their parents in Achkhoi-Martan with their respective families. Arbi Chitaev, a thirty-six-year-old engineer, had moved his family from the Grozny suburb of Staraia Sunzha after their house was destroyed by the bombing in October 1999. His brother, a thirty-three-year-old schoolteacher, had returned with his family from Kazakhstan to Chechnya in 1999. Both brothers were seized by officers of the Temporary Office of the Interior of the Achkhoi-Martan District (Achkhoi-Martan VOVD) on April 12, 2000.

Three months prior, the VOVD had searched the house of their parents, at 28 Matrosov Street, where the two brothers and their families had moved. With no formal search warrant, the officers stole a new cordless telephone set with batteries and an antenna. VOVD officers returned on April 12 and again searched the house, this time taking some electronic equipment and personal documents. The two brothers were asked to accompany the officers to the VOVD office. They were charged with kidnapping and participation in an unlawful armed group under Articles 126 (2) and 208 (2) of the Russian Criminal Code. Three hours later, an estimated thirty officers appeared at the house and seized all the electronic equipment, including a printer, television sets, and video and tape recorders.[53]

For the first two weeks of detention, Arbi and Adam Chitaev were kept at the Achkhoi-Martan VOVD. As the court reported:

> The applicants were subjected to various forms of torture and ill-treatment. In particular, they were fettered to a chair and beaten; electric shocks were applied to various parts of their bodies, including their fingertips and ears; they were forced to stand for a long time in a stretched position, with their feet and hands spread wide apart; their arms were twisted; they were beaten with rubber truncheons

> and with plastic bottles filled with water; they were strangled with adhesive tape, with a cellophane bag and a gas mask; dogs were set on them; parts of their skin were torn away with pliers.[54]

Transferred to Chernokozovo on April 28, the two brothers testified that they were blindfolded, put into a vehicle, and threatened with execution. At Chernokozovo, the questioning and torture occurred every two days and then about once a week, in an effort to force the brothers to confess to involvement in the Chechen separatist movement. Again they were forced into swallow position; their fingers and toes were beaten with a mallet or put in the door of a safe; they were beaten and subjected to electric shock.[55] The conditions in the cells were dire, only improving after a visit from the International Red Cross in June. On October 9, the two brothers were informed that the charges had been dropped for failure to prove their involvement. On release, they were examined by a general physician, a surgeon and a neuropathologist from the Achkhoi-Martan hospital. Both Adam and Arbi Chitaev were diagnosed with craniocerebral traumas, hypertension, posttraumatic stress, and numerous blunt injuries to the head, body, and extremities.[56] Adam Chitaev moved to Ust-Ilimsk, in Russia's Irkutsk region, where he worked as an English teacher. His brother, Arbi, sought asylum in Germany. They had been detained for over six months.

From the date of their detainment, Salaudi Chitaev complained repeatedly about his sons' abduction and the looting of their property. The case was profiled by Anna Politkovskaia in *Novaia Gazeta*. And once the brothers were released, they joined their father in the complaint process. The Achkhoi-Martan District Prosecutor's Office threatened to reopen criminal proceedings against both applicants if Adam Chitaev refused to withdraw the complaint of "illicit methods of investigation."[57] Adam Chitaev did so under duress, and the District Prosecutor's Office subsequently decided not to open criminal proceedings in the absence of sufficient evidence.[58] No investigation was undertaken. No medical examination was performed by the Prosecutor's Office, nor was any attempt made to identify and question officials who worked with the Achkhoi-Martan VOVD and Chernokozovo filtration point at the time of the Chitaevs' detention.[59]

The Russian defense essentially discounted the charge of torture. It argued only that Adam Chitaev had retracted his initial complaint and that his brother, Arbi, had arrived at Chernokozovo with a preexisting head trauma. With regard to the medical documents from the Achkhoi-Martan hospital submitted to the court, the Russian side simply refused to give them any credence. As a result, the court concluded: "On the basis of the materials before it, the Court does not find the Government's arguments convincing, since neither the authorities at domestic level, nor the Government in the proceedings before the Court, made any comments as regards the medical documents attesting to the applicant's injuries or advanced any plausible explanation as to the origin of those injuries."[60]

The court judged that the ill treatment inflicted on the brothers was torture. The pain was of "severe" proportions, inflicted with the specific purpose of obtaining a confession, and it was done so with the consent of state officials.[61]

The court's arguments by no means discounted the right of the Russian armed forces to detain suspected members of the Chechen separatist movement. The Russian side argued that during the first search on April 12 VOVD officers had confiscated tapes of televised interviews with Shamil Basaev, a videorecording of a documentary called *Nokhcho Chechnya: The Day of Freedom*, photographs of exhumations, photographs of the first applicant armed, a computer and diskettes with information concerning taped telephone conversations of members of the government of the Chechen Republic of Ichkeria in 1998, and lists of the cell phone numbers of the top-ranking officials of Chechnya, among other items. When asked to present this evidence, the defense was unable to provide the court with any of the listed material. The court ruled, however, that holding of the Chitaev brothers for two months had been a valid action under national law. The subsequent four months of detention, however, were arbitrary and unlawful. Sufficient evidence was not provided as to a reason for the prolonged detention, nor evidence that the brothers had been given the right to a trial.[62]

The court concluded that the Russian state was guilty of violating Article 5 of the European Convention on Human Rights: the right to liberty and security. The state was found guilty of violating Article 3, on torture, and of denying effective remedy under Article 13. Each of the brothers was awarded EUR 35,000 in compensation.[63]

Public Hearings

There is a growing consensus that the European Court of Human Rights should institute fact-finding hearings in the Chechen cases.[64] This strategy gained significant ground after the Kurd cases were tried in Turkey. With the repeated failure of the Russian government to disclose information from the investigation files, it has grown increasingly difficult for the court to draw satisfying conclusions. As the judgments illustrate, the court can *infer* from nondisclosure of documents—but just how far inferences can act as confirmation that state authorities are responsible for a particular crime is a complex problem and is determined on a case-by-case basis. The fact-finding hearing is a formal private hearing that draws together the applicants to tell their stories before a European judge. The court requests that the national authorities call on identified state witnesses, who may either have witnessed events or be suspected of having information about the case, to appear before the judge, to listen to the testimony of the applicants, to give their own statements, and to respond to questions.

The fact-finding hearing symbolizes a shift in the reach of the court, well beyond its declaratory role. Summoning witnesses to answer directly in front of a judge from the European Court of Human Rights is essentially an interrogation procedure. This is certainly a far larger step over the border of state sovereignty than has previously been taken by the court.[65] The issue now is to convince the court that this strategy is essential both on a pragmatic level, for gaining further evidence, and as a psychological tool in dealing with the Chechen cases. The failure to disclose documents from the Russian side has been of an order far greater and far more systemic than with the Turkish government in the Kurdish cases.[66] Of course the court is anxious about the political implications of fact-finding hearings held on any state territory. There is the problem of safety for the applicants and the judges, especially after Luzius Wildhaber, the former president of the European Court of Human Rights, claimed that he may have been poisoned during a visit to Russia in October 2006.[67] There is the problem, also experienced in Turkey, of whether the state witnesses selected by the court would actually appear or testify in a way that was other than evasive or misleading to protect either themselves or a military unit. But what the hearings may do is provide an opportunity for victims and state actors to meet in a one-to-one environment that may have a psychological resonance capable of disclosing new evidence.

The Russian government has fulfilled its obligations to the applicants on a number of levels. It has paid the required financial compensation on time and in full.[68] It has distributed the judgments of the court to the appropriate bodies. The problem, however, rests with the *substantive* obligations. The first responsibility relates to the reopening of domestic criminal proceedings on the cases in question to ensure the prosecution of the responsible parties.[69] With regard to *Isaeva, Iusupova and Bazaeva v. Russia,* the Chief Military Prosecutor's Office reopened the investigation in late 2005. Yet serious questions lingered. Who exactly was responsible for the investigation of the case and who would guarantee the type of impartiality a new investigation would require? What legal options were available if and when a state official simply refused to give adequate responses to questions about a serious violation? And what means were available to the victim if a prosecutor refused to prosecute?[70]

The Chechen legal teams have urged the Committee of Ministers of the Council of Europe to continue pressuring Russia to implement domestic measures to prevent a repeat of the violations in question—to provide training to the armed forces, security forces, and law enforcement agencies, prosecutors, and judges using the standards in the European Convention on Human Rights—and called for an overhaul of the *Army Field Manual*.[71] The Russian government claimed, in its strikingly oblique and sweeping response, that it had complied with most measures and was in the process of revising an army manual on international humanitarian law, and that it showed videos on law and provided other published materials as part of general army training. No titles or copies of these documents and videos were provided. No details on what progress had been made in the investigation of the case of *Isaeva, Iusupova and Bazaeva v. Russia* have been provided. By 2007, still no new material on the investigation had emerged.[72]

There is no doubt that a more sophisticated and rigorous approach to the enforcement of the court's judgments is needed. The Committee of Ministers has a collective responsibility to exert pressure. The point is that the Russian state is merely *invited* to inform the Committee of Ministers of the measures it intends to take.[73] No time frame is instituted for the reply, and greater transparency is urgently needed.[74] The committee secretariat needs to be staffed appropriately to provide a unified front of peer pressure.[75] The PACE Rapporteur Erik Jurgens has recommended that a special mechanism of interagency cooperation be established to monitor the implementation of the Strasbourg judgments.[76] Furthermore, a special monitoring commission should be established in Russia, as in Ukraine, with the specific and sole purpose of monitoring the domestic response to the judgments.[77]

The main issue now is to prove to the court that there is a *systemic* failure in Russia to investigate cases of serious human rights violations in Chechnya.[78] The questions, of course, remain: What is motivating this failure? How much is the center pulling the strings? How much of the inaction is based on fear, inadequate education, inexperience, or lack of political will? The question of mere disorganization in the regional and federal bodies cannot be dismissed. Nor can the role of fear. Local prosecutors have confessed that they have greatly feared for their lives and those of their families in the course of pursuing a case.[79] Some internal power structure, whether the military prosecutor or the FSB, is ensuring that individual complaints are closed or indefinitely investigated. There is definitely a strategy in place to check and hold potentially damaging evidence that would identify either individuals or military units. Who exactly is orchestrating this and to what degree it is federal or local are almost impossible to determine. Too much is still to be disclosed.

The leading lawyers for the Chechen applicants, Bill Bowring and Philip Leach, appealed to the Committee of Ministers to institute criminal proceedings against two senior Russian officers, Major General Vladimir Shamanov and Major General Yakov Nedobitko. The court has already concluded that both are responsible for the "massive use of indiscriminate weapons."[80] Moreover, Bowring and Leach called for the prosecution of the pilots "Ivanov" and "Petrov" and the air traffic controller "Sidorov," responsible for the attack on the Red Cross IDP convoy.

An impressive demonstration of the challenges faced by the Russian judicial system in prosecuting war criminals was the case of Colonel Yuri Budanov, a senior officer who murdered eighteen-year-old Elza Kungaeva. The second case was that of Captain Ulman and his three colleagues, who executed five Chechen civilians at a checkpoint in the village of Dai in the Shatoi region. Both cases had strong bodies of evidence but were plagued by obvious struggles behind the scenes. Even with the strong evidence against Budanov, and several retrials, the general was declared temporarily insane at the time of the murder. The Russian Supreme Court finally overturned the decision, and the colonel was finally convicted and sentenced to ten years in prison. Captain Ulman and his colleagues were twice acquitted by a jury in Rostov-on-Don before being tried in absentia. They were convicted after they failed to show up for the trial—they had all fled.

Finally, there is still the unresolved question of national reconciliation. Will fact-finding hearings or the court judgments play a role in reconciliation in Chechnya? How do the rulings affect the likelihood of national reconciliation between Russians and Chechens? They may ameliorate some of the pain of the victims; at the very least, international bodies are acknowledging injustice. Despite its palpable limitations, the court no doubt offers moral compensation, a vital fact. And while Chechens are denied the benefits of citizenship in Russia, the court has managed to give them the sense that, at the very least, there is one international body that recognizes the violence inflicted upon them. But the pain was not eased by the culture that imposed it. After the judgments, civilians remain in an environment where the perpetrators remain free and in a landscape still shaped by humiliation and violence.

The crimes of the separatists have not been addressed either, nor have those of the current Chechen government of Ramzan Kadyrov. One of the major problems is that the court deals *only* with state crimes, and the Chechen separatist movement has been exempt from these judgments. One of the future problems for the European Court of Human Rights will be the question of reconciliation inside Chechnya, between Russians and Chechens and among Chechens themselves. There will be long-term consequences if the Russian government, civil society, and the international community fail to begin thinking about a process and the repercussions of a policy that accords Chechens a place in the European Court of Human Rights while denying them the right to criminal justice in Russia.

CONCLUSION

The military war may be over but the psychological one continues.
—Rashid, Grozny, 2006

THIS BOOK HAS SOUGHT to describe the wide-ranging human rights violations of the second Chechen war—the bombings, summary executions, disappearances, and torture perpetrated by the Russian armed forces—and Chechen retaliation. The point of this work has been to move beyond a single interpretation of the crimes of the second conflict in Chechnya as an unfortunate consequence of a civil war. By illuminating the disproportionate violence and evaluating the motivating factors that drove the Russian government to inflict such pain and humiliation on the Chechen people, this book seeks to generate and contribute to a deeper discussion of exactly those factors that prevailed at the center of this conflict.

There are several models or metaphors that might help us understand the practices of the Russian government beginning in 1999. In the first place, the violence in Chechnya may be conceptualized as part of a dramatic reassertion of the Russian state. By September 1999, aligning his rhetoric with that of international counterterrorist debates, the president-in-waiting, Vladimir Putin, launched a more decisive campaign to rejuvenate Russia, both internally and abroad. This campaign took various forms and, as Andrei Illarionov has argued, reached its completion in 2005 with the takeover and formation of quasi-state corporations in energy and major infrastructure to form a corporatist state.[1] This consolidation of economic power demanded the centralization and management of the state bureaucracy and the takeover of assets from individual oligarchs. It witnessed the appointment of regional leaders and the extensive rebuilding of the Federal Security Service, which today has 40 percent more officers per citizen than it had in Soviet times.[2] It was the second Chechen war, therefore, that provided such a momentous opportunity for the seizure and consolidation of state power. The aim of centralizing power and restoring the integrity of the Russian state through nationalist discourse was matched with the familiar idea of foreign enemies—this time international terrorists—in an effort to ease the transition of Prime Minister Putin to the presidency in March 2000. The antiterrorism agenda was no doubt legitimate, but its extreme magnification sought to heighten long-held fears related to state security and foreign enemies that had dominated so much of the Soviet Union's political landscape.

The new government under President Putin and the state's deflated military stood to gain enormously from the conflict in Chechnya. The success of President Putin's statist exercise was intimately linked to the restoration of the military and its success in the region. If the new president was serious about asserting Russia's dominance in the international arena and restoring national pride, he had to prove that the Russian army was still capable of victory despite the humiliation of the first Chechen war. A newly assertive state suited the posturing of the Russian military hawks, most notably Colonel General Valerii Manilov, Major General Vladimir Shamanov, and Lieutenant General Gennadii Troshev, who led the second war, albeit at the provocation of radical Chechen separatists. The public statements of the Russian generals confirmed the extraordinary spirit of revenge that lay at the heart of much of the campaign. This pattern of reckless violence, however, had been well established with the first Chechen war. No personnel were ever held to account for the excesses of that conflict and such protection only contributed to the culture of immunity that defined the second campaign. Similarly, the recalcitrance of the new Russian government with regard to negotiations with the moderate Chechen side and its decision to send 120,000 troops over the border into Chechnya in pursuit of a long and destructive campaign displayed the obsessive desire of the *siloviki* for control over the state at any human cost.

This idea of strengthening Russian statehood was intimately linked to a rise in state-sponsored nationalism. At first, the nationalist frame was linked to decorative gestures such as reinstating the melody of the Soviet national anthem and may well have been accepted as the harmless consequence of a declining Russian state, keen to reassert itself. But the frame grew to encompass serious misrepresentations, such as honoring Joseph Stalin for making Russia "great" and dismissing his mistakes as no greater than those of his Western counterparts to censoring the history of the Great Terror and the Gulag in school textbooks.[3] To feed this need for control, the government launched a massive takeover of the major media outlets to channel information and nationalist propaganda to its own ends. Reprisals against those seeking freedom of expression and information became commonplace. And the new nationalism sought to internalize Russian experience by generating an increasingly inward-looking vision.

It was this nationalist frame that helped reforge the emotional foundation for an already deep-seated mood of prejudice against Chechens. This mood of intolerance was significantly enhanced by the provocative incursion into Dagestan in August by radical Chechen actors, by the apartment bombings in Moscow, regardless of who was responsible for them, the rise in minority migration to major cities, and the toll of prolonged warfare. Conceptualizing the second Chechen war through the prism of racism, therefore, is a necessary and important contribution to this debate. The full extent of this prejudice was disguised by the Russian government's perpetuation of international terrorism as the idée fixe of the conflict. This strategy was ingenious on two fronts. On one level, it succeeded in uniting the country against a common enemy and urged Russians to shift their loyalty to the mission of the state. On another level, it concealed the internal nature of the conflict and deflected the idea that Russia was engaged in a conflict motivated in part by racial prejudice. Igor Ivanov, Russia's foreign minister, was astute enough to insist as early as 2000 that "The war in Chechnya is against international terrorism—not Chechens, but international bandits and terrorists."[4] It was a subtle campaign. Foreign mercenaries were in Chechnya, supporting the radical wing of the separatist movement, but not on the scale purported. Chechens were cast as victims of a force they could not control and this was to a large degree true—but the war was not a war of liberation. The Chechen population ended up the victim of two political agendas: latent Russian neo-imperialism and Wahhabi extremism. The crudity of power drove both.

Apportioning blame to an outside faction of Islamic fundamentalists was in itself a strategy of disempowerment. The aim of the Russian government was to avert control away from President Aslan Maskhadov, who had been duly elected to power in 1997, and back to the Russian state. In completely disenfranchising the Chechen government and casting it as a supporter of international terrorism, the Russian government legitimated its strong tactics as the price and rigors of a counterterrorist operation. While historical memory remained important in relation to the construction and perpetration of Chechen stereotypes, as well as a legacy of discrimination at the level of social and professional relations, I would argue that these constructs gained new momentum in 1999. The resonant subtext of this antiterrorism propaganda was that all Chechens, as latent or active supporters of the separatist movement, were in some form or another supporters of international terrorists. The population was cast, as it had been historically, as "bandits" and recast in modern parlance as "terrorists." When asked how he would describe "the wife of a Chechen fighter," General Shamanov responded, "She is a female bandit."[5] This process of association goes a long way toward explaining the collective punishment inflicted on the Chechen population. Yet this broader context, as Babchenko's memoir reminds us, was also reinforced by the strong cultural differences the troops experienced on the ground, including the small domestic objects, symbols of another worldview that incited an incongruous rage among certain Russian troops.

The language around this war provides some vital clues to this growing atmosphere of intolerance. Language often expresses particular stereotypes or deeply held racial views, and it is important to remember that words like "bandits" and "terrorists" and discriminatory attitudes were not circulating on the margins of Russian society. They existed at the very center of Russian political and military life. We witnessed such prejudice on two fronts: on an institutional level, as embodied in government statements like those of Yuri Luzhkov, the mayor of Moscow, and President Putin; and in everyday practices as testified by civilians on their treatment by Russian soldiers, as well as the graffiti on the walls across Chechnya that the Russian journalist Anna Politkovskaia poignantly emphasized. The emergence of the term *zachistka* is especially important here and is to a large degree an extension of this prejudice. While I have argued that it constituted a mind-set as much as a set of practices that encompassed varying degrees of violations, its ubiquitous nature and crude tone did set a conscious agenda. The corresponding militarization of language in everyday discourse in Russian society was one of a variety of factors that helped shape the articulation of latent racism and aggression in Chechnya.

We do not know how the events in Chechnya were coordinated by the Russian administration. We do not know to what degree the Kremlin coordinated action with the Ministry of Defense, or whether departments were acting alone, notably the Ministry of the Interior (MVD) and the Federal Security Service (FSB). Yet the bombings were not spontaneous, random acts of violence, nor were the sweep operations, the disappearances, the torture, the looting, or the humiliation. The widespread practices of disappearances and torture did at the very least form a consistent pattern, whether we are able to prove the existence of a formal policy or not. What we do know is that the impunity of the perpetrators did not disturb the Russian command or the pro-Moscow Chechen administration enough for either to insist that it be stopped. The category of crimes against humanity against the civilian population of Chechnya, therefore, most notably the bombing campaign of 1999–2000, the policy of enforced disappearances, and the torture, does allow us to capture more poignantly the dimensions of what occurred as crimes against the whole of humanity as such. The degree to which particular practices attack our sensibilities as human beings is one of the most important criteria in identifying crimes against humanity. Such practices must certainly be at issue with regard to Chechnya.

A sharp dividing line does appear to separate conscript soldiers from the Special Forces. The reticence of some conscript soldiers to engage violently in this war stems from their own mistreatment and an empathy for Chechen civilians also disempowered by the Russian state. This landscape of humiliation shared by Russian conscripts and Chechen civilians does undercut on some level the argument for an all-pervasive racism. Degrees of racism can change, dependent as they are on the political environment; they are also a function of personality, and there were always exceptions in this war. The racism displayed by contract soldiers and by OMON, SOBR, and GUIN officers was clearly a form of ego defense that served to bolster their own self-esteem and justify their actions, but this should not exclude the possibility that some within the Russian armed forces might have wished for a different, less brutal outcome. The reasons compelling soldiers to loot reflected, I would argue, a number of confluent social concerns in Russian life more generally. There was a financial crisis within the Russian army, which was incapable of providing adequate equipment and wages to or boosting the morale of its soldiers. Trying, therefore, to determine the motivating line between economic hardship and racial prejudice is more complex in this instance, but the mere readiness of the Russian command to allow conspicuous looting suggests, at the very least, a callous indifference. In the extreme, it was a gesture aimed at disempowerment and humiliation—the removal of the lingering items of personal value, symbols of self-respect and identity, that defined Chechen civilian culture and everyday life.

In the number of bodies and the amount of property destroyed there is little comparison between what the Russian government did to Chechens and what, in retaliation, the radical Chechens did to Russians. Yet Chechen war crimes played a decisive role in the conflict and they, too, should be subject to analysis. The parallel authority within the Maskhadov government that grew into a fundamentalist faction was indeed a response to the brutality of the 1994–96 war. Yet it was also a result of the extremist views and personal agendas of ideologues like Zelimkhan Yandarbiev and Movladi Udugov, who aggravated an already tense political environment. The crimes committed by the Chechen radicals, especially those at Dubrovka and Beslan, are complex. They suggest both a deepening desperation on the part of members of the civilian population, notably women, and a growing cooperation with more fundamentalist ideas and ideological support, as well as the formation of corresponding *jamaats* across the region in Ingushetia, Dagestan, and Kabardino-Balkariia. The threat posed by the extremists was real, while their interactions with Al Qaeda networks, from the evidence available, were real, though not substantial, and it is extremely difficult to sustain an argument that they were working on behalf of Al Qaeda or the Taliban. Yet the motivating agendas of the radical Chechen separatists had become highly questionable by the time of the Dubrovka and Beslan tragedies. For this very reason, the crimes committed by these extremists stand not only as atrocious war crimes but as crimes that mark the death knell of public sympathy for the cause of the Chechen separatists, radical and moderate.

The desire for control embodied in the Putin presidency extended also to Russia's civil society and to the broader international community. While Chechens remain the ultimate victims of this era, this book has sought to provide an extensive critique of the ways in which the reassertion of Russian statehood was exemplified in the treatment of journalists and human rights activists who worked on exposing the breadth of the war and protecting where possible the rights of those on the ground. The treatment of Russian journalists Andrei Babitskii and Anna Politkovskaia exemplified this most profoundly, as did the harassment of the Russian-Chechen Friendship Society. In addition, the Putin administration, although never intending to close the door completely on Western countries—in relation to any criticism of its actions in Chechnya—remained recalcitrant. Public statements by government representatives, notably Dmitrii Rogozin in PACE, the Russian foreign minister, Igor Ivanov, and the minister of justice, Yuri Chaika, were more than disarming in both their gross misrepresentation of the crisis and their one-sided portrayal of events. As Mike Hancock, the British Liberal MP, ruefully concluded after Ivanov's speech to PACE in 2001, "His account of the facts would have put the leading acrobat in the Moscow state circus to shame."[6]

If the stakes had not been so high, the taunts and polemics in Europe might well have been interpreted as embarrassing displays of hubris. Yet they were crude counterattacks that buttressed, time and time again, any question of a serious and productive discussion on the question of Chechnya. The modus operandi of the Russian emissaries to Western Europe was to prove that "normalization" was taking place in the republic, and the Russian government did ostensibly cooperate with human rights organizations, the OSCE, and the Council of Europe on human rights issues. But the cooperation was a gesture without substance, effectively illustrating how well the presidential administration had learned to adopt the language of human rights while simultaneously pursuing its own agenda.

* * *

Where does this leave us in relation to the human rights question of Chechnya? One of the only ways to pressure the Russian government to initiate further criminal trials is to continue consolidating a strong body of evidence of human rights violations in the republic. With each judgment, the European Court of Human Rights is building up the argument for a more thorough and more comprehensive investigation into events in Chechnya from 1999 onward. And the proposed fact-finding hearings would undoubtedly assist this process. There is an urgent need, however, for an independent international commission on Chechnya, based on the model of the Kosovo Commission led by Judge Richard Goldstone. This commission would be nongovernment, led by leaders of human rights groups, academics, and lawyers, and its mandate would be to address the scale of the human rights violations that have taken place in Chechnya. It would deal with individuals guilty of crimes from *both* parties, an important reality that the European Court of Human Rights is unable to address. The specific purpose of the commission would be to establish the facts and identify grave breaches of the 1949 Geneva Conventions, including war crimes and crimes against humanity. It should also address the role of racial discrimination in the conflict and the rise of racism and xenophobia more generally in Russia. The commission should be supported by a documentation project that would include extensive interviews with Chechens and Russians, as well as the collation of documentation, video footage, and photographs from both the first and second wars. An accompanying research program would assist the commission in establishing the facts and analyzing them. While this book has elaborated on the human rights crisis in Chechnya from 1999 onward, it has also sought to uncover and expose the depth of research that still urgently needs to be undertaken.

The European Court of Human Rights on its own is not sufficient to address the gross human rights violations in Chechnya. It is not the solution to the problem, but one of several methods of dealing with states like Russia that refuse to accept responsibility for large-scale state crimes. Power has to be exerted more fully in the third sector in relation to conflicts like those that took place in Chechnya, where the international community has little or no power to exert its influence. This is precisely where documentation projects and nongovernment war crimes tribunals must be supported by philanthropic organizations. While the Ford Foundation and the Open Society Institute have continued their vital support of Memorial in Moscow, the groundwork has to go beyond monitoring to a more comprehensive program that embodies sound research in conjunction with a political agenda. And this agenda is to awaken others to the crimes, to keep the dialogue open, and to prove that the third sector exists as a power within itself that not only can genuinely threaten state recalcitrance but in this instance can threaten state obstructionism. The point is that when governments reject either retributive or restorative justice, it is the role of the third sector to make the record public.

This project is all the more urgent since the introduction of a public program in Grozny titled "No Traces of War." Instituted by the Moscow-backed Chechen president Ramzan Kadyrov, the initiative carries the slogan "By 2008, we shall be free of all traces of war."[7] While on the surface this campaign ostensibly relates to the rebuilding of Grozny, the implication extends further. It would be disingenuous to suggest that Chechen society *cannot* move on from its past, for it is doing so and it can. Although there are those who believe that the legacy of violence can never be swept away, the crude truth is that societies can and do move forward with material concerns and aspirations for peace as understandable life objectives despite latent and past violence. The point therefore rests in our obligation to ensure that the memory of these wars is *not* countered by government slogans or the urban sounds of construction, promising a prosperous future at the expense of a tragic past.

NOTES

Introduction

The epigraphs to this chapter come from S. Kovalev, "Kovalev Takes Grim Message to U.S.," *Moscow Times*, February 18, 2003, and V. Putin, cited in Memorial Human Rights Center, "Zdes' Zhivut Liudi" (Moscow: Memorial, 2003), 3.

1. A. Glucksmann, "Chechnya's Antiterrorists," *Wall Street Journal*, May 14, 2004.
2. S. Kovalev, "Ne znat', ne slyshat', ne ponimat': Khronika—pozitsiia—mnenie" (Moscow: Memorial, 1995), 23.
3. "Russia: Explosive Politics," *Economist*, September 18, 1999.
4. "Ekonomika terrorizma 'Chechenskii' shet," *Profil'*, no. 036, September 27, 1999; "Velikaia Chechenskaia Stena," *Izvestiia*, August 7, 2003.
5. A. Politkovskaia, "Deti Chechenskikh 'Spetsoperatsii,'" *Novaia Gazeta*, March 4, 2002.
6. "Developments in Chechnya—Round Up," ITAR-TASS Weekly News, February 21, 2003.
7. Kovalev, "Kovalev Takes Grim Message to U.S."
8. "RIA Reports Results of Successful Crime Fighting in Chechnya in 2000," RIA News Agency/BBS Monitoring, May 28, 2000.
9. Human Rights Watch, "'Welcome to Hell.'"
10. Estimate by the Memorial Human Rights Center, "Chechnya, 2004: Abductions and 'Disappearances' of People" (Moscow: Memorial Archive, 2005).
11. Rome Statute of the International Criminal Court, http://www.un.org/law/icc/statute/romefra.htm (accessed July 2005).
12. Denber, "Glad to Be Deceived."
13. A secret report on crimes committed in Chechnya, written by the Chechen Temporary Administration, was leaked to the press in April 2003. See Memorial Human Rights Center, "The 'Cleansing' Operations in Sernovodsk and Assinovskaia Were Punishment Operations (5.07.2001)."
14. Memorial Human Rights Center, "Poteri grazhdanskogo naseleniia v Chechenskikh voinakh (10.12.2004)."
15. Bowring telephone interview.
16. This quote is from the father of a young man who was summarily executed in June 2004. See Human Rights Watch, "Worse Than a War."
17. "Priamaia Rech," *Kommersant Daily*, no. 216, November 23, 1999; "Daite nam pravo voevat' na storone Rossii," *Kommersant Daily*, no. 077, March 5, 2000; "Okhota za tarakanami na minnom pole," *Slovo*, no. 005, January 26, 2000; "Nado razmazat' etikh 'klopov' po stene: Ivan Rybkin znaet, kak dobit'sya mira v Chechne," *Kommersant Daily*, no. 146, August 19, 2002.
18. Ivanov, cited in Council of Europe, Parliamentary Assembly (PACE), "Conflict in Chechnya and Credentials of the Russian Federation and Address by Mr. Ivanov, Minister of Foreign Affairs of the Russian Federation"; "Conflict in Chechnya and Credentials of

the Delegation of the Russian Federation [resumed debate]"; and "Letter from the Minister of Foreign Affairs of the Russian Federation to the Secretary General of the Council of Europe."

19. V. Havel, Mary Robinson, Prince Hassan bin Talal, George Soros, Frederik Willem de Klerk, Yohei Sasakawa, Desmond Tutu, and Karel Schwarzenberg, editorial, *Daily Star*, http://www.dailystar.com.lb/article.asp?edition_id=10&categ_id=5&article_id=22567# (accessed May 2004).

20. See M. Boot, *Genocide, Crimes against Humanity, War Crimes: Nullum Crimen Sine Lege and the Subject Matter Jurisdiction of the International Criminal Court* (Antwerp: Intersentia, 2002).

21. "Public Statement Concerning the Chechen Republic of the Russian Federation," press release, July 10, 2003, Council of Europe Archive, http://www.coe.org/ (accessed May 2004).

22. Human Rights Watch, "Swept Under."

23. R. Kaliyev, "The Particulars of a 'Cleansing,'" *Perspective* 12, no. 1 (September–October 2001), http://www.bu.edu/iscip/vol12/kaliyev2.html (accessed March 2009).

24. U. Dudaev, "Chechen Rebels Radicalize: Radicals and Islamists Now Dominate the Ranks of Chechen Rebel Fighters," Institute for War and Peach Reporting's Caucasus Reporting Service, no. 330, March 9, 2006.

25. LAM Center Grozny, "Appeal to United Nations Security Council," http://www.idee.org/genocideappeal.htm (accessed January 2005). See also Bisultanov interview and Subject 8A interview.

26. Convention on the Prevention and Punishment of the Crime of Genocide, Adopted by Resolution 260 (III) A of the United Nations General Assembly on 9 December 1948, http://www.hrweb.org/legal/genocide.html (accessed April 2004).

27. Maura Reynolds, "War Has No Rules for Russian Forces Fighting in Chechnya," *Los Angeles Times*, September 17, 2000.

28. Convention on the Prevention and Punishment of the Crime of Genocide.

29. Footage available at http://bi.gazeta.pl/im/2095/m2095011.rm (accessed January 2006); a copy also resides with the author.

30. Rome Statute.

31. See Boot, *Genocide*.

32. Ibid.

33. Ref 3/180.01, 16.01.2001, letter to Rudolph Bindig from Yuri Abazov.

34. Ref 3/179.01, 16.01.2001, letter to Rudolph Bindig from Yuri Abazov.

35. Council of Europe, "Conflict in the Chechen Republic—Recent Developments."

36. See Kramer, "The Perils of Counterinsurgency."

37. Ibid.

38. V. Putin, cited in Jean Michel Carré's documentary film, *The Putin System: From the KGB to the Kremlin* (Paris: Les Films Grain De Sable, 2008).

39. A. Zakaev, "Chechnya: We Are Not Your Enemy in the War on Terror," *International Herald Tribune*, June 19, 2001.

40. Ibid.

41. "Russia Helps U.S. Hunt Down Terrorists, Sees Vindication for Chechnya," Agence France-Presse, September 12, 2001.

42. See European Committee for the Prevention of Torture and Inhuman or Degrading Treatment or Punishment (CPT), "Public Statement Concerning the Chechen Republic of the Russian Federation, July 2003," http://www.cpt.coe.int/documents/rus/2003-33-inf-eng.htm (accessed December 2004).

Chapter 1. The Bombing, 1999–2000

The epigraphs to this chapter come from "Pause in the Russian War on Chechnya," National Public Radio from the "Sputnik" Refugee Camp, Ingushetia, January 9, 2000, and M. Abdulaeva, "Evropogrom, ili reportazh iz byvshego goroda?" *Novaia Gazeta*, no. 64, September 2, 2002.

1. Hughes, *Chechnya*, 20.
2. Ibid., 25.
3. Ibid., 29.
4. Ibid., 68.
5. J. Hughes, "Chechnya: The Causes of a Protracted Post-Soviet Conflict," *Civil Wars* 4, no. 4 (Winter 2001): 11–48.
6. V. Kogan-Yasni, *Perekresta Chechenskie* (Moskva: Yrebus, 1995), 19–20.
7. Hughes, *Chechnya*, 57.
8. Ibid., 76.
9. Ivan Rybkin apparently appeared on television stating that President Dudaev had met with Defense Minister Pavel Grachev and proposed such a discussion. Eliza Moussaeva, e-mail correspondence with the author, October 29, 2008.
10. E. Gilligan, *Defending Human Rights in Russia: Sergei Kovalyov, Dissident and Human Rights Commissioner, 1969–2001* (London: Routledge, 2004).
11. *Report of the President's Commission on Human Rights (1994–1995)* (New York: Kline Archive, 1996), 29.
12. Frederick Cuny concluded that approximately 30,000 civilians were still left in Grozny. See F. Cuny, *An Assessment of the Humanitarian Situation in Chechnya, Ingushetia and Ossetia* (New York: Kline Archive, 1995), 7.
13. Human Rights Watch, "Russia's War in Chechnya: Victims Speak Out," vol. 7, no. 1 (New York: Human Rights Watch, 1995), 3, http://www.unhcr.org/refworld/publisher,HRW,,RUS,3ae6a7d2c,0.html (no longer available).
14. Baiev, *The Oath*, 131.
15. Hughes, *Chechnya*, 91.
16. Cherkasov, "Zalozhnichestvo na Kavkaze v kontse 90-kh."
17. "How We Met: Jon James & Camilla Carr," *Independent*, January 11, 2004.
18. "Why Did I Survive and Other Hostages Didn't?" interview with Vincent Cochetel, *Refugees Magazine*, no. 114 (1999), http://www.unhcr.org/publ/PUBL/3b8130d49.html (accessed May 2006).
19. See Souleimanov, "Chechnya, Wahhabism and the Invasion of Dagestan," 57, and Hughes, *Chechnya*.
20. Baiev, *The Oath*, 213.
21. D. Dudaev, cited in Souleimanov, "Chechnya, Wahhabism and the Invasion of Dagestan," 57. See also "President of Chechnya Backs Islamic State," *New York Times*, November 21, 1994.
22. Souleimanov, "Chechnya, Wahhabism and the Invasion of Dagestan," 57.
23. "In the Spotlight: The Special Purpose Islamic Regiment," Center for Defense Information: Terrorism Project, Washington, DC, May 2, 2003, http://www.cdi.org/terorrorism/spir-pr.cfm (accessed August 2005).
24. Ibid.
25. Souleimanov, "Chechnya, Wahhabism and the Invasion of Dagestan," 57.
26. I. Shevelev, "My Foxhole Was Out in Front: A Thursday Morning with Aslan Maskhadov," *Obshchaia Gazeta*, February 18, 1998.

27. A. Maskhadov, cited in Souleimanov, "Chechnya, Wahhabism and the Invasion of Dagestan," 56.

28. Souleimanov, "Chechnya, Wahhabism and the Invasion of Dagestan," 56.

29. This is the expression of Chechen human rights activist Eliza Moussaeva. E-mail discussion with author, October 28, 2008.

30. Hughes, *Chechnya*.

31. "Congress of Peoples of Dagestan and Chechnya Deemed Illegal," ITAR-TASS, Moscow, in Russian, 1110 GMT, April 20, 1999.

32. "Russia: Possible Culprits of Dagestan Attack Named," Interfax News Agency, Moscow, in English, 1102 GMT, May 28, 1999.

33. "7 Troops Killed in Chechen Gunfight," *Moscow Times*, June 19, 1999.

34. According to Eliza Moussaeva, the Chechen public had been waiting for Maskhadov to come out publicly against Basaev and his radical supporters. This declaration seemed, in the end, too late. Eliza Moussaeva, e-mail discussion with the author, October 28, 2008.

35. *Sovershenno Sekretno*, October 5, 1999.

36. Aslan Maskhadov, cited in *Moscow News*, no. 21, June 9–15, 1999. There was also suspicion that Maskhadov was planning a meeting with President Yeltsin. There is speculation that it was the chance of this meeting that finally pushed Basaev and his Dagestani supporters into leading the incursion into Dagestan. Eliza Moussaeva, e-mail discussion with the author, October 28, 2008.

37. The estimates on the number of fighters ranges from 300 to 2,000.

38. "'Islamic Republic' Proclaimed in Russian North Caucasus," Interfax News Agency, Moscow, in Russian, 0757 GMT, August 10, 1999.

39. *New York Times*, September 6, 1999, September 7, 1999. See also "Dagestan Blast Death Toll Rises to 61," Agence France-Presse, September 7, 1999.

40. An ethnic Karachai was prosecuted.

41. NTV News coverage, September 1999, http://www.youtube.com.

42. Ibid.

43. "Chechnia: Krovavyi schet," *Sovetskaia Rossiia*, no. 010, January 27, 2000.

44. "Yeltsin Foes Urge an End to Campaign in Chechnya," *New York Times*, September 29, 1999.

45. V. Putin, cited in Politkovskaia, *A Dirty War*, 58. See also Wide Angle PBS, "Greetings from Grozny," http://www.pbs.org/wideangle.

46. Eliza Moussaeva, e-mail discussion with the author, October 28, 2008.

47. V. Putin, "PM Putin Vows to Stay the Course," *Moscow News*, September 29, 1999.

48. I. Ivanov, cited in PACE debates: "Address by Mr. Ivanov, Minister of Foreign Affairs of the Russian Federation"; "Conflict in Chechnya and Credentials of the Delegation of the Russian Federation [resumed debate]"; "Letter from the Minister of Foreign Affairs of the Russian Federation to the Secretary General of the Council of Europe."

49. "Address by Mr. Ivanov."

50. Malinkina and McLeod, "From Afghanistan to Chechnya."

51. "Imitating NATO: A Script Is Adapted for Chechnya," *New York Times*, September 28, 1999.

52. R. Evans, "The Use of Russian Air Power in the Second Chechen War, Report by Fort Leavenworth School of Advanced Military Studies," http://www.red-stars.org/ (accessed November 2007). See also "'Tochechnyi Udary.'"

53. Ibid.

54. "Convention on Prohibitions or Restrictions on the Use of Certain Conventional Weapons Which May Be Deemed to Be Excessively Injurious or to Have Indiscriminate Effects, Geneva, 10 October 1980." Ratified by the Soviet Union, now Russian Federation, on June 10, 1982, http://www.icrc.org/.

55. "While no comprehensive surveys have been done to document unexploded cluster munitions, clearance specialists have encountered them with regularity, and press accounts and human rights groups have documented many deaths and injuries caused by cluster bomb duds." See report "Chapter 3: Cluster Munitions Use by Russian Federation Forces in Chechnya," http://www.mcc.org/clusterbombs/resources/research/death/chapter3.html (accessed March 2009).

56. "The Destruction of Chechnya," Prima News Agency, February 9, 2004.

57. Médecins Sans Frontières, "Chechnya: The Tracking of Civilians." See also "Evidence of War Crimes in Chechnya," by Diederik Lohman, Rachel Denber, and Jean-Paul Marthoz.

58. "Kto stoit za potokom 'bezhentsev' iz Chechni," *Rossiskaia Gazeta*, no. 194, October 1, 1999.

59. Witness testimony by Saidan, age sixty-two, in Médecins Sans Frontières, "Chechnya: The Tracking of Civilians."

60. Witness testimony by Abdulkhader, in Médecins Sans Frontières, "Chechnya: The Tracking of Civilians."

61. Ibid.

62. Dmitrii Shalganov, "Russian Pilots Jubilant as Chechnya Toll Mounts," *Boston Globe*, November 3, 1999.

63. Deputy Commander of the North Caucasus Military District, Lieutenant Colonel Gennady Troshev, cited in "Round-Up: Heavy Fighting Reported as Chechens Engage Russian forces," Deutsche Presse-Agentur, December 2, 1999.

64. "Colonel General Viktor Kazantsev," *Krasnaia Zvezda*, no. 014, January 26, 2000.

65. "Kazantsev: I Will Go to the Limit in Chechnya," *Trud*, November 10, 1999.

66. "Kuznitsov Krovnikov," *Itogi*, March 7, 2000.

67. See Sergei Yastrezhembskii, "My zashchishchaem mirovuiu tsivilizatsiiu," *Krasnaia Zvezda*, no. 017, January 29, 2000.

68. "Usually Silent, the Military Urges Hard Line on Chechnya," *New York Times*, November 7, 1999.

69. "Russia Rebuffs Chechen Peace Overture," *The Guardian*, October 12, 1999.

70. "Russia Seizes Major Chechen City," *Ottawa Citizen*, November 14, 1999.

71. "Maskhadov: If I Were Allowed to Speak with Yeltsin We Would Negotiate," *Vremia MN*, October 13, 1999.

72. "Ruslan Aushev: I Strongly Feel That the Kremlin and Maskhadov Should Strive for an Agreement," *Komsomolskaia Pravda*, November 2, 1999.

73. "Maskhadov Calls for Halt to Military Operations in Chechnya," Interfax, December 15, 1999.

74. Bouckaert, "Testimony before the Senate Committee on Foreign Relations."

75. "Flee or Die, Chechens Warned," *The Guardian*, December 7, 1999.

76. Associated Press Worldstream, December 1, 1999.

77. "Russia Hits Chechen Strongholds," *International News*, December 14, 1999. See also "Rasskaz ochevidtsa o sobytiyakh v Groznom: Yanvar'–Fevral' 2000" (Moscow:

Memorial Archive, 2000); "Zaiavleniia zhitelei Chechni"; M. Abdulaeva, "Zdes' khoteli zhit'," *Novaia Gazeta*, February 2, 2000.

78. "No Way out of Grozny for Its Terrified, Elderly Residents," Associated Press, December 9, 1999. See also Memorial Human Rights Center, "Soobshchenie nabliudatel'noi missii Pravozashchitnogo Tsentra 'Memorial' v zone konflikta v Chechne (17.12.1999)."

79. "Chechens in Peace Talks Shot by Islamist Extremists," *Independent*, December 2, 1999.

80. "Chechens Pull Back towards Grozny Center in 'Tactical' Retreat," *International News*, December 29, 1999.

81. "Civilians Tell of Executions," *St. Petersburg Times*, December 24, 1999.

82. Human Rights Watch, "No Happiness Remains." See also Memorial Human Rights Center, "K sobytiiam v sele Alkhan-Iurt (24.12.1999)."

83. Memorial Human Rights Center, "K sobytiiam v sele Alkhan-Iurt (24.12.1999)."

84. Ibid.

85. Ibid.

86. Chadaeva interview no. 2.

87. "Chechnya: Ecological Woes: Unchecked Oil Spills and Radiation Leaks Are Threatening the Health of Chechens," Institute for War and Peace Reporting, June 5, 2003.

88. "Russia Hits Chechnya with Scuds, Tank Fire," *Star-Ledger*, January 1, 2000.

89. "Putin Asserts National Pride Is at Stake in Chechen War," *New York Times*, December 31, 1999.

90. "Chechnia: Boi v Argune i Shali," ITAR-TASS, January 10, 2000.

91. General V. Kazantsev, quoted in Human Rights Watch, "Russia Closes Borders to Chechen Males."

92. Human Rights Watch, "Civilian Killings in Staropromyslovsky District of Grozny."

93. Baiev, *The Oath*, 300.

94. Memorial Human Rights Center, "'Counterterrorism Operation' by the Russian Federation in the Northern Caucasus throughout 1999–2006."

95. Ibid. See also European Court of Human Rights, *Isaeva, Iusupova and Basaeva v. Russia*, http://www.echr.coe.int/ (accessed March 2005).

96. "Main Street, Grozny," *Toronto Star*, February 7, 2000.

97. Memorial Human Rights Center, "Zdes' Zhivut Liudi" (Moscow: Memorial Archive, 2003), 13.

98. "On the Situation in Chechnya," *What the Papers Say*, February 25, 2000.

99. Article 3 common to all four 1949 Geneva Conventions, http://www.crimesofwar.org/thebook/article3.html (accessed May 2005).

100. Rome Statute.

101. Memorial Human Rights Center, "Rasskazy ochevidtsev bombardirovki kolonny bezhentsev 29 oktiabria 1999 goda (26.11.1999)."

102. Rome Statute.

103. Evangelista, *The Chechen Wars*, 61.

Chapter 2. The *Zachistka*, 2000–2002

The epigraphs to this chapter come from V. Kazantsev, *Krasnaia Zvezda*, no. 014, January 26, 2000, and "Only You Can Save Your Sons," *New York Times*, July 8, 2001.

1. This is the term taken from the Protocol Additional to the Geneva Convention of 12 August 1949, and Relating to the Protection of Victims of Non-International Armed Conflicts (Protocol II), June 8, 1977.

2. "Order: Commanding United Forces in the North Caucasus Region of the Russian Federation, No. 80 March 27, 2002" (Moscow: Memorial Archive, 2002).

3. Memorial Human Rights Center, "Appeal to the UN Commission for Human Rights, 59th Session 2003 (27.03.2002)."

4. I derived this figure from a database search of 7,236 articles in 63 Moscow central newspapers run on the Eastview Database of Russian Newspapers from 1999 to 2005. The search term was *zachistk*[a] from January 1, 1999, to February 12, 2005.

5. Robert Lagerberg, Department of Russian, University of Melbourne, Australia, e-mail discussion with the author, December 15, 2006.

6. *Tikhookeanskaia Vakhta*, no. 041, October 14, 2004.

7. Dr. Robert Lagerberg, Department of Russian, University of Melbourne, Australia, e-mail discussion with the author, December 16, 2006.

8. Norman Naimark makes this link between "chistki" in the Russian context and the German word "Sauberung." He notes that German racial thinking did create the term "völkische Flurbereinigung," which was an agricultural metaphor indicating the cleansing, in this case of alien ethnic elements, from the soil. See *Fires of Hatred*, 4.

9. See *Moskovskii Komsomolets*, no. 11, February 18, 2001.

10. See *Voennyi Vestnik Yuga Rossii*, no. 037, September 4, 2000.

11. See *Moskovskii Komsomolets*, no. 217, November 11, 1999.

12. See *Novaia Gazeta*, no. 068, September 15, 2005; *Novaia Gazeta*, no. 012, March 27, 2000.

13. See *Izvestiia*, no. 106, June 25, 2005.

14. See *Nezavisimaia Gazeta*, no. 074, April 25, 2001.

15. See *Agenstvo Voennykh Novostei*, November 28, 2000.

16. See "Filologiya," *Itogi*, no. 47, November 23, 1999.

17. See *Trud*, no. 188, October 7, 1999.

18. Sergei Kovalev, "Na moikh glazakh on pogibal dvazhdi," *Obshchaia Gazeta*, no. 050, December 15, 1999.

19. Getty, *Origins of the Great Purges*, 40.

20. Ibid., 38.

21. Peter Holquist, e-mail discussion with the author, December 9, 2006. See also S. Singleton, "The Tambov Revolt—(1920–21)," *Slavic Review*, no. 3 (1966): 497–512; Erik-C Landis, "Between Village and Kremlin: Confronting State Food Procurement in Civil War Tambov, 1919–1920," *Russian Review* 63 (January 2004): 70–88.

22. See Holquist, "State Violence as Technique," 30. Sheila Fitzpatrick, Arch Getty, and Peter Holquist have not come across the word *zachistka* in their work on either the revolutionary or Stalinist period (author's conversations with Fitzpatrick, Getty, and Holquist).

23. Memorial Human Rights Center, "Vsemi imeiushchimisia sredstvami: Operatsii MVD RF v sele Samashki 7–8 Aprelia 1995 g." (Moscow: Memorial, 1995), 41.

24. Ibid.

25. P. Grachev, cited in *Segodnia*, no. 028, February 22, 1996.

26. Search conducted from January 1, 1995, to December 30, 1995, using Eastview database.

27. *Zavtra*, no. 018, April 30, 1996. See also *Segodnia*, no. 036, June 5, 1996.

28. "Slova Goda," *Moskovskie Novosti*, no. 050, December 28, 1999.

29. Press release, Department of Defense, *Krasnaia Zvezda*, October 30, 1999. See also *Krasnaia Zvezda*, no. 217, October 9, 1999; *Krasnaia Zvezda*, no. 219, October 13, 1999; *Krasnaia Zvezda*, no. 224, October 20, 1999; *Krasnaia Zvezda*, no. 230, October 28, 1999.

30. Press release, Department of Defense, *Krasnaia Zvezda*, no. 218, October 12, 1999.

31. Volga Military District.

32. North Caucasus Military District.

33. Siberian Military District Command.

34. Daily of the Leningrad Military District.

35. Moscow Air Defense Force and Air Force Command.

36. Magazine published by General Staff of Russia's armed forces.

37. Newspaper of the Russian Federation Railway Troops.

38. Pain, "The Second Chechen War."

39. Memorial Human Rights Center, "Zachistka Poselok Novye Aldy, 5 Fevralia 2000—prednamerennye prestupleniia protiv mirnovo naseleniia" (henceforth *Zachistka*).

40. Three witnesses testify to the use of cluster bombs. See Human Rights Watch, "February 5."

41. Documentary by Viktor Popkov, February 9, 2000 (Moscow: Memorial Archive, 2000).

42. *Zachistka*.

43. Other witnesses talk of them arriving after lunch. Some claim they were older than twenty-five.

44. *Zachistka*.

45. Ibid.

46. Chadaeva interview no. 2.

47. Human Rights Watch, "February 5."

48. *Zachistka*.

49. Documentary by Viktor Popkov, February 9, 2000.

50. *Zachistka*.

51. Chadaeva interview no. 2.

52. Ibid.

53. Ibid.

54. Ibid.

55. Ibid.

56. Ibid.

57. Chadaeva interview no. 3.

58. *Zachistka*.

59. Chadaeva interview no. 4.

60. Human Rights Watch, "February 5."

61. Medical Foundation for the Care of Victims of Torture, "Rape and Other Torture in the Chechnya Conflict." There is a short summary in this report of a man who witnessed the events at Novye Aldy and was tortured during detainment.

62. Documentary by Viktor Popkov, February 9, 2000.

63. *Zachistka*.

64. Human Rights Watch, "February 5." This woman's name has been changed to protect her identity.

65. Medical Foundation for the Care of Victims of Torture, "Rape and Other Torture in the Chechnya Conflict."

66. Under the Ministry of Justice.

67. Under the Ministry of the Interior.

68. Although "filtration point" was not an official term, Lieutenant General Vladimir Moltenskoi used it in a meeting with human rights organizations in Znamenskoe on January 12, 2002. See Memorial Human Rights Center, "Myths and Truths about Tsotsin-Iurt: December 30, 2001–January 3, 2002 (16.01.2002)."

69. Interview with Oleg Orlov, "Crimes of War Project," April 18, 2003, http://www.crimesofwar.org/chechnya-mag/chech-interview.html (accessed July 2004).

70. "Chelovek iz drugogo ushchel'ia: Beseda v bronetransportere s nachal'nikom razvedki po doroge na Duba-Iurt," *Izvestiia (Rossiia)*, no. 054, March 28, 2003.

71. "The purposeful infliction of severe pain." This is the definition offered by Parry, "Escalation and Necessity," 153.

72. This letter was originally published in *Le Monde* on February 4, 2000. The full text was published in "Esli est' 'ad', to eto mozhno uvidet' zdes'—Fil'tratsionnye lageria v Chechne i sud'ba Andreia Babitskogo," on Radio Svoboda/LibertyLive, February 10, 2000, http://www.memo.ru/Search/search.pl?q=%E0%F3%EB%E5&s=R&cache=290311&stpos (accessed March 2009). See also *Moskovskie Novosti*, no. 007, February 22, 2000.

73. "Esli est' 'ad', to eto mozhno uvidet' zdes'—Fil'tratsionnye lageria v Chechne i sud'ba Andreia Babitskogo."

74. *Kommersant Daily*, no. 216, November 23, 1999. See also *Komsomolskaia Pravda*, no. 039, March 1, 2000. The allegations were echoed by the World Organization against Torture, which issued a statement in Geneva, Associated Press, February 18, 2000.

75. Memorial Human Rights Center, "Fil'tratsionnye lageria v Chechne (14.03.2000)."

76. Testimony of Khassan Abdullaev in *Novye Izvestiia*, March 1, 2000.

77. Human Rights Watch, "'Welcome to Hell.'"

78. Ibid.

79. Ibid. See also "Obyknovennyi Genotsid," *Versiia*, March 7–13, 2000.

80. Ibid.

81. No last name provided.

82. Memorial Human Rights Center, "'Zachistka' v Shami-Iurte, Fevral' 2000" (Moscow: Memorial Archive, 2000).

83. "Moscow Keeps Firm Lid on Chechnya's Human Rights Outcry," Deutsche Presse-Agentur, February 23, 2000.

84. *Krasnaia Zvezda*, no. 031, February 18, 2000.

85. *Vremia MN*, no. 034, March 3, 2000.

86. "Chechens Say Russian Are Torturing Refugees; U.S. Official Urges Moscow to Investigate Reports from Detention Camps," Associated Press, February 18, 2000.

87. Memorial Human Rights Center, "To Members of the Parliamentary Assembly of the Council of Europe by Human Rights Centre, Memorial, Moscow, September 25, 2000."

88. O. Orlov, "Chlenam Parlamentskoi Assamblei Soveta Evropy, June 28, 2000" (Moscow: Memorial Archive, 2000).

89. *Sevodnia*, March 13, 2000.

90. V. Kartashkin, cited in "Check Your Facts, Snaps Moscow's Human Rights Commissioner as Rubin Reports Chechnya Atrocities," Ria Novosti, February 23, 2000.

91. Memorial Human Rights Center, "Swept Under—The Sernovodsk Sweep: July 2–3, 2001" (Moscow: Memorial Archive, 2001).

92. Memorial Human Rights Center, "Myths and Truths about Tsotsin-Iurt: December 30, 2001–January 3, 2002 (16.01.2002)."

93. Ibid.

94. Memorial Human Rights Center, "'Zachistka' sela Avtury" (Moscow: Memorial Archive, 2002).

95. Of the eighty-nine sweeps studied for this book, these were the most common forms of torture. See also Memorial Human Rights Center, "Doklad: Pytki v Chechne: 'Stabilizatsiia Koshmara'" (Moscow: Memorial Archive, 2006), and Memorial Human Rights Center, "The First 'Cleansing' Operation in the Village of Mairtup, June 2001" (Moscow: Memorial Archive, 2001).

96. Ibid.

97. Testimony of Malika Ortsueva, in Memorial Human Rights Center, "Testimonies of the Inhabitants of the Village of Tsotsin Iurt" (Moscow: Memorial Archive, 2002).

98. See testimony of "Salambel Sulumov" in Human Rights Watch, "Swept Under." See also *Moskovskie Novosti*, no. 31 (July 31–August 6 2001).

99. Memorial Human Rights Center, "'Cleansing Operations' in the Village of Chiri-Iurt: May–June 2001 (30.07.2001)."

100. Memorial Human Rights Center, "Zachistka v sele Shuani: 24 iiulia i 11 avgusta 2000 g." (Moscow: Memorial Archive, 2000).

101. Memorial Human Rights Center, "Zachistka v sele Gekhi: 8–10 Avgusta, 2000" (Moscow: Memorial Archive, 2000).

102. Memorial Human Rights Center, "'Zachistka' v poselke Chernorech'e: 30 Avgusta–1 Sentiabria, 2000 g." (Moscow: Memorial Archive, 2002).

103. A. Seierstad, *The Angel of Grozny: Orphans of a Forgotten War* (New York: Basic Books, 2008), 234.

104. Kaliyev, "The Particulars of a 'Cleansing.'"

105. Memorial Human Rights Center reported that the number was closer to 300. The head of the local administration, Vakha Arsamakov, said to HRW that 438 locals were detained, plus 182 IDPs. See Human Rights Watch, "Swept Under."

106. Ibid.

107. Memorial Human Rights Center, "The 'Cleansing' Operations in Sernovodsk and Assinovskaia Were Punishment Operations, 09.07.2001" (Moscow: Memorial Archive, 2002).

108. Human Rights Watch, "Swept Under."

109. "Order: Commanding United Group Forces in the North Caucasus Region of the Russian Federation, No. 80, 27 March 2002." Cited in "Zachistki goes Bureaucratic," *Chechnya Weekly* 3, no. 10 (April 1, 2002).

110. "Zachistki Goes Bureaucratic."

111. "I budet mir cherez nedeliu posle 'zachistki' Groznogo, utverzhdaet rossiiskoe voennoe rukovodstvo," *Literaturnaia Gazeta*, no. 001, January 1, 2000.

112. Memorial Human Rights Center, "Myths and Truths about Tsotsin-Iurt: December 30, 2001–January 3, 2002 (16.01.2002)."

113. Medical Foundation for the Care of Victims of Torture, "Rape and Other Torture in the Chechnya Conflict."

114. Ibid.

115. Memorial Human Rights Center, "'Zachistka' v sele Tsotsin-Iurt: 25–29 iiulia 2002 goda (9.08.2002)."

116. Ibid.

117. *Dispatches from Chechnya*, no. 22, February 27, 2002.

118. M. Lazreg, *Torture and the Twilight of Empire* (Princeton: Princeton University Press, 2008), 254.

119. General Kvashnin, cited in Pavel Felgenhauer, "Degradation of the Russian Military: General Anatoli Kvashnin," *Perspective* 15, no. 1 (October–November 2004), http://www.armscontrol.org/act/2004_12/acprint (accessed October 2005).

120. Ibid.

121. S. Main, "North Caucasus Military District: Defending Russia's Interests in the Caucasus, (1996–August 1999)," June 2000, http://www.globalsecurity.org/ (accessed October 2005).

122. Memorial Human Rights Center, "Cleansing Operation in the Village of Chernorech'e, June 29, 2001," interview with Avalu Ajdamirov, a resident of the village of Chernorech'e, July 6, 2001 (Moscow: Memorial Archive, 2001).

123. Memorial Human Rights Center, "Myths and Truths about Tsotsin-Iurt: December 30, 2001–January 3, 2002 (16.01.2002)."

124. Memorial Human Rights Center, "'Clean-up' Operations in the Village of Tsotsin-Iurt: October to November 2001 (8.01.2002)."

125. Ibid.

126. Ibid.

127. Eyewitness testimony from the "mopping up" at Chechen-Aul, in Memorial Human Rights Center, "'Mopping Up' Operation in the Village of Chechen-Aul, 24–26 December 2001 (23.01.2002)."

128. Politkovskaia, *A Dirty War*, 234.

129. Signed by the 101st Otriad (Ot) (of the) Brigrada osobogo naznacheniia (BroN). Photograph by Natal'ia Medvedeva, http://exhibition.ipvnews.org/images/028b.jpg (accessed October 2008).

130. Photograph (untitled), http://www.fmso.leavenworth.army.mil/ . . . /grozny2000.htm (accessed October 2008).

131. A. Babchenko, *One Soldier's War* (New York: Grove Press, 2007), 276.

132. Ibid., 201.

133. "Contract Soldiers Are Discharged," *Chechnya Weekly* 4, no. 38 (October 23, 2003).

134. Babchenko, *One Soldier's War*, 186.

135. Ibid., 102.

136. Memorial Human Rights Center, "'Clean-up' Operations in the Village of Tsotsin-Iurt: October to November 2001 (8.01.2002)."

137. Memorial Human Rights Center, "The First 'Cleansing' of the Village of Mairtup, June 2001."

138. Kaliyev, "The Particulars of a Cleansing."

139. Memorial Human Rights Center, "Cleansing Operation in the Village of Alleroy: August 16–27, 2001" (Moscow: Memorial Archive, 2001).

140. Ibid.

141. Testimony by Dukaev Vakha Sharpudinovich, Memorial Human Rights Center, "'Mopping Up' Operation in the Village of Chechen-Aul: 24–26 December 2001 (23.01.2002)."

142. See Memorial Human Rights Center, "'Zachistka' v sele Tsotsin-Iurt: 25–29 iiulia 2002 goda (9.08.2002)."

143. K. Slawner, "Interpreting Victim Testimony: Survivor Discourse and the Narration of History." As Karen Slawner has argued in the case of Argentina, "accounts of

broken bodies contradict the claims of the perpetrators to be pursuing noble goals." http://www.yendor.com/vanished/karenhead.html (accessed February 2009).

144. A. Cherkasov, cited in Sakwa, *Chechnya*, 139–41.

Chapter 3. The Disappearances, 2002–5

The epigraphs to this chapter come from "Chelovek iz drugogo ushchel'ia"; International Helsinki Federation, "Chechnya: More of the Same: Extrajudicial Killings, Enforced 'Disappearances,' Illegal Arrests, Torture," International Helsinki Federation for Human Rights, March 30, 2005; and Human Rights Watch, "The 'Dirty War' in Chechnya," http://www.ihf-hr.org/ (accessed March 2009).

1. This was not a uniform policy, however. The Urus-Martan region was subject to twenty-seven sweeps over the course of 2005, but overall the dynamic of the conflict had changed.
2. "Chelovek iz drugogo ushchel'ia."
3. Only 24 of a sample of 113 disappearances from 1999–2001 were targeted sweeps. Human Rights Watch, "The 'Dirty War' in Chechnya."
4. Memorial Human Rights Center, "Situatsiia s sobliudeniem prav cheloveka v Chechenskoi Respublike osen'iu 2000 g. (25.12.2000)."
5. European Court of Human Rights, *Khamila Isaeva v. Russia* (Application no. 6846/02), Judgment, Strasbourg, November 15, 2007. See http://www.echr.coe.int/ (accessed December 2007).
6. Ibid.
7. Ibid.
8. Human Rights Watch, "Last Seen."
9. Ibid.
10. See photo gallery by Chechen photographer Musa Sadulaev, http://www.hamburger-stiftung.de/sites_eng/start.html (accessed June 2007).
11. European Court of Human Rights, *Khamila Isaeva v. Russia*.
12. "Memorial's Poll Shows Only 12% of Chechens Had Intended Taking Part in the Referendum," Prague Watchdog, March 27, 2003. See also "Chechen Rights Defenders Cast Doubt on Referendum Results," Prague Watchdog, March 24, 2003.
13. Sokirianskaia interview.
14. "Chelovek iz drugogo ushchel'ia."
15. E. Moussaeva, e-mail correspondence with the author, October 29, 2008.
16. *Vremia Novostei*, May 17, 2002.
17. Sokirianskaia interview.
18. International Helsinki Federation, "Chechnya: More of the Same."
19. Sokirianskaia interview.
20. Human Rights Watch, "Last Seen."
21. Sokirianskaia interview.
22. "Vicious Practice Mars Russia's COE Membership," *Caucasian Knot News*, June 13, 2005.
23. Ramzan Kadyrov, NTV, June 9, 2004, cited in "From the Conflict Zone: Bulletin of Human Rights Center 'Memorial,' March 17, 2005" (Moscow: Memorial Archive, 2005).
24. "Fixers" is a term used by human rights groups for locals who work and collate material on their behalf.

25. "Rights Activists: Kadyrovtsy Are Chechnya's Main Problem," *Chechnya Weekly* 6, no. 6 (February 9, 2005).

26. Neistat interview.

27. Human Rights Watch, "Worse Than a War."

28. Memorial Human Rights Center, "The Chechen Republic: Consequences of 'Chechenization' of the Conflict" (Moscow: Memorial Archive, 2006).

29. A. Seierstad, *The Angel of Grozny: Orphans of a Forgotten War* (New York: Basic Books, 2008), 99.

30. Ibid., 152.

31. "To Smother Rebels, Arson Campaign in Chechnya," *New York Times*, September 28, 2008.

32. For 2003, 497 were abducted, 157 freed, 52 murdered, and 288 disappeared. For 2004, 448 were abducted, 213 freed, 24 murdered, and 203 disappeared. For 2005, 320 were abducted, 154 freed, 24 murdered, and 127 disappeared.

33. Memorial Human Rights Center, "Praktika provedeniia 'kontrterroristicheskoi operatsii' Rossiiskoi Federatsiei na Severnom Kavkaze v 1999–2006 gg." (Moscow: Memorial Archive, 2007). Memorial collated information on 1,650 cases of disappearances in Chechnya.

34. *Ekho Moskvy*, March 26, 2003.

35. "Chechnya: Disappearances Mount," Chechnya Reporting Service, no. 178, May 9, 2003.

36. "Stern, But Kind," *Vremia Novostei*, October 26, 2004.

37. Human Rights Watch, "Worse Than a War."

38. Memorial Human Rights Center, "Praktika provedeniia 'kontrterroristicheskoi operatsii' Rossiiskoi Federatsiei na Severnom Kavkaze v 1999–2006 gg." (Moscow: Memorial Archive, 2007).

39. "Sifting a Human Dumping Ground in Chechnya," *Washington Post*, April 13, 2001.

40. Memorial Human Rights Center, "Bodies Discovered Near Khankala—Irrefutable Evidence of War Crimes Committed by Federal Forces." Materials from a press conference held on March 5, 2001, in Moscow at the Institute of Press Development (Moscow: Memorial Archive, March 29, 2001).

41. Human Rights Watch, "The 'Dirty War' in Chechnya."

42. Ibid. This information pertains to bodies discovered near Khankala.

43. Ibid.

44. Ibid.

45. "On Places of Mass Graves of Civilians on the Territory of the Chechen Republic [Spravka]," February 26, 2002, signed by Sh.B. Abdurakhmanov. This document was leaked to Natalie Nougayrede of *Le Monde* in April 2003. Author's collection, Storrs, CT.

46. Petrovlovskii Shosse (10), January 2002; Krasnostepanovsk (7), September 2002; Dachnyi, Khankala (4), March 2001; Argun (3), March 2002; Novye Atagi (2), January 2001; Iliskhan-Iurt (4), January 2001; Argun (4), March 2001; Mesker Iurt (2), June 2002; Starye Atagi (3 graves, 6 bodies), September 2000; Serzhen'-Iurt (9), April 2004.

47. FEDEFAM, "Fighting against Forced Disappearances in Latin America," http://www.desaparecidos.org/fedefam/eng.html (accessed June 2007).

48. "Russian Cooperation with International Human Rights Organizations over the Situation in the Chechen Republic" (press statement by the Russian Foreign Ministry), no. 34, September 12, 2000, http://www.great-britain.mid.ru/pressrel/pr34.htm (accessed

March 2009). A Commission for Prisoners of War, Interned and Missing Persons under the President of the Russian Federation was set up to begin what the Russian Foreign Ministry described as a "systematic search for missing people."

49. Memorial Human Rights Center, "Chechnya, 2004."

50. Subject 6A interview.

51. Ibid.

52. Sokirianskaia interview.

53. "The Human Rights Situation in the Chechen Republic, Doc. 10283, September 20, 2004 Report," Committee on Legal Affairs and Human Rights Rapporteur: Mr. Rudolf Bindig, Germany, Socialist Group. See Article 4 of Draft Resolution, Council of Europe, Strasbourg, http://www.coe.org/ (accessed March 2009).

54. See Constitution of the Chechen Republic, March 27, 2003, http://www.servat.unibe.ch/icl/cc00000_.html (accessed October 2004).

55. Memorial Human Rights Center, "Reports of Human Rights Organizations Are Supported by Evidence from Other Sources (25.04.2003)."

Chapter 4. Finding Refuge

The epigraphs to this chapter come from Médecins Sans Frontières, "Médecins Sans Frontières Activity Report 2003: North Caucasus"; Norwegian Refugee Council, "Whose Responsibility?"; and Levin, "Chechen Migration and Integration in Ukraine."

1. Memorial Human Rights Center, "Spravka o polozhenii v lageriakh vynuzhdennykh pereselentsev, pokinuvshikh mesta postoiannogo prozhivaniia v rezul'tate provedeniia 'antiterroristicheskoi operatsii' (23.12.1999)."

2. *Vremia MN*, no. 180, September 30, 1999.

3. *Novye Izvestiia*, no. 182, October 1, 1999.

4. *SPB Vedomosti*, no. 180, October 2, 1999.

5. A. Politkovskaia, "Obstoiatel'stva: Kabardino-Balkariia otdelilas' ot Rossii; Deportatsiia chechenskikh bezhentsev iz RF naznachena na 2 ianvaria," *Novaia Gazeta*, no. 047, December 14, 1999.

6. Common Action Initiative Group, "Letter to the UN High Commissioner for Refugees Concerning Attempts to Forcefully Return Refugees to Chechnya," June 7, 2001, author's collection, Storrs, CT.

7. *Novaia Gazeta*, no. 46, December 6, 1999.

8. Baiev, *The Oath*, 253.

9. Subject 6A interview.

10. "Aushev: Kremlin Wrong on Chechnya," *Moscow Times*, no. 1835, November 11, 1999. See also "Tret'ia otechestvennaia; Ruslan Aushev: Esli mne ob'iaviat voinu, ya tozhe budy voevat'," no. 039, October 18, 1999.

11. "Aushev: Kremlin Wrong on Chechnya."

12. "Antiingushkii Sindrom: Polemika s Dmitriem Rogozinym," *Nezavismaia Gazeta*, January 22, 2000. See also Memorial Human Rights Center, "Zaiavleniia PTS 'Memorial' o kampanii v presse protiv Ausheva (2.12.1999)."

13. Stepan Dvornikov and Anna Feofilaktova, "Ingusheskaia Zona," *Vremia MN*, no. 204, November 3, 1999.

14. Memorial Human Rights Center, "Obrashchenie pravleniia mezhdunarodnogo obshchestva 'Memorial' po povodu ul'timatuma zhiteliam Groznogo (6.12.1999)."

15. "MSF Joins Protest Over Chechnya," Agence France-Presse, December 10, 1999.

16. Memorial reports that witness testimonies indicated that the Federal Ministry of Emergency Situations worked well in getting them out and moving them to Znamenskoe. See Memorial Human Rights Center, "Gumanitarnyi Koridor: Vykhod mirnykh zhitelei iz Groznogo: Dekabr' 1999 g. (25.12.1999)."

17. "Russian Warplanes Resume Shelling of Chechnya," Associated Press, November 20, 1999. See also "Heavy Fighting Reported as Chechens Engage Russian Forces," Deutsche Presse-Agentur, December 2, 1999; "Elderly Flee Hell of Grozny as Onslaught Continues," *Herald (Glasgow)*, December 20, 1999.

18. See President Putin's statements in "Liudi begut ne iz Chechni, a begut ot banditov," *SPB Vedomosti*, no. 180, February 10, 1999.

19. Médecins Sans Frontières, "Chechnya: The Tracking of Civilians—Interview with Chechen Refugees in Georgia, December 1999."

20. "Chechen Refugees in Ingushetia (1999–2002)," Prague Watchdog, November 8, 2002.

21. Memorial Human Rights Center, "Spravka o polozhenii v lageriakh vynuzhdennykh pereselentsev, pokinuvshikh mesta postoiannogo prozhivaniia v rezul'tate provedeniia 'antiterroristicheskoi operatsii' (23.12.1999)."

22. UNHCR figures quoted in Catherine A. Fitzpatrick, "Chechen Refugees Face Forced Return," Radio Free Europe/Radio Liberty 3, no. 23 (June 5, 2002), http://www.rferl.org/content/Article/1347266.html (accessed March 2009).

23. Dunn interview. The International Rescue Committee (IRC) worked with up to 55 spontaneous settlements. Dunn noted that the number of settlements was probably closer to 200.

24. It had 2,136 people living there.

25. *Stroitel'no-montashnogo upravleniia* in Sleptsovskaia.

26. *Molochno-tovarnaia ferma* in the town of Karabulak.

27. Médecins Sans Frontières, "Chechnya/Ingushetia: A Deliberate Strategy of Non-Assistance to People in Crisis" (Special Report, February 2002).

28. This was in Sleptsovskaia.

29. As of February 2000, there were 4,900 civilians.

30. This camp was in Karabulak.

31. Lanzer telephone interview.

32. Dunn interview.

33. Ibid.

34. For the IDPs in the southern camps of Chechnya, the conditions were calamitous. After the sweep operations and complete annihilation of the village of Duba-Iurt in December 1999, 11,000 IDPs moved to Chiri-Iurt at the foothills of the mountains. Confined to a cement factory and High School No. 3, they lived on paltry aid of evaporated milk and processed meat from EMERCOM. The village was essentially unable to cope with the sudden influx. As Aishat Junaidova, head of the Shali Regional Migration Service, said to journalist Anna Politkovskaia, "Call Moscow's attention to the fact that this government handout is not enough to live on. Many of our refugees are for all intents and purposes condemned to starvation." Politkovskaia, *A Small Corner of Hell*.

35. Memorial Human Rights Center, "O situatsii v mestakh kompaktnogo razmeshcheniia vynuzhdennykh pereselentsev: Respublika Ingushetiia; Chechenskaia Respublika, Dekabr' 2000–ianvar' 2001" (Moscow: Memorial Archive, 2001); Memorial Human

Rights Center, "O situatsii v mestakh kompaktnogo razmeshcheniia vynuzhdennykh pereselentsev: Respublika Ingushetiia, Chechenskaia Respublika: 17–21 noiabria 2000 g. (24.11.2000)."

36. Memorial Human Rights Center, "Violations of Humanitarian Law and Human Rights; Situation of Civilians Who Have Fled the Conflict Zone: Report on the Visit to Ingushetia and Chechnya by Representatives of the Memorial Human Rights Centre (MHRC) from 12 to 20 January 2000 (20.01.2000)."

37. Memorial Human Rights Center, "Action of the Federal Migration Service on the Provision of Aid to Those Who Suffered as a Result of Warfare in the Chechen Republic" (Moscow: Memorial Archive, 2000).

38. United Nations Human Rights Commission, Guiding Principles on Internal Displacement.

39. Ibid.

40. Russian Federation, "Law on the Introduction of Amendments and Additions to the Law of the Russian Federation on 'Forced Migrants,'" December 20, 1995.

41. Norwegian Refugee Council, "Profile of Internal Displacement." See also S. A. Gannushkina, "The Internally Displaced Persons from Chechnya in the Russian Federation" (Moscow: Memorial Archive, 2002).

42. Cited in *Moscow Times*, July 10, 2002.

43. Ibid.

44. Gannushkina, "The Internally Displaced Persons from Chechnya in the Russian Federation." See also Gannushkina, "The Internally Displaced Persons from Chechnya in the Russian Federation, 2003" (Moscow: Memorial Archive, 2003).

45. Memorial Human Rights Center, "Violations of Humanitarian Law and Human Rights."

46. Gannushkina, "On the Situation of Residents of Chechnya in the Russian Federation: July 2005–July 2006."

47. *Moscow Times*, July 10, 2002.

48. Subject 2A interview; Subject 2A interview no. 2.

49. See Sergei Ivanov, "Letter from Minister of Foreign Affairs of the Russian Federation to the Chairman of the Committee of Ministers and the Secretary General of the Council of Europe," June 24, 2000.

50. Letter to the UN High Commissioner for refugees concerning attempts to forcefully return refugees to Chechnya from the "Common Action" Initiative Group, Moscow, June 7, 2001 (Moscow: Memorial Archive, 2001). On December 17, 1999, the chief of the FMS issued order no. 110 banning Form No. 7 to those from safe zones.

51. S. Shoigu, cited in "Russians Propose Special Enclaves for Chechens," *Independent*, November 6, 1999.

52. Memorial Human Rights Center, "Violations of Humanitarian Law and Human Rights." See also "Skorei by konchilas' eta proklyataia voina," *Literaturnaia Gazeta*, February 2, 2000.

53. Politkovskaia, *A Dirty War*, 131. See also Memorial Human Rights Center, "Spravka o polozhenii v lageriakh vynuzhdennykh pereselentsev, pokinuvshikh mesta postoiannogo prozhivaniia v rezul'tate provedeniia 'antiterroristicheskoi operatsii' (23.12.1999)."

54. Memorial Human Rights Center, "To Sadake Ogate, Supreme Commissar of the UNO for the Affairs of Refugees from the Chairman of the Council of the Memorial Human Rights Centre, O. Orlov and the Chairman of 'Civic Assistance' S. Gannushkina, 29.12.99" (Moscow: Memorial Archive, 1999).

55. Memorial Human Rights Center, "Violations of Humanitarian Law and Human Rights."

56. *Moscow Times*, April 8, 2002. For more on the removal of Khamzat Gutseriev as the opposing candidate, see Politkovskaia, *A Small Corner of Hell*, 190.

57. Politkovskaia, *A Small Corner of Hell*, 194.

58. "Chechen Refugees Evicted from Refugee Camp," Prima News Agency, September 11, 2002.

59. "Displaced Chechens Anxious as Troops Move Near Ingushetia Camps," UNHCR press release, November 1, 2002.

60. "Chechen Refugees in Ingushetia Protest against Russian Soldiers in Neighborhood," Prague Watchdog, November 5, 2002.

61. "Chechen Refugees in Ingushetia (1999–2002)," Prague Watchdog, November 8, 2002.

62. "UN Worried by Refugee Checkpoints," *Moscow Times*, November 4, 2002.

63. "Chechen Refugees in Ingushetia Protest against Russian Soldiers in Neighborhood."

64. Lanzer interview.

65. Ibid.

66. Subject 1A interview.

67. Ibid.

68. Ibid.

69. "First Ingush Tent Camp Torn Down," Reuters, December 4, 2002.

70. "Refugees Fear Death in War-Torn Chechen Homeland," Reuters, November 29, 2002.

71. Ibid.

72. Cited in "Persecution of Chechens Is Growing in Russia," *Gazeta Wyborcza*, December 3, 2002.

73. "North Caucasus: UNHCR Asks for Camp Closures Postponement," UNHCR spokesperson Ron Redmond, press briefing at the Palais des Nations in Geneva, November 29, 2002.

74. Médecins Sans Frontières, "Left without a Choice."

75. Ibid.

76. Information Center of the Society of Russian-Chechen Friendship, press release no. 332, "Report from Ingushetia," December 30, 2002.

77. Ibid.

78. Depiction from the UNHCR Handbook on Voluntary Repatriation, cited in the Norwegian Refugee Council, "Whose Responsibility?"

79. Human Rights Watch, "Last Seen."

80. Médecins Sans Frontières, "Left without a Choice."

81. Ibid.

82. Lanzer telephone interview.

83. "Chechen Refugees in the Dark on Constitutional Referendum," Agence France-Presse, January 23, 2003.

84. The rest were told that they would be considered later on. See *Chechnya Weekly* 5, no. 6 (February 10, 2004). The issue of compensation soon became tainted with the bribes that were necessary to process the application, taking up to one half of the full amount. By the beginning of 2004 there were 37,000 houses on the list, but only 1,500 families had received compensation. The 35,000 rubles was far from sufficient to rebuild a house in Chechnya, and as soon as they received money they lost their place in the temporary accommodation center.

85. "Key Western Diplomat Endorses Referendum," *Jamestown Reports* 4, no. 5 (February 20, 2003).

86. *Chechnya Weekly* 4, no. 8 (2003).

87. Memorial Human Rights Center, "Respublika Ingushetiia."

88. "Voina Palatkam," *Russkyi Kurier*, January 26, 2004.

89. S. A. Gannushkina, "On the Situation of Chechnya Residents in the Russian Federation: June 2003–May 2004" (Moscow: Memorial Human Rights Center, Migration Rights Network, 2004). See Gannushkina, "The Internally Displaced Persons from Chechnya in the Russian Federation" (2003); Gannushkina, "On the Situation of Residents of Chechnya in the Russian Federation: July 2005–July 2006."

90. Rochowanski interview.

91. "War in Chechnya Boosts Refugees Seeking Asylum," *Chechnya Weekly* 4, no. 43 (November 26, 2003). As of 2007, approximately 4,000 Chechen refugees had been registered and granted protection in Georgia. There were around 2,500 refugees from Chechnya mostly residing in Pankisi Gorge, and around 8,500 Chechen refugees in Azerbaijan. See European Council on Refugees and Exiles, "Guidelines on the Treatment of Chechen Internally Displaced Persons (IDPs), Asylum Seekers and Refugees in Europe."

92. Keil interview; Rochowanski interview.

93. Levin, "Chechen Migration and Integration in Ukraine."

94. Ibid.

95. Keil interview.

96. European Council on Refugees and Exiles, "Guidelines on the Treatment of Chechen Internally Displaced Persons (IDPs), Asylum Seekers and Refugees in Europe."

97. Keil interview.

98. Ibid.

99. "Poland: Chechen Refugees Grateful for Protection But Need Integration Support," *Refugees International*, June 12, 2005.

100. Eßer, Gladysch, and Suwelack, "Report on the Situation of Chechen Asylum Seekers and Refugees in Poland and Effects of the EU Dublin II Regulation."

101. European Council on Refugees and Exiles, "EU 'Dublin' Rules on Asylum Claims Cause Misery and Put Refugees at Risk."

Chapter 5. Chechen Retaliation

The epigraphs to this chapter come from *Kommersant*, no. 012, January 28, 2000; Maskhadov cited in "Maskhadov Seeks Negotiations," Institute for War and Peace Reporting, Caucasus Reporting Service, no. 133, June 13, 2002; and Bin Laden, *Osama Messages to the World*, 175.

1. See Hahn, *Russia's Islamic Threat*.

2. Grau and Smith, "A 'Crushing' Victory."

3. See Uppsala Conflict Data Program, Department of Peace and Conflict Research.

4. Ibid.

5. Politkovskaia, cited in "Chechnya's 'Black Widow' Bombers," Friday, July 11, 2003, posted 11:14 AM EDT (1514 GMT), CNN World.

6. Nikolay Zagnoyko, ITAR-TASS Report, 1148 GMT, June 14, 1995, as reported in FBIS-SOV-95-114, June 14, 1995.

7. "From Gallantry to Savagery," *Moscow Times*, January 12, 1996.

8. "Terroristicheskie Akty za predelami Chechni."

9. "We Set Off for Budennovsk with a One Way Ticket," *Prism*, Jamestown Foundation, October 25, 1995.

10. "Terroristicheskie Akty za predelami Chechni."

11. Kovalev, "Speech by Sergei Kovalev at Human Rights Watch Meeting, New York, March 9, 1996."

12. "Terroristicheskie Akty za predelami Chechni."

13. Kovalev, "Stenogramme of interview with Sergei Kovalev, New York," 6. See also Kovalev, "Speech by Sergei Kovalev at Human Rights Watch Meeting, New York, March 9, 1996."

14. See Yakov's account of Kovalev's arrival at the hospital. (Yakov was a journalist with *Izvestiia* who was also a hostage.) *Izvestiia*, June 23, 1995.

15. S. Kovalev, *Novoe Vremia*, no. 26, July 1995.

16. S. Basaev, cited in "Shamil Basayev: We Will Soon Go to Budennovsk to Repent," *Russian Press Digest*, January 16, 1997.

17. "Pervomaiskoe Debacle in Retrospect," *Jamestown Foundation* 2, no. 14 (January 22, 1996).

18. "Chechen Rebels Free All 2,000 Hostages in Southern Russia," *International News*, January 9, 1996.

19. Ibid.

20. Article 3 Common to the Four Conventions and Additional Protocol II, http://www.icrc.org/Web/Eng/siteeng0.nsf/html/57JMJU (accessed October 20, 2007).

21. Subject 8A interview.

22. M. Lanskoy, "Daghestan and Chechnya: The Wahhabi Challenge to the State," *SAIS Review* 22, no. 2 (2002): 167–92.

23. V. Putin, quoted in by Pavel Felgenhauer, "Was It Just a Warning Shot?" *Moscow Times*, October 31, 2002.

24. Hahn, *Russia's Islamic Threat*, 40.

25. Ibid., 41.

26. He was killed in April 2004. See "Chechnya's Abu Walid and the Saudi Dilemma," *Jamestown Foundation* 2, no. 1 (January 15, 2004).

27. Stahl, "Hostage A Stahl Tells about the Events."

28. Mozhegova, "Hostage G. Mozhegova Tells about the Events."

29. "Gunmen Release Chilling Video," Friday, October 25, 2002, CNN.com, posted 5:36 AM EDT (0936 GMT).

30. *Terror in Moscow*, HBO documentary film by Dan Reed and Mark Franchetti, 2003.

31. Ibid.

32. Speckhard and Akhmedova, "Black Widows."

33. J. Dunlop, "The October 2002 Moscow Hostage-Taking Incident" (Part II), Radio Free Europe/Radio Liberty 4, no. 1 (January 8, 2004).

34. Ibid., 152.

35. "The Genealogy of Chechen Terrorism," *Sueddeutsche Zeitung*, December 23, 2002.

36. *Terror in Moscow.*

37. *"Nord Ost" Investigation Unfinished: Events, Facts, Conclusions.* The book was published with assistance from "Terrorism Victims Support Fund," Moscow, April 26, 2006.

38. Lokshina, "Hostage L. Lokshina Recalls the Events."

39. *Terror in Moscow.*

40. Ibid.

41. Hearings by the Russian opposition party Union of Right-Wing Forces (SPS) on the Nord-Ost hostage rescue operation, October 29 and November 1, 2002, English text available at http://www.geocities.com/svetlana.gubareva/other/125.html (accessed August 2003). For Russian text, see *Novaia Gazeta*, no. 86, November 21, 2002.

42. Tamara Starkova, cited in *Terror in Moscow*. See also "Interview with Svetlana Gubareva," Radio Svoboda, October 31, 2003, http://www.svoboda.org/II/russia/1003/II.103103-5.asp (accessed March 2005).

43. A. Stahl, "A Chronicle of Three Nights at 'Nord-Ost,'" December 26, 2002, http://nord-ost.org/vospominaniya/rasskazyivaet-zalozhnik-a.stal.html (accessed August 2007).

44. Speckhard and Akhmedova, "Black Widows," 46.

45. "Aslan Maskhadov: After 'Nord-Ost,' Basaev Has Been Acting on His Own," interview in *Novaia Gazeta*, October 2, 2003.

46. "Why Didn't the Russians Negotiate?" *Chicago Tribune*, November 3, 2002.

47. G. Yavlinskii, cited in J. Dunlop, "The October 2002 Moscow Hostage-Taking Incident," Parts I, II, III, December 18, 2003, January 8, 2004, January 15, 2004, Radio Free Europe/Radio Liberty, http://www.rferl.org/content/Article/1342329.html (accessed March 2009).

48. See "FSB Says Barayev Acted on Orders from Above," November 1, 2002, http://www.gazeta.ru/print/2002/11/01/FSBsaysBaray.shtml (accessed September 2007).

49. Bin Laden, *Osama Messages to the World*, 153.

50. Ibid., 136.

51. Hughes, *Chechnya*, 157.

52. Ibid., 157–58.

53. Ibid, 159.

54. Andrew McGregor, "'Operation Boomerang': Shamid Basaev's Justification for Terrorism," *Terrorism Monitor* 2, no. 4 (February 26, 2004), http://www.jamestown.org/single/?no_cache=1&tx_ttnews%Btt_news%5D=26313 (accessed March 2009).

55. "Excerpts: Basayev Claims Beslan," BBC Monitoring, September 17, 2004.

56. Philips, *Beslan*, 27.

57. Ibid., 49.

58. R. Aushev, Ren TV, Moscow, 0855 GMT, August 29, 2005.

59. "Confusion Surrounds Beslan Band," Caucasus Reporting Service, no. 254, September 23, 2004.

60. Philips, *Beslan*, 86–87. See *Moskovskie Komsomolets*, September 11, 2004.

61. Dunlop, *The 2002 Dubrovka and 2004 Beslan Hostage Crises*, 65.

62. V. Putin, cited in "Media Gone Soft on Terror; 'Militant' and 'Insurgent' Are Mealy Mouthed Words for Child-Killers, Says Peter Worthington," *Toronto Sun*, September 9, 2004.

63. Quotes in "Official Statements on Beslan: A Study in Obfuscation," *Chechnya Weekly*, September 2004.

64. M. Litvinovich, "The Truth about Beslan," http://www.pravdabeslana.ru/truth.htm (accessed October 2008).

65. "Beslan Killing Frenzy Was Sparked by Accidental Bomb Blast in School," *Independent*, Wednesday, October 6, 2004.

66. "Special Report; Beslan—The Search for the Truth Goes on," Caucasus Reporting Service, no. 300, August 18, 2005. See also "Beslan: The Hostages' Truth—A Report

Compiled by Yurii Savel'ev," http://www.pravdabeslana.ru/english.htm (accessed October 2008).

67. See Oleg Kuskov, "Materi Beslana poluchili videopodtverzhdneie svoei pravoty," Svobodanews.ru, July 27, 2007.

68. "New Video of Beslan School Terror," CBS News, January 21, 2005.

69. Dunlop, *The 2002 Dubrovka and 2004 Beslan Hostage Crises*, 39.

70. See "Feelings of Revenge Have Eclipsed Reason," announcement to the Chechen people, September 5, 2004, http://www.primanews.ru/eng/news/articles/2004/9/13/29354.html (accessed September 2004).

71. Ibid.

72. Matthew B. Ridgway Center for International Security Studies at the University of Pittsburgh, "Anatomy of a Terrorist Attack: Terror at Beslan: A Chronicle of an Ongoing Tragedy and a Government's Failed Response" (Pittsburgh: Ridgway Center for International Security Studies, 2007), http://www.ridgway.pitt.edu/docs/working_papers/BeslanFINALreport12-3-07.pdf (accessed August 2008).

73. Hughes, *Chechnya*.

74. Hahn, *Russia's Islamic Threat*, 72–74.

75. R. Zhadaev, "'Fiery Summer' of Shamil Basayev," *Chechen Society*, no. 10, May 24, 2005.

76. See M. Grove, "Ideology, Not Tribal Hate, Spurred Massacre—Russia Mourns," *The Times*, September 8, 2004.

Chapter 6. Civil Society Reacts

The epigraphs to this chapter come from Elena Bonner's letter of May 21, 2000, ASF Archive Documents, read at the Moscow Conservatoire during the celebration and gala concert on the occasion of the 79th anniversary of Andrei Sakharov's birth, http://asf.wdn.com/ (accessed March 2008), and interview with *Novaia Gazeta* deputy editor Vitali Yaroshevskii on Anna Politkovskaia: "Many People Saw Her as Their Last Hope," Reporters Without Borders, October 31, 2006, http://www.rsf.org/print.php3?id_article=19517 (accessed July 2007).

1. Hunter interview.

2. "On the Fight against Terrorism: Russian Federation Federal Law No. 130-FZ, 25 July 1998."

3. Ugolovnyi kodeks RF (UK RF) ot 13.06.1996 N.63-FZ, http://www.consultant.ru/ (accessed April 2008).

4. V. Putin, *Kommersant*, March 10, 2000.

5. E. Batuev, "The War in Chechnya Has Taken a Severe Toll on the Hearts and Minds of the Russian Journalistic Community," Caucasus Reporting Service, no. 63, December 22, 2000.

6. Ognianova, "Rewriting the Law to Make Journalism a Crime."

7. Theodore Gerber and Sarah Mendelson, "Casualty Sensitivity in a Post-Soviet Context: Russian Views of the Second Chechen War, 2001–2004," *Political Science Quarterly* 123, no. 1 (Spring 2008): 39–68.

8. Ibid.

9. Ibid. See also the Levada Center, Moscow (Centre for the Study of Public Policy, University of Aberdeen), slide nos. 283, 157, 161, 409, 147, 227, 141, 223, 245, 305, 146, 380, 253, 371, 143, 335, 282, http://www.russiavotes.org (accessed October 2008).

10. Seierstad, *The Angel of Grozny*, 308–9.

11. J. Dwyer, "Telling the 'Real' Story: Interpretation of Contemporary Events in Viktor Dotsenko's Superboeviki," *Soviet and Post-Soviet Review* 29, no. 3 (2002): 221–40.

12. "Nation Non Grata: Interview with Anna Politkovskaia," *Rzeczpospolita*, April 27, 2002.

13. Politkovskaia, *A Dirty War*, 67.

14. Politkovskaia, *A Small Corner of Hell*, 216.

15. Politkovskaia, *A Dirty War*, 105.

16. Ibid., 45.

17. Politkovskaia, *A Small Corner of Hell*, 148.

18. "Voina—osnovnoi instinct imperii," *Novaia Gazeta*, no. 044, November 22, 1999.

19. Politkovskaia, *A Dirty War*, 151.

20. Politkovskaia, *A Small Corner of Hell*, 40.

21. Ibid., 43.

22. Ibid., 178.

23. This is my own assessment that her criticisms were often too harsh. For two examples, see Inki interview; Sokirianskaia interview.

24. Politkovskaia, *A Dirty War*, 83.

25. Politkovskaia, *Putin's Russia*, 224.

26. "Threatened Journalist Flees from Russia," Gazeta.ru, October 18, 2001.

27. A. Politkovskaia, "Liudi ischezaiushchie," *Novaia Gazeta*, no. 65, September 10, 2001.

28. S. Levine, *Putin's Labyrinth: Spies, Murder and the Dark Heart of the New Russia* (New York: Random House, 2008), 113–14.

29. Umalt Dudaev is a pseudonym for a Chechen journalist.

30. "Zdes' Khoteli Zhit','" *Novaia Gazeta*, February 7, 2000.

31. Ibid.

32. Abdulaeva interview.

33. "On the Beat in Battered Grozny," *Christian Science Monitor*, May 2, 2001.

34. "Interview with Musa Muradov in Moscow," Center for the Protection of Journalists, September 26, 2003.

35. T. Aliev, "The Risks of Independent Reporting in Chechnya" (Cambridge, MA: Nieman Foundation for Journalism at Harvard, 2004), 90.

36. "Closure of the Independent Weekly Chechen Society and the Strong Pressure on Editor, Timur Aliev," IHF press release, August 5, 2004.

37. O. Orlov, Caucasus Reporting Service, no. 7, November 19, 1999. Orlov noted that there had been much internal debate about this. See "O Chechenskoi voine govoriat pravozashchitniki: Beseda s Elenoi Bonner i Sergeem Kovalevym," in *Kavkazskii krizis: Liberty Live: Press-konferentsiia rossiiskikh i chechenskikh pravozashchitnikov*. See also Memorial Human Rights Center, "Positsiia obshchestva 'Memorial' v sviazi s vooruzhennym konfliktom v Chechne (9.12.1999)."

38. Orlov then later called for negotiations with Maskhadov.

39. Neistat interview no. 2.

40. A. Kiva, "Blesk i nishcheta dvizheniia pravozashchitnikov," *Rossiiskaia Gazeta*, no. 36, February 21, 1997.

41. Elena Bonner said this in an interview published in *Yezhenedelnyi Zhurnal*: see Politkovskaia, *A Russian Diary*, 187.

42. Evans, "President Putin's Design for Civil Society," 150.

43. Ibid., 151.

44. Kovalev, "Ugroza pravovomu gosudarstvu i konstititsionnyim osnovam demokratii v strane."

45. General Resolution of All-Russia Extraordinary Congress in Defense of Human Rights, http://www.gdf.ru/arh/file009e.shtml (accessed September 2003).

46. "Rezolyutsiia vserossiiskogo chrezvychainogo s'ezda v zashchity prav cheloveka o situatsii v Chechne," ASF Archive Documents, Moskva, 21 ianvaria 2001 goda, http://asf.wdn.com/ (accessed March 2008).

47. Ibid.

48. Memorial Human Rights Center, "Communiqué on the Third Meeting of Non-governmental Human Rights Organizations and Representatives of State Authorities of the Chechen Republic (30.04.2002)."

49. Memorial Human Rights Center, "Soobshchenie pravoshchitnogo tsentra 'Memorial' o prekrashchenii uchastiia nepravitel'stvennykh organizatsii v zasedanniiakh postiannoi rabochei gruppy (12.07.2002)."

50. Moussaeva interview.

51. International Helsinki Federation for Human Rights, "The Silencing of Human Rights Defenders in Chechnya and Ingushetia."

52. These included 4 abductions, 19 instances of torture/beatings, 19 illegal detentions, and 69 counts of harassment or threats.

53. Amnesty International, IOR 30/14/2005, September 20, 2005.

54. Human Rights First, "Russian Human Rights Activist Convicted in Politically Motivated Case." See also Amnesty International, "The Risk of Speaking Out."

55. Memorial Human Rights Center, "Peaceful Mass Protests in Chechnya: Spring–Early Summer 2001" (Moscow: Memorial Archive, 2001).

56. Memorial Human Rights Center, "'Clean-up' Operations in the Village of Tsotsin-Iurt: October to November 2001 (8.01.2002)."

Chapter 7. International Failure

The epigraphs to this chapter come from an interview with Chechen refugee, Wide Angle "Greetings from Grozny," PBS documentary, http://www.pbs.org/wnet/wideangle/shows/chechnya/ (accessed December 2004), and "Yevgeny Voronin, Deputy Spokesman of Russia's Ministry of Foreign Affairs, Answers a Russian Media Question about the Intention of the PACE Legal Committee to Create an International Tribunal for Chechnya," March 5, 2003. Posted on Web site of the Russian Embassy of the Slovak Republic, http://www.slovakia.mid.ru/ch_9.html (accessed December 2004).

1. M. Robinson, "Mary Robinson: A Career in Quotes," BBC News, November 28, 2001.

2. Press release #9, "Statement by Russian Foreign Ministry Spokesman," Ministry of Foreign Affairs, February 25, 2000, http://www.great-britain.mid.ru/pressrel_00.htm (accessed July 2004).

3. Ibid.

4. "The Fifty-Sixth Session of the UN Commission on Human Rights," *American Journal of International Law* 95, no. 1 (January 2001): 213–21.

5. Memorial Human Rights Center, "On the Passing by the UN Human Rights Commission of a Resolution on the Situation in the Chechen Republic (3.05.2001)."

6. Press release #21, "Statement by the Russian Ministry of Foreign Affairs," April 27, 2000.

7. "Human Rights in 2002: The Annual Sessions of the UN Commission on Human Rights and the Economic and Social Council," *American Journal of International Law* 97, no. 2 (April 2003): 364–86.

8. On May 4, 2004, U.S. ambassador Sichan Siv walked out of the commission following the uncontested election of Sudan to the commission. See "Sudan Retains U.N. Human Rights Post; U.S. Ambassador Walks out to Protest Reappointment," Associated Press, May 4, 2004.

9. D. Rogozin, cited in "Russia Slams the Door—But Leaves It Ajar," *Trud*, April 13, 2000.

10. "Playful Feast behind Closed Doors," *Chechen Times*, March 22, 2000, http://www.chechentimes.org/en/comments/?id=27401 (accessed May 2004).

11. Inki interview; Moussaeva interview.

12. Elena Bonner said this in an interview in *Yezhenedelnyi Zhurnal*: see Politkovskaia, *A Russian Diary*, 187.

13. There never was a public document outlining the official mandate of the office.

14. "On Certain Measures of the Russian Federal Authorities to Normalize the Political, Human Rights and Socio-Economic Situation in the Chechen Republic of the Russian Federation, June 24, 2000." This appears to be a memo from the Ministry of Foreign Affairs to the Council of Europe, Council of Europe Archive, Strasbourg. Only the title is given on the document.

15. Council of Europe, SG/Inf (2000): 27 Revised September 5, 2000.

16. Ibid.

17. Inki interview.

18. Lohman interview.

19. Council of Europe, SG/Inf (2000): Statistical data/27 September 2000.

20. Council of Europe, SG/Inf (2000): 27 Revised September 5, 2000.

21. Council of Europe, SG/Inf (2000): Statistical data/27 September 2000.

22. Ibid.

23. Ibid.

24. Council of Europe, SG/Inf (2001): 8/13 March 2001.

25. Ibid.

26. Inki interview.

27. Over a period of thirty months, the experts produced thirty-one reports.

28. Council of Europe, SG/Inf (2001): 12/17 April 2001.

29. Council of Europe, SG/Inf (2000): 51/11 December 2000.

30. Council of Europe, SG/Inf (2001): 8 Addendum/13 March 2001.

31. Kalamanov, cited in "Forgotten Terror: Chechnya," Norwegian Helsinki Committee, September 27 to October 7, 2001, http://www.reliefweb.int/ (accessed June 2005).

32. Subject 4A interview.

33. "Russian Human Rights Envoy Denies Use of Torture in Chechnya," CNSNews.com, July 15, 2003.

34. Lohman interview.

35. Council of Europe, "Conflict in Chechnya and the Credentials of the Russian Delegation."

36. Council of Europe, "Ordinary Session, Thursday September 27, 2001 at 3 P.M.," Council of Europe Archive, Strasbourg, http://www.coe.int/ (accessed March 2009).

37. "Human Rights Champion Blasts PACE, Says No Real Improvement in Chechnya," *Ekho Moskvy* Moscow, in Russian, 0915 GMT, January 26, 2001.

38. Council of Europe, SG/Inf (2004): 3/16 January 2004.

39. Valentinas Mite, "Chechnya: Moscow Scraps Human-Rights Post," January 23, 2004, Radio Free Europe/Radio Liberty, http://www.rferl.org/Content/Article/1051305.html (accessed March 2009).

40. E. Moussaeva, private communication with the author, April 6, 2008, Boston.

41. Guldimann, "Supporting the Doves against the Hawks."

42. Organization for Security and Co-operation in Europe, "The OSCE Assistance Group to Chechnya: Basic Decisions."

43. Inki interview.

44. "OSCE's Chechnya Mission Packs Up," *Moscow Times*, January 9, 2003.

45. "Moscow to End OSCE Mandate in Chechnya," Deutsche Presse-Agentur, December 21, 2001.

46. "Bush and Putin: Best of Friends," BBC World, June 16, 2001.

47. "The Bush-Putin Summit; New Allies: One Trusts, the Other's Not So Sure," *New York Times*, November 14, 2001.

48. "A Nation Challenged: The Russians; Schröder Urges Milder View of Moscow Role in Chechnya," *New York Times*, September 26, 2001.

49. Ibid.

50. V. Putin, "Ministry of Foreign Affairs of the Russian Federation: Daily News Bulletin," September 18, 2001, address at Yerevan State University, Armenia. See also "I Feel Guilty about What Happened in the USA," Russian Public TV (ORT), Moscow, in Russian, 1400 GMT, September 15, 2001.

51. "Russia Chides U.S. over Chechen Contacts," Reuters, January 24, 2002.

52. "9/11 'Twinned' with Beslan Horror," BBC News, September 11, 2004.

53. *The Times*, March 26, 1999.

54. "Russian Steps up Action over Kosovo, Sends Warships to Zone," Agence France-Presse, March 31, 1999.

55. "Russia Warns NATO: 'Don't Push Us,'" Press Association, April 9, 1999, Friday.

56. At no time, except by Tomasz Wojcik, did the deputies insist on a UN peacekeeping force, a suggestion later formulated by Ilyas Akhmadov in his 2003 Peace Plan.

57. *Voina v Chechne: Mezhdunarodnyi Tribunal* (Moskva: Glasnost', 1996).

58. Haslam, "Non-governmental War Crimes Tribunals."

59. Eliza Moussaeva, private communication with the author, May 15, 2008, Boston.

60. Council of Europe, Recommendation 1600 (2003).

61. "Rudolph Bindig: Moscow Has Yet to Refute Human Rights Abuse Allegations," *Nezavisimaia Gazeta*, March 31, 2003.

62. V. Smirnov, "Russian Expert Says International Tribunal for Chechnya Is Invalid Idea," Ria Novosti, March 5, 2003.

63. "PACE Backs a Chechnya Tribunal," *Moscow Times*, April 3, 2003.

Chapter 8. Seeking Justice in Europe: Chechens at the European Court of Human Rights

The epigraph to this chapter comes from Bowring, telephone interview.

1. Buchanan telephone interview.

2. Chadaeva interview no. 4.

3. B. Bowring, "Russia's Relations with the Council of Europe under Increasing Strain," *EU Russia Centre Review*, Brussels, February 2007, http://www.eu-russiacentre.org/ (accessed January 2008).

4. "Putin Calls European Rights Court Rulings 'Political,'" January 11, 2007, Radio Free Europe/Radio Liberty, http://www.rferl.org/content/Article/1073951.html (accessed March 2009).

5. Bowring, "Russia's Relations with the Council of Europe under Increasing Strain."

6. Kornilina interview.

7. Ibid.; Bowring telephone interview.

8. "Letter to Sergei Kovalev from S. N. Fridinsky, Office of the Prosecutor General of the Russian Federation, April 25, 2003."

9. Memorial Human Rights Center, "Deceptive Justice (10.06.2003)."

10. Ref 3/180.01, 16.01.2001, letter to Rudolph Bindig from Yuri Abazov. "Information on criminal case no. 12038." Full text in addendum to Council of Europe, "Conflict in the Chechen Republic—Recent Developments."

11. Council of Europe, "Conflict in the Chechen Republic—Recent Developments."

12. See Amnesty International, "Russian Federation: Chechen Republic Applicants to the European Court of Human Rights Must Be Protected."

13. See the case of Aslambek Salmanovich Utsaev.

14. For more information on the harassment of applicants, see http://www.srji.org/en/ (accessed February 2009).

15. See European Court of Human Rights, *Estamirov and Others v. Russia; Bazorkina v. Russia.*

16. European Court of Human Rights, *Isaeva, Iusupova and Basaeva v. Russia.*

17. Ibid.

18. Ibid.

19. Bowring telephone interview.

20. Ibid.

21. European Court of Human Rights, *Isaeva, Iusupova and Basaeva v. Russia.*

22. Ibid.

23. Ibid.

24. Ibid.

25. Ibid.

26. Abresch, "A Human Rights Law of Internal Armed Conflict."

27. Leach interview.

28. Abresch, "A Human Rights Law of Internal Armed Conflict."

29. Referenced in European Court of Human Rights, "Applicants' Submissions Regarding Compliance with the Judgments of the European Court of Human Rights."

30. Ibid.

31. See Baiev, *The Oath,* 293–306.

32. European Court of Human Rights, *Bazorkina v. Russia.*

33. Ibid.

34. Ibid.

35. See YouTube CNN Report by Ryan Chilcote, http://www.youtube.com/watch?v=oZW1uwMma5w (accessed July 25, 2007).

36. European Court of Human Rights, *Bazorkina v. Russia.*

37. Ibid.

38. Ibid.

39. Ibid.

40. Ibid.

41. Ibid.

42. UNHCR, Fact Sheet no. 6 (Rev. 2), Enforced or Involuntary Disappearances, http://www.unhchr.ch/html/menu6/2/fs6.htm (accessed March 2007).

43. European Court of Human Rights, *Luluev and Others vs. Russia.*

44. Memorial Human Rights Center, "Persons Detained in Chechnya by Military and Internal Affairs Agents Become Victims of Summary Executions (19.03.2001)."

45. European Court of Human Rights, *Luluev and Others vs. Russia.*

46. Ibid.

47. Ibid.
48. Ibid.
49. Ibid.
50. Ibid.
51. Ibid.
52. See European Court of Human Rights, *Anguelova v. Bulgaria*, §§ 161–62.
53. European Court of Human Rights, *Chitaev & Chitaev v. Russia*.
54. Ibid.
55. Ibid.
56. Ibid.
57. Ibid.
58. Ibid.
59. Ibid.
60. Ibid.
61. Ibid.
62. Ibid.
63. Ibid.
64. Leach interview.
65. Ibid.
66. Ibid.
67. Bowring interview.
68. European Court of Human Rights, Official Statement.
69. Council of Europe, CM/Inf/DH(2006)32.
70. Ibid.
71. European Court of Human Rights, "Applicants' Submissions Regarding Compliance with the Judgments of the European Court of Human Rights."
72. European Court of Human Rights, Official Statement.
73. Leach, "The Effectiveness of the Committee of Ministers in Supervising the Enforcement of Judgments of the European Court of Human Rights," 451.
74. Ibid., 452.
75. Ibid., 455.
76. Leach, "Strasbourg's Oversight of Russia."
77. Leach interview.
78. European Court of Human Rights, "Applicants' Submissions Regarding Compliance with the Judgments of the European Court of Human Rights."
79. Inki interview.
80. European Court of Human Rights, "Applicants' Submissions Regarding Compliance with the Judgments of the European Court of Human Rights," October 4, 2005.

Conclusion

The epigraph to this chapter comes from A. Nivat, "Chechnya Only Seems Normal," *Le Monde Diplomatique*, May 20, 2006.

1. A. Illarionov, "Q&A: Putin's Critical Adviser," *Time Magazine*, December 31, 2005.
2. O. Figes, "Vlad the Great," *New Statesman*, November 29, 2007.
3. Ibid.
4. Ivanov, cited in Council of Europe, "Conflict in Chechnya and Credentials of the Russian Federation and Address by Mr. Ivanov, Minister of Foreign Affairs of the Russian Federation." See also "Conflict in Chechnya and Credentials of the Delegation of the

Russian Federation [resumed debate]"; "Letter from the Minister of Foreign Affairs of the Russian Federation to the Secretary General of the Council of Europe."

5. Shamanov, quoted in interview with Anna Politkovskaia. See *A Dirty War,* 179.

6. Council of Europe, "Conflict in Chechnya and Credentials of the Delegation of the Russian Federation [resumed debate]."

7. "Sledy Voiny," *Chechenskoe Obshchestvo,* August 17, 2007.

BIBLIOGRAPHY

Newspapers and Other Media

Agence France-Presse
Agenstvo Voennykh Novostei
Associated Press
BBC Monitoring International Report
Caucasus Reporting Service (CRS)
CBS News
Chechenskoe Obshestvo
Chechen Press
Chechnya Weekly
Christian Science Monitor
Deutsche Presse-Agentur
Dispatches from Chechnya
The Economist
Ekho Moskvy
Financial Times
Groznenskii Rabochii
The Guardian
Independent (London)
Information Center of the Society of Russian-Chechen Friendship
Interfax
ITAR-TASS
Izvestiia
Kommersant Daily
Komsomolskaia Pravda
Krasnaia Zvezda
LAM
Literaturnaia Gazeta
Le Monde
Moskovskie Novosti
Moskovskii Komsomolets
Moscow Times
New York Review of Books
New York Times
Nezavisimaia Gazeta
Novaia Gazeta
Novye Izvestiia
Obshchaia Gazeta
Perspective
Prague Watchdog
Prima News Agency
Radio Free Europe/Radio Liberty (RFE/RL)

Reuters
Refugees Magazine
Ria Novosti
Rossiskaia Gazeta
Rzeczpospolita
Segodnia
Sovershenno Sekretno
Sovetskaia Rossiia
SPB Vedomosti
Der Spiegel
St. Petersburg Times
Die Suddeutsche Zeitung
Tikhookeanskaia vakhta
The Times (London)
Trud
Voennyi Vestnik Yuga Rossii
Vremia MN
Vremia Novostei
Wall Street Journal
Washington Post
Zavtra

Books, Articles, Reports

Abresch, William. "A Human Rights Law of Internal Armed Conflict: The European Court of Human Rights in Chechnya." *European Journal of International Law* 16, no. 4 (2005): 741–67.

Aliev, Timur. "The Risks of Independent Reporting in Chechnya." *Nieman Reports: Nieman Foundation for Journalism at Harvard* (Summer 2004): 90. http://www.nieman.harvard.edu.

Amnesty International. "Real Scale of Atrocities in Chechnya: New Evidence of Cover-Up." AI Index: EUR 46/20/00.

———. "The Risk of Speaking Out." AI Index: EUR 46/059/2004.

———. "Russian Federation: Chechen Republic Applicants to the European Court of Human Rights Must Be Protected." AI Index: EUR 46/055/2004, October 1, 2004.

Baiev, Khassan. *The Oath: A Surgeon under Fire*. New York: Walker and Company, 2003.

Bassiouni, M. Cherif. *Crimes against Humanity in International Criminal Law*. 2nd rev. ed. Dordrecht: Kluwer Academic Publishers Group, 1999.

Bennett, Vanora. *Crying Wolf: The Return of War to Chechnya*. London: Macmillan, 1998.

Bennigsen, Marie. "Chechnia: Political Developments and Strategic Implications for the North Caucasus." *Central Asian Survey* 18, no. 4 (1999): 535–74.

Bin Laden, Osama. *Osama Messages to the World: The Statements of Osama Bin Laden*. Ed. Bruce Lawrence. London: Verso, 2005.

Bouckaert, Peter. "Testimony before the Senate Committee on Foreign Relations." Human Rights Watch Emergencies Researcher. March 1, 2000. http://www.hrw.org/campaigns/russia/chechnya/peter-testimony.htm (accessed July 2005).

Bowring, Bill. "Russia's Relations with the Council of Europe under Increasing Strain." *EU Russia Centre Review*, February 2007. http://www.eu-russiacentre.org/assets/files/15%20Feb%20Bowring%20article%20EU-RC.pdf (accessed March 2009).

———. "Tensions Multiply between Russia and Council of Europe: Could the Malaise Be Terminal?" *EU Russia Centre Review* 6 (April 2008): 4–12.

Cherkasov, Alexander. "Zalozhnichestvo na Kavkaze v kontse 90-x: Istoricheskie kornu." Moscow: Memorial, 1999. http://www.memo.ru/hr/hotpoints/N<->Caucas/zalozhn.htm.

Cornell, Svante. "International Reactions to Massive Human Rights Violations: The Case of Chechnya." *Europe-Asia Studies* 51, no. 1 (January 1999): 85–100.

Council of Europe. Parliamentary Assembly (PACE). CM/Inf/DH(2006)32. "Violation of the ECHR in the Chechen Republic: Russia's Compliance with the European Court's Judgments." June 29, 2006. http://www.coe.int/.

———. "Conflict in Chechnya." Doc. 8631, January 25, 2000. Opinion 1, Committee on Legal Affairs and Human Rights: Rudolph Bindig. http://www.coe.int/.

———. "Conflict in Chechnya and the Credentials of the Delegation of the Russian Federation." Thursday, January 27, 2000. Resumed debate. http://www.coe.int/.

———. "Conflict in Chechnya and the Credentials of the Russian Delegation." Thursday, April 6, 2000, 10 A.M. Ordinary Session. http://www.coe.int/.

———. "Conflict in Chechnya and the Credentials of the Russian Federation." Thursday, April 6, 2000, 10 A.M. Addendum 1. http://www.coe.int/.

———. "Conflict in Chechnya and Credentials of the Russian Federation and Address by Mr. Ivanov, Minister of Foreign Affairs of the Russian Federation." Thursday, January 27, 2000, 10 A.M. http://www.coe.int/.

———. "Conflict in the Chechen Republic—Recent Developments." Doc. 8948, January 23, 2001. http://www.coe.int/.

———. "Credentials of the Delegation of the Russian Federation." Doc. 8956, January 25, 2001. Opinion: Committee on Legal Affairs and Human Rights. http://www.coe.int/.

———. "High Level Russian Message." Moscow, January 18, 1995. Signed by the President, Boris Yeltsin, Prime Minister, V. Chernomyrdin, Chairman of the Federation Council, V. Shumeyko, and Chairman of the State Duma, I. Rybkin. Full text of message in "Russia's Request for Membership of the Council of Europe." Doc. 7443, January 2, 1996. http://www.coe.int/.

———. "The Human Rights Situation in the Chechen Republic." Doc. 9732, March 13, 2003. Report of the Committee on Legal Affairs and Human Rights. http://www.coe.int/.

———. "Letter from the Minister of Foreign Affairs of the Russian Federation to the Chairman of the Committee of Ministers and the Secretary General of the Council of Europe." June 24, 2000. http://www.coe.int/.

———. "Letter from the Minister of Foreign Affairs of the Russian Federation to the Secretary General of the Council of Europe." February 29, 2000. http://www.coe.int/.

———. "Motion for a Resolution: Chechen People's Right to Live in Safety from Inhuman Treatment and Extermination." Doc. 8961, February 1, 2001. Signed by Landsbergis (Lithuania), Baumet (FR), Bjorck (Sweden), Bartos (Czech), Jackson (UK), Knight (UK), Krzaklewski (Poland), Olekas (Lithuania), Ouzky (Czech), Ragnarsdottir (Iceland), Sinka (Latvia), Stankevic (Lithuania), Vahtre (Estonia), Wojcik (Poland). http://www.coe.int/.

———. Ordinary Session (First Part) Report. Fifth sitting, Wednesday, January 29, 2003, 3 P.M. http://www.coe.int/.

———. "Progress Report on the Activities of the Joint Working Group on Chechnya." Doc. 9038, April 23, 2001. http://www.coe.int/.

———. "Progress Report on the Activities of the Joint Working Group on Chechnya." Doc. 9227, September 24, 2001. http://www.coe.int/.

———. Recommendation 1456 (2000) 1. "Conflict in Chechnya: Implementation by the Russian Federation of Recommendation 1444 (2000)." Council of Europe, Strasbourg. http://www.coe.int/.

———. Recommendation 1600 (2003). "The Human Rights Situation in the Chechen Republic." Council of Europe Archive, Strasbourg. http://www.coe.int/.

———. Ref 3/179.01, 16.01.2001. Letter to Rudolph Bindig from Yuri Abazov. "Information on Criminal Case No. 12009, Instigated with Regard to the Murder of Civilians in the Settlements of Noviye Aldy, Chernoreche Zavodskiy [*sic*] Rayon, Grozny." Full text in addendum to "Conflict in the Chechen Republic—Recent Developments." Doc. 8948, January 23, 2001. Council of Europe Archive, Strasbourg. http://www.coe.int/.

———. Ref 3/180.01, 16.01.2001. Letter to Rudolph Bindig from Yuri Abazov. "Information on Criminal Case No. 12038, Instigated on 3 May with Regard to the Murder of Civilians in the Mikrorayon of Novaya Katayama, Grozny." Full text in addendum to "Conflict in the Chechen Republic—Recent Developments." Document 8948. January 23, 2001. Council of Europe Archive, Strasbourg. http://www.coe.int/.

———. Report by Mr. Alvaro Gil-Robles, Commissioner for Human Rights on his visit to the Russian Federation (in particular Ingushetia and Chechnya—Grozny, February 24–29, 2000). Council of Europe Archive, Strasbourg. http://www.coe.int/.

———. Resolution 1055 (1995) on Russia's request for membership in light of the situation in Chechnya. Text adopted by the Assembly on February 2, 1995 (7th sitting). Council of Europe Archive, Strasbourg. http://www.coe.int/.

———. SG/Inf (2000) Statistical data/27 September 2000. "Secretary General's Interim Report on the Presence of Council of Europe Experts in the Office of the Russian President's Special Representative for Human Rights in Chechnya." Council of Europe Archive, Strasbourg. http://www.coe.int/.

———. SG/Inf (2000) 51/11 December 2000. "Fourth Interim Report to the Secretary General on the Presence of Experts of the Council of Europe in the Office of the Special Representative of the Russian Federation for Ensuring Human Rights and Civil Rights and Freedoms in the Chechen Republic. Period from 2 November to 10 December 2000." Council of Europe Archive, Strasbourg. http://www.coe.int/.

———. SG/Inf (2000) 51 Addendum/11 December 2000. Addendum to the Fourth Interim Report. Council of Europe Archive, Strasbourg. http://www.coe.int/.

———. SG/Inf (2001) 8/13 March 2001. Sixth Interim Report. "Interim Report to the Secretary General on the Presence of Experts of the Council of Europe in the Office of the Special Representative of the Russian Federation for Ensuring Human Rights and Civil Rights and Freedoms in the Chechen Republic." Council of Europe Archive, Strasbourg. http://www.coe.int/.

———. SG/Inf (2001) 8 Addendum/13 March 2001. "Addendum to the Sixth Interim Report by the Secretary General on the Presence of Experts of the Council of Europe in the Office of the Special Representative of the Russian Federation for Ensuring Human Rights and Civil Rights and Freedoms in the Chechen Republic." Council of Europe Archive, Strasbourg. http://www.coe.int/.

———. SG/Inf (2001) 12/17 April 2001. "Seventh Interim Report to the Secretary General on the Presence of Experts of the Council of Europe in the Office of the Special Representative of the Russian Federation for Ensuring Human Rights and Civil Rights and Freedoms in the Chechen Republic." Council of Europe Archive, Strasbourg. http://www.coe.int/.

———. SG/Inf (2001) 41/12 December 2001. "Fifteenth Interim Report by the Secretary General on the Presence of Experts of the Council of Europe in the Office of the Special

Representative of the Russian Federation for Ensuring Human Rights and Civil Rights and Freedoms in the Chechen republic." Council of Europe Archive, Strasbourg. http://www.coe.int/.

———. SG/Inf (2004) 3/16 January 2004. "Russian Federation: Council of Europe's Response to the Situation in the Chechen Republic. Report by the Secretary General on the Presence of Council of Europe's Experts in the Chechen Republic and Overview of the Situation since June 2000." Council of Europe Archive, Strasbourg. http://www.coe.int/.

———. "Walter Schwimmer to the Minister of Foreign Affairs of the Russian Federation." December 25, 2003. Appendix 1, SG/Inf (2004) 3/16 January 2004. Council of Europe Archive, Strasbourg. http://www.coe.int/.

———. "Who Is POA to Rogozin? Situation in the Republic of Chechnya—Implementation of Recommendation 1456 (2000) Doc. 8777, June 27, 2000." Communication—POA to Dmitry Rogozin, June 8, 2000. Council of Europe Archive, Strasbourg. http://www.coe.int/.

Crook, John. "The Fifty-First Session of the UN Human Rights Commission." *American Journal of International Law* 90, no. 1 (January 1996): 126–38.

Denber, Rachel. "Glad to Be Deceived: The International Community and Chechnya." New York: Human Rights Watch World Report, 2004. Available at: http://www.hrw.org/wr2k4/7.htm#_Toc58744956 (accessed May 2005).

Dennis, Michael. "The Fifty-Sixth Session of the UN Commission on Human Rights." *American Journal of International Law* 95, no. 1 (January 2001): 213–21.

———. "The Fifty-Seventh Session of the UN Commission on Human Rights." *American Journal of International Law* 96, no. 1 (January 2002): 181–97.

———. "Human Rights in 2002: The Annual Sessions of the UN Commission on Human Rights and the Economic and Social Council." *American Journal of International Law* 97, no. 2 (April 2003): 364–86.

Dickson, Captain Keith D. U.S. Army Reserve. "The Bamzachi and the Lkfujahidin: Soviet Responses to Insurgency Movements." *Military Review* (n.d.).

Dunlop, John. "How Many Soldiers and Civilians Died during the Russo–Chechen War of 1994–1996?" *Central Asian Survey* 19, no. 3/4 (2000): 329–39.

———. "The October 2002 Moscow Hostage-Taking Incident" (Parts I and II). *RFE/RL Organized Crime and Terrorism Watch* 3, no. 42 (December 18, 2003). http://www.rferl.org/content/Article/1342329.html (accessed March 2009).

———. "The October 2002 Moscow Hostage-Taking Incident" (Part III). *RFE/RL Organized Crime and Terrorism Watch* 4, no. 2 (January 15, 2004). http://www.rferl.org/content/Article/1342329.html (accessed March 2009).

———. *Russia Confronts Chechnya: Roots of a Separatist Conflict*. Cambridge: Cambridge University Press, 1998.

———. *The 2002 Dubrovka and 2004 Beslan Hostage Crises: A Critique of Russian Counter-Terrorism*. Foreword by Donald N. Jensen. Stuttgart: Ibidem-Verlag, 2006.

East/West Institute. *Conflict Prevention in the Caucasus: Actors, Response Capacities and Planning Processes*. London: East/West Institute and Forum on Early Warning and Early Response, December 2001.

Ehrenreich Brooks, Rosa. "War Everywhere: Rights, National Security Law, and the Law of Armed Conflict in the Age of Terror." *University of Pennsylvania Law Review* 153 (2004–5): 675–761.

Eßer, Barbara, Barbara Gladysch, and Benita Suwelack. "Report on the Situation of Chechen Asylum Seekers and Refugees in Poland and Effects of the EU Dublin II

Regulation." February 1995. http://www.chechnyaadvocacy.org/refugees/Refugees%20in%20Poland%2002-2005.pdf (accessed February 2009).

European Committee for the Prevention of Torture. Press release. "European Committee for the Prevention of Torture: Public Statement Concerning the Chechen Republic." July 10, 2001. Council of Europe Archive, Strasbourg. http://www.coe.int/ (accessed March 2009).

Evangelista, Matthew. *The Chechen Wars: Will Russia Go the Way of the Soviet Union?* Washington, DC: Brookings Institution Press, 2002.

European Council on Refugees and Exiles. "EU 'Dublin' Rules on Asylum Claims Cause Misery and Put Refugees at Risk." PR1/3/2006/Ext/RW, March 16, 2006. http://www.echr.coe.int/ (accessed February 2009).

European Court of Human Rights. *Anguelova v. Bulgaria*. No. 38361/97. Judgment, ECHR, Strasbourg, 2002-IV. http://www.echr.coe.int/ (accessed February 2009).

———. "Applicants' Submissions Regarding Compliance with the Judgments of the European Court of Human Rights (Rule 6 of the Committee of Ministers' Rules)." http://www.echr.coe.int/ (accessed February 2009).

———. *Bazorkina v. Russia*. No. 69481/01. Judgment, ECHR, Strasbourg, July 27, 2006. http://www.echr.coe.int/ (accessed February 2009).

———. *Chitaev & Chitaev v. Russia*. No. 59334/00. Judgment, ECHR, Strasbourg, January 18, 2007. http://www.echr.coe.int/ (accessed February 2009).

———. *Estamirov and Others v. Russia*. No. 60272/00, Judgment, ECHR, Strasbourg, October 12, 2006. http://www.echr.coe.int/ (accessed February 2009).

———. *Isaeva, Iusupova and Basaeva v. Russia*. Nos. 57947/00, 57948/00, and 57949/00. Judgment, ECHR, Strasbourg, February 24, 2005. http://www.echr.coe.int/ (accessed February 2009).

———. *Luluev and Others vs. Russia*. No. 69480/01, Judgment, ECHR, Strasbourg, February 9, 2007. http://www.echr.coe.int/ (accessed February 2009).

———. Official statement of the permanent representative of the Russian Federation to the Council of Europe at the meeting of the Committee of Minister of the Council of Europe concerning the action plan as regards execution by the Russian Federation of the judgment of the European Court of Human Rights in the cases of *Khashiev and Akaeva v. Russia*, Nos. 57942/00 and 57945/00, *Isaeva, Iusupova and Bazaeva v. Russia*, Nos. 57947/00, 57948/00 and 57949/00, and *Isaeva v. Russia*, No. 57950/00. http://www.echr.coe.int/ (accessed February 2009).

Evans, A. "President Putin's Design for Civil Society." In *Russian Civil Society: A Critical Assessment*, ed. Alfred B. Evans, Laura A. Henry, and Lisa McIntosh Sundstrom. New York: M. E. Sharpe, 2006.

Gall, Carlotta, and Thomas De Waal. *Chechnya: A Small Victorious War*. New York: New York University Press, 1998.

Gammar, Moshe. *The Lone Wolf and the Bear: Three Centuries of Chechen Defiance of Russian Rule*. Pittsburgh: University of Pittsburgh Press, 2006.

Gannushkina, S., ed. "On the Situation of Residents of Chechnya in the Russian Federation: July 2005–July 2006." Moscow: Memorial Human Rights Center Migration Rights Network, 2006.

German, Tracey. *Russia's Chechen War*. London: Routledge, 2003.

Getty, Arch. *Origins of the Great Purges: The Soviet Communist Party Reconsidered, 1933–1938*. New York: Cambridge University Press, 1985.

Goltz, Thomas. *Chechnya Diary: A War Correspondent's Story of Surviving the War in Chechnya*. New York: St. Martin's Press, 2003.

Grau, Lester, and Timothy Smith. "A 'Crushing' Victory: Fuel Air Explosives and Grozny, 2000." *Foreign Military Studies Office*, August 2000. http://fmso.leavenworth.army.mil/documents/fuelair/fuelair.htm (accessed September 2006).

———. "Russian Snipers in the Mountains and Cities of Chechnya." *Infantry* (Summer 2002): 7–11.

Guldimann, Tim. "Supporting the Doves against the Hawks: Experiences of the OSCE Assistance Group to Chechnya." Hamburg: CORE Center for OSCE Research, 1997. http://www.core-hamburg.de/documents/yearbook/english/97/Guldimann.pdf (accessed April 2008).

Hahn, Gordon. *Russia's Islamic Threat*. New Haven: Yale University Press, 2007.

Haslam, Emily. "Non-governmental War Crimes Tribunals." In *Renegotiating Westphalia: Essays and Commentary on the European and Conceptual Foundations of Modern International Law*. Netherlands: Martinus Nijhoff, 1999.

Hodgson, Q. E. "Is the Russian Bear Learning? An Operational and Tactical Analysis of the Second Chechen War, 1999–2002." *Journal of Strategic Studies* 26, no. 2 (2003): 64–91.

Holquist, Peter. "State Violence as Technique: The Logic of Violence in Soviet Totalitarianism." In *Landscaping the Human Garden*, ed. Amir Weiner. Stanford: Stanford University Press, 2003.

Hughes, James. *Chechnya: From Nationalism to Jihad*. Philadelphia: University of Pennsylvania Press, 2007.

Human Rights First. "Russian Human Rights Activist Convicted in Politically Motivated Case." February 3, 2006. http://www.humanrightsfirst.org/media/2006_alerts/hrd_0203_rus.htm (accessed April 2008).

Human Rights Watch. "Burying the Evidence: The Botched Investigation into a Mass Grave in Chechnya." Human Rights Watch 13, no. 3(D) (May 2001). http://www.hrw.org/.

———. "Chechnya: Council of Europe Must File Complaint against Russia—Open Letter to Council of Europe Foreign Ministers." October 25, 2000. http://www.hrw.org/en/news/2000/11/02/chechnya-council-europe-must-file-complaint-against-russia (accessed March 2009).

———. "Civilian Killings in Staropromyslovski District of Grozny." Human Rights Watch 12, no. 2(D) (February 2000). http://www.hrw.org/.

———. "The 'Dirty War' in Chechnya: Forced Disappearances, Torture, and Summary Executions." Human Rights Watch 13, no. 1(D) (March 2001). http://www.hrw.org/.

———. "Evidence of War Crimes in Chechnya." Press release, November 3, 1999. http://www.hrw.org/.

———. "February 5: A Day of Slaughter in Novye Aldi." Human Rights Watch 12, no. 9(D) (June 2000). http://www.hrw.org/.

———. "Into Harm's Way: Forced Return of Displaced People to Chechnya." Human Rights Watch 15, no. 1(D) (January 2003). http://www.hrw.org/.

———. "Last Seen . . . Continued 'Disappearances' in Chechnya." Human Rights Watch 14, no. 3(D) (April 2002). http://www.hrw.org/.

———. "'No Happiness Remains': Civilian Killings, Pillage and Rape in Alkhan-Iurt, Chechnya." Human Rights Watch 12, no. 5(D) (April 2000). http://www.hrw.org/.

———. "Russia Closes Borders to Chechen Males: Blanket Ban Traps Men in War Zone." Press release, January 12, 2000. http://www.hrw.org/.

———. "Spreading Despair: Russian Abuses in Ingushetia." Human Rights Watch 15, no. 8(D) (September 2003). http://www.hrw.org/.

———. "Swept Under: Torture, Forced Disappearances and Extrajudicial Killings during Sweep Operations in Chechnya." Human Rights Watch 14, no. 2(D) (2002). http://www.hrw.org/.

———. "'Welcome to Hell': Arbitrary Detention, Torture, and Extortion in Chechnya." October 2000. http://www.hrw.org/.

———. "Worse Than a War: 'Disappearances' in Chechnya—A Crime against Humanity." Human Rights Watch Briefing Paper, March 2005. http://www.hrw.org/.

International Helsinki Federation for Human Rights (IHF). "Chechnya: Terror and Impunity: A Planned System." No. 329/2, March 2002. http://www.fidh.org/spip.php?article1714 (accessed March 2009).

———. "Closure of the Independent Weekly Chechen Society and the Strong Pressure on Editor, Timur Aliev." IHF press release, August 5, 2004. http://www.ihf-hr.org/viewbinary/viewhtml.php?doc_id=6066 (accessed March 2009).

———. "The Silencing of Human Rights Defenders in Chechnya and Ingushetia." International Helsinki Federation for Human Rights (IHF) and the Norwegian Helsinki Committee (NHC), September 15, 2004. http://www.ihf-hr.org/documents/doc_summary.php?sec_id=3&d_id=3965 (accessed March 2009).

Jakobsen, P. V. "National Interest, Humanitarianism or CNN: What Triggers UN Peace Enforcement after the Cold War?" *Journal of Peace Research* 33, no. 2 (May 1996): 205–15.

Kovalev, Sergei. "Press Conference with State Duma Deputy Sergei Kovalev." *Petrovka* 26, no. 2 (April 18, 2000).

———. "Speech by Sergei Kovalev at Human Rights Watch Meeting, New York, March 9, 1996." Author's collection, Storrs, CT.

———. "Stenogramme of Interview with Sergei Kovalev. New York, October 22, 1995." New York: Kline Archive, unpublished. No author's name provided.

———. "Ugroza pravovomu gosudarstvu i konstititsionnyim osnovam demokratii v strane." http://www.hro.org/ngo/congress (accessed March 2003).

Kramer, Mark. "The Perils of Counterinsurgency: Russia's War in Chechnya." *International Security* 29, no. 3 (Winter 2004–5): 5–63.

Lanskoy, Miriam. "Daghestan and Chechnya: The Wahhabi Challenge to the State." *SAIS Review* 22, no. 2 (2002): 167–92.

Lapidus, Gail. "Contested Sovereignty: The Tragedy of Chechnya." *International Security* 23, no. 1 (Summer 1998): 5–49.

Leach, Philip. "The Effectiveness of the Committee of Ministers in Supervising the Enforcement of Judgments of the European Court of Human Rights." *Public Law*, no. 3 (2006): 443–56.

———. "Strasbourg's Oversight of Russia: An Increasingly Strained Relationship." Working paper, European Human Rights Advocacy Centre. London, 2007.

Levin, Mariah. "Chechen Migration and Integration in Ukraine." Working paper, November 2006. http://www.chechnyaadvocacy.org/refugees.html (accessed August 2007).

Lieven, Anatol. *Chechnya: Tombstone of Russian Power.* New Haven: Yale University Press, 1998.

Lokshina, L. "Hostage L. Lokshina Recalls the Events." http://nord-ost.org/vospominaniya/rasskazyivaet-zalozhnik-l.lokshina.html (accessed August 2007).

Malinkina, Olga, and Douglas McLeod. "From Afghanistan to Chechnya: News Coverage by *Izvestiia* and the *New York Times.*" *Journalism and Mass Communication Quarterly* 77, no. 1 (Spring 2000): 37–49.

Maskhadov, Aslan. "Open Letter to the French Philosopher Andre Glucksmann." *Central Asian Survey* 19, no. 3/4 (2000): 309–14.

May, Larry. *Crimes against Humanity: A Normative Account*. Cambridge: Cambridge University Press, 2005.

McFaul, Michael. "A Precarious Peace: Domestic Politics in the Making of Russian Foreign Policy." *International Security* 22, no. 3 (Winter 1997–98): 5–35.

Médecins Sans Frontières (MSF). "Chechnya: The Tracking of Civilians—Interviews with Chechen Refugees in Georgia," December 15, 1999. http://www.doctorswithoutborders.org/publications/article.cfm?id=1461&cat=special-report (accessed March 2009).

———. "Left without a Choice: Chechens Forced to Return to Chechnya." Special Report, April 2003. http://www.msf.org.au/resources/reports/report/article/left-without-a-choice-chechens-forced-to-return-to-chechnya.html (accessed March 2009).

———. "Médecins Sans Frontières Activity Report 2003: North Caucasus." Special Report, 2003. http://www.doctorswithoutborders.org/publications/ar/report.cfm?id=1080&cat=activity-report (accessed March 2009).

———. "The Trauma of Ongoing War in Chechnya: Quantitative Assessment of Living Conditions, and Psychosocial and General Health Status among War Displaced in Chechnya and Ingushetia." Special Report, August 2004. http://fieldresearch.msf.org/msf/handle/10144/27877 (accessed March 2009).

Medical Foundation for the Care of Victims of Torture. "Rape and Other Torture in the Chechnya Conflict: Documents Evidence from Asylum Seekers Arriving in the United Kingdom." United Kingdom: Medical Foundation for the Care of Victims of Torture Report, April 2004.

Meier, Andrew. *Chechnya: To the Heart of the Conflict*. London: W. W. Norton, 2005.

Memorial Human Rights Center. *"Counterterrorism Operation" by the Russian Federation in the Northern Caucasus throughout 1999–2006*. Moscow: Memorial Archive, 2007.

———. *Liudi Zhyvut Zdes'*. Moscow: Memorial Archive, 2003.

———. "Terroristicheskie akty za predelami Chechni: Zakhvaty zalozhnikov, prednamerennye napadeniya na grazhdanskoe naselenie i meditsinskie uchrezhdeniya, bessudnye kazni, ispol'zovanie "zhivogo shita." In *Rossiya-Chechnya—Tsel' Oshibok i Prestupleniya*. Moscow: Memorial Archive, 1997.

Meron, Theodor. "The Humanization of Humanitarian Law." *American Journal of International Law* 94, no. 2 (April 2000): 239–78.

Mozhegova, G. "Hostage G. Mozhegova Tells about the Events." http://nord-ost.org/vospominaniya/rasskazyivaet-zalozhnik-g.mozhegova.html (accessed August 2007).

Naimark, Normam. *Fires of Hatred: Ethnic Cleansing in Twentieth-Century Europe*. Cambridge, MA: Harvard University Press, 2001.

Nivat, Anne. *Chienne de Guerre: A Woman Reporter behind the Lines of War in Chechnya*. Trans. Susan Darnton. New York: Public Affairs, 2001.

Nord-Ost [Al Stahl]. "Hostage A Stahl Tells about the Events." December 26, 2002. http://nord-ost.org/vospominaniya/rasskazyivaet-zalozhnik-a.stal.html (accessed August 2007).

"Nord Ost" Investigation Unfinished: Events, Facts, Conclusions. With assistance from "Terrorism Victims Support Fund," Moscow, April 26, 2006. http://www.pravdabeslana.ru/nordost/dokleng.htm (accessed March 2007).

Norwegian Refugee Council. "Whose Responsibility? Protection of Chechen Internally Displaced Persons, Asylum Seekers and Refugees." Norway: Norwegian Refugee Council, May 2005.

———. "Profile of Internal Displacement: Russian Federation." Norway: Norwegian Refugee Council and Global IDP Project, March 14, 2005.

Norwegian Helsinki Committee. "Forgotten Terror: Chechnya." Norway: Norwegian Helsinki Committee, September 27 to October 7, 2001. http://www.nhc.no/php/index.php?module=fatcat&fatcat%5Buser%5D=viewCategory&fatcat_id=107 (accessed March 2009).

Ognianova, Nina. "Rewriting the Law to Make Journalism a Crime." Center for the Protection of Journalists, undated. http://www.cpj.org/ (accessed April 2008).

Organization for Security and Cooperation in Europe. "The OSCE Assistance Group to Chechnya: Basic Decisions." Establishment: 16th Meeting of the Permanent Council, April 11, 1995, PC.DEC/35. New York: Kline Archive, 1995.

Orlov, Oleg, and Alexander Cherkasov. "Russia and Chechnya: A Chain of Errors and Crimes." *Russian Studies in History* 41, no. 2 (Fall 2002): 77–99.

Pain, Emil. "The Second Chechen War: The Information Component." *Military Review*, July–August 2000. http://fmso.leavenworth.army.mil/documents/secchech/secchech.htm (accessed December 2006).

Parry, John T. "Escalation and Necessity; Defining Torture at Home or Abroad." In *Torture: A Collection*, ed. Sanford Levinson. Oxford: Oxford University Press, 2004.

Petrovic, Drazen. "Ethnic Cleansing—An Attempt at Methodology." *European Journal of International Law* 1, no. 359 (1994): 1–19.

Philips, Timothy. *Beslan: The Tragedy of School No. 1*. London: Granta Books, 2007.

Politkovskaia, Anna. *A Dirty War: A Russian Reporter from Chechnya*. London: Harvill Press, 2001.

———. *Putin's Russia*. London: Harvill Press, 2004.

———. *A Russian Diary*. New York: Random House, 2007.

———. *A Small Corner of Hell: Dispatches from Chechnya*. Chicago: University of Chicago Press, 2003.

Refugees International. "Poland: Chechen Refugees Grateful for Protection But Need Integration Support." Refugees International Report, June 12, 2005. http://www.unhcr.org/refworld/country,,RI,,RUS,4562d8b62,47a6eecc15,0.html (accessed March 2009).

Russian Federation Federal Law No. 130-FZ. "O bor'be s terrorizmom." *Rossiskaia Gazeta*, August 4, 1998.

———. "Law on the Introduction of Amendments and Additions to the Law of the Russian Federation on 'Forced Migrants.'" December 28, 1995. http://www.internal-displacement.org/8025708F004CE90B/(httpDocuments)/CE55AE0666755CE7802570B70059F578/$file/LawForcedMigrants.pdf (accessed March 2009).

Russian Foreign Ministry. Press release. Deputy Official Spokesman of Russia's Ministry of Foreign Affairs, "Otvet zamestitelya ofitsialnogo predstavitelya MID Rossii E.R Boronina na vopros Rossiiskikh SMI." http://www.slovakia.mid.ru/ch_9.html (accessed March 2004).

———. Press release no. 9. "Statement by Russian Foreign Ministry Spokesman," Ministry of Foreign Affairs, February 25, 2000. http://www.great-britain.mid.ru/pressrel_00.htm (accessed March 2009).

———. Press release no. 16. "Russia's Reaction to the PACE Resolution in Connection with the Situation in the Chechen Republic." April 7, 2000. http://www.great-britain.mid.ru/pressrel_00.htm (accessed March 2009).

———. Press release no. 19. "Open Letter by a Number of Prominent Russian Arts and Culture Figures on the Situation in the Northern Caucasus Region of Russia." April 21, 2000. http://www.great-britain.mid.ru/pressrel_00.htm (accessed March 2009).

———. Press release no. 21. "Statement by the Russian Ministry of Foreign Affairs." April 27, 2000. http://www.great-britain.mid.ru/pressrel_00.htm (accessed March 2009).

Said, Edward. *From Oslo to Iraq and the Road Map*. New York: Vintage Books, 2005.

———. *The Politics of Dispossession*. New York: Vintage Books, 1995.

———. *The Question of Palestine*. New York: Vintage Books, 1992.

Sakwa, Richard, ed. *Chechnya: From Past to Future*. London: Anthem Press, 2005.

Slawner, Karen. "Interpreting Victim Testimony: Survivor Discourse and the Narration of History." http://www.yendor.com/vanished/karenhead.html (accessed March 2009).

Souleimanov, Emil. "Chechnya, Wahhabism and the Invasion of Dagestan." *Middle East Review of International Affairs* 9, no. 4 (December 2005): 48–71.

Speckhard, Anne, and Khapta Akhmedova. "Black Widows: The Chechen Female Suicide Terrorists." In *Female Suicide Terrorists*, ed. Yoram Schweitzer. Tel Aviv: Jaffe Center Publication, 2005.

Staar, Richard. *KGB & Other Buddies in Putin Apparat*. Boston: Institute for the Study of Conflict, Ideology, and Policy, 2000.

Thomas, Timothy. "Grozny 2000: Urban Combat Lessons Learned." *Military Review*, July–August 2000.

———. "A Tale of Two Theaters: Russian Actions in Chechnya in 1994 and 1999." *Analysis of Current Events* 12, nos. 5–6 (September 2000). http://leav-www.army.mil/fmso/documents/chechtale.htm (accessed March 2009).

Tishkov, Valery. *Chechnya: Life in a War-Torn Society*. Berkeley: University of California Press, 2004.

Tomuschat, Christian. *Human Rights: Between Idealism and Realism*. Oxford: Oxford University Press, 2003.

Ugolovnyi kodeks RF (UK RF) ot 13.06.1996 N 63-F3. http://www.consultant.ru (accessed April 2008).

Union of Right-Wing Forces. "Minutes of the Sessions of the Public Commission of the 'SPS' on Questions of Rendering Medical Aid to the Injured Hostages." October 29 and November 1, 2002. http://2002.novayagazeta.ru/nomer/2002/86n/n86n-s02.shtml (accessed March 2009).

United Nations High Commissioner for Refugees. Fact Sheet No. 6 (Rev.2). Enforced or Involuntary Disappearances. http://www. unhchr.ch/html/menu6/2/fs6.htm (accessed March 2007).

———. "North Caucasus: UNHCR Asks for Camp Closures Postponement." UNHCR spokesperson Ron Redmond, press briefing, November 29, 2002, Palais des Nations, Geneva.

United Nations Human Rights Commission, Distr. General E/CN.4/1998/53/Add.2. February 11, 1998. Commission on Human Rights, Fifty-Fourth Session. Item 9 (d) of the Provisional Agenda: Guiding Principles on Internal Displacement.

Uppsala Conflict Data Program. Department of Peace and Conflict Research, Uppsala University, Sweden. http://www.pcr.uu.se (accessed August 2007).

Williams, Brian Glyn. "Commemorating 'The Deportation' in Post-Soviet Chechnya: The Role of Memorialization and Collective Memory in the 1994–1996 and 1999–2000 Russo-Chechen Wars." *History and Memory: Studies in Recollections of the Past* 12, no. 1 (Spring/Summer 2000).

Yo'av Karny. *Highlanders: A Journey to the Caucasus in Quest of Memory*. New York: Farrar Straus, 2000.

Zelkina, Anna. *In Quest for God and Freedom: The Sufi Naqshbandi Brotherhood of the North Caucasus*. London: Hurst, 1999.

Memorial Human Rights Center archive

All documents itemized in chronological order. No amendments have been made to translations of Russian text into English by Memorial. Archive available online at http://www.memo.ru/.

Year 1999

———. Pis'mo pravleniia rossiikogo obshchestva "Memorial" Predsedateliu Pravitel'stva RF Putinu (28.10.1999)
———. Pis'mo pravleniia rossiikogo obshchestva "Memorial" v mezhdunarodnye organizatsii (28.10.1999)
———. Tekst vystupleniia A. Cherkasova v Stambule 9 noiabria 1999 g. (9.11.1999)
———. Pis'mo Natsional'nogo Soveta Chechentsev Dagestana (9.11.1999)
———. K sobytiiam v Chechne: Press-reliz 16.11.99 (16.11.1999)
———. Mezhdunarodnaia Amnistiia (18.11.1999)
———. Chelovechestvo nedelimo (18.11.1999)
———. K vstreche glav gosudarstv v Stambule (18.11.1999)
———. Rasskazy ochevidtsev bombardirovki kolonny bezhentsev 29 oktiabria 1999 goda (26.11.1999)
———. Zaiavlenie initsiativnoi gruppy "Obshchee Deistvie" (26.11.1999)
———. Zaiavleniia zhitelei Chechni (28.11.1999)
———. Zaiavleniia PTS "Memorial" o kampanii v presse protiv Ausheva (2.12.1999)
———. O chislennosti naseleniia Chechni v iiule 1999 g. (2.12.1999)
———. Obrashchenie pravleniia mezhdunarodnogo obshchestva "Memorial" po povodu ul'timatuma zhiteliam Groznogo (6.12.1999)
———. Positsiia obshchestva "Memorial" v sviazi s vooruzhennym konfliktom v Chechne (9.12.1999)
———. Pis'mo Predsedateliu Pravitel'stva Rossiiskoi Federatsii Putinu (9.12.1999)
———. Soobshchenie nabliudatel'noi missii Pravozashchitnogo Tsentra "Memorial" v zone konflikta v Chechne (17.12.1999)
———. Pis'mo PTS "Memorial" i Komiteta "Grazhdanskoe Sodeistvie" rukovoditeliam mezhdunarodnykh organizatsii o polozhenii bezhentsev (19.12.1999)
———. Spravka o polozhenii v lageriakh vynuzhdennykh pereselentsev, pokinuvshikh mesta postoiannogo prozhivaniia v rezul'tate provedeniia "antiterroristicheskoi operatsii" (23.12.1999)
———. K sobytiiam v sele Alkhan-Iurt (24.12.1999)
———. Gumanitarnyi Koridor: Vykhod mirnykh zhitelei iz Groznogo: Dekabr' 1999 g. (25.12.1999)
———. "Tochechnye Udary": Kratkaia khronika bombardirovok i obstrelov, 1 noiabria–14 dekabria 1996 g. (25.12.1999)
———. Letter to Sadake Ogate, Supreme Commissar of the UNO for the affairs of refugees; Mary Robinson, Supreme Commissar of the UNO for human rights; Alvaro Gil Robles, Commissioner for Human Rights of the Council of Europe (29.12.1999)

Year 2000

———. Pis'mo PTS "Memorial" i Komiteta "Grazhdanskoe Sodeistvie" rukovoditeliam mezhdunarodnykh organizatsii o polozhenie mirnogo naseleniia (18.01.2000)
———. Violations of humanitarian law and human rights; situation of civilians who have fled the conflict zone: Report on the visit to Ingushetia and Chechnya by representa-

tives of the Memorial Human Rights Centre (MHRC) from 12 to 20 January 2000 (20.01.2000)

———. Prikaz FMS No. 110 (20.01.2000)

———. Zaiavlenie ob "obmene" zhurlanista Babitskovo na rossiiskikh soldat, vziatykh v plen Chechentsami (4.02.2000)

———. Svidetel'stva o zachistke Groznogo (10.02.2000)

———. Sovmestnoe zaiavlenie PTS "Memorial" i FIDH o polozhenie v Chechne (11.02.2000)

———. Information of the supervisory mission in the zone of the armed conflict in Chechenia (15.02.2000)

———. Situatsiia v lageriakh (gorodkakh) vynuzhdennykh pereselentsev iz Chechni, raspolozhennykh na territorii Ingushetii (24.02.2000)

———. Fil'tratsionnye lageria v Chechne (14.03.2000)

———. Riad rossiiskikh pravozashchitnykh organizatsii napravil pis'mo k ministram inostrannykh del stran-chlenov Soveta Evropy (16.03.2000)

———. New Aldy settlement—February 5, 2000, intentional killings of civilians (21.03.2000)

———. Gruziia: bezhentsy iz Chechni (24.03.2000)

———. Fil'tratsionnye lageria v Chechne—Urus-Martan (07.04.2000)

———. Zaiavlenie PTS "Memorial" po povodu rezoliutsii Komissii OON po pravam cheloveka "Polozhenie v Chechenskoi Respublike" (26.04.2000)

———. Chechnya: Got missed in "filtration" procedure (26.04.2000)

———. Zaiavlenie PTS "Memorial" ob ubiistve plennykh sotrudnikov OMON (02.05.2000)

———. Dva dokumental'nykh dokazatel'stva grabezhei i unichtozheniia domov voennosluzhashchimi v sele Duba-Iurt (11.05.2000)

———. "Novaia Zhizn'": Sobytiia vokrug sela Geldagana (11.05.2000)

———. There were found dead corpses of the people who had disappeared after detention held for the purpose of identity check (19.05.2000)

———. Chechnya: Prestupleniia protiv chelovechestva; Kogda sostoitsia sud? (30.05.2000)

———. Urus Martan commandant introduces a preliminary censorship and willfully declares an extraordinary position (15.06.2000)

———. Chechnya: People disappear; no court hearings prior to executions (17.06.2000)

———. Urus-Martan—arbitrariness, beating, tortures (20.06.2000)

———. Fil'tratsionnaia sistema in Chechne (20.06.2000)

———. Obrashchenie Pravozashchitnogo Tsentra "Memorial" k chlenam Parlamentskoi Assamblei Soveta Evropy (28.06. 2000)

———. Situation with violations of human rights in Chechnya, June–July 2000 (6.07.2000)

———. Zachistka: Poselok Novye Aldy, 5 fevralia 2000—prednamerennye prestupleniia protiv mirnovo naseleniia g. (22.07.2000)

———. V ozhidanii oseni: Nadvigaiushchaiasia katastrofa; Polozhenie vynuzhdennykh pereselentsev na territorii Respubliki Ingushetiia (31.07.2000)

———. Otpravlenie v Starykh Atagakh: Neschastnyi sluchai? Vspyshka zabolevaniia? Primenenie oruzhiia (14.09.2000)

———. Podborka pokazanii o sobytiiakh v Chechne, dekabr' 1999 g.–mart 2000 g. (15.09.2000)

———. To members of the Parliamentary Assembly of the Council of Europe by Human Rights Centre, Memorial, Moscow (25.09.2000)

———. Terroristicheskii akt v Groznom (16.10.2000)

———. Polozhenie vynuzhdennykh pereselentsev iz zony voennykh deistvii: Ingushetiia, avgust–sentiabr' 2000 g. (19.10.2000)
———. Polozhenie vynuzhdennykh pereselentsev iz zony voennykh deistvii: Ingushetiia, Konets sentiabria–seredina oktiabria 2000 g. (20.10.2000)
———. Letter to the special presidential representative for the protection of human rights and freedoms of the citizens of the Republic of Chechnya, V. A. Kalamanov (27.10.2000)
———. Pravozashchitnyi Tsentr "Memorial" napravil pis'mo Spetsial'nomu predstaviteliu Prezidenta RF po obespecheniiu prav i svobod cheloveka i grazhdanina v Chechenskoi Respublike (27.10.2000)
———. Rasskaz zhitelia Naurskogo raiona, soderzhavshegosia v sisteme "fil'tratsii" (3.11.2000)
———. "Zachistki" naselennykh punktov: Konets iiulia–sentiabr' 2000 g. (16.11.2000)
———. O situatsii v mestakh kompaktnogo razmeshcheniia vynuzhdennykh pereselentsev: Respublika Ingushetiia, Chechenskaia Respublika: 17–21 noiabria 2000 g. (24.11.2000)
———. "Chechenskie" dela rassmatrivaiutsia Strasburgskim sudom (27.11.2000)
———. Situatsiia s sobliudeniem prav cheloveka v Chechenskoi Respublike osen'iu 2000 g. (25.12.2000)
———. Address given by Oleg Orlov, representative of the HRC "Memorial" at the meeting of the Committee for Legal Affairs and Human Rights Council of Europe in Paris, December 2000.

Year 2001

———. Dekabr' 2000: Sobytiia v sel'skikh raionakh Chechni (15.01.2001)
———. Zachistka na Kataiame (15.01.2001)
———. Vizit delegatsii PACE v Chechniu i vstrecha v predstavitel'stve "Memoriala" v Groznom (16.01.2001)
———. O situatsii v mestakh kompaktnogo razmeshcheniia vynizhennykh pereselentsev: Respublika Ingushetiia i Chechenskaia Respublika, dekabr' 2000–ianvar' 2001 (22.01.2001)
———. Vserossiiskii chrezvychainyi s'ezd v zashchitu prav cheloveka (Moskva, 20–21 ianvaria 2001 g.) o situatsii na Severnom Kavkaze (5.02.2001)
———. Pis'mo k chlenam Parlamentskoi Assamblei Soveta Evropy (8.02.2001)
———. Information on the situation in the Urus-Martan region, Chechen Republic (9.02.2001)
———. Zaiavlenie zhitelei s. Alleroi Kurchaloevskogo raiona CR (15.02.2001)
———. Prodolzhaiutsia sluchai ischeznoveniia liudei, zaderzhannykh predstaviteliami federal'nykh sil (15.02.2001)
———. V Urus-Martanovskom vremennom otdele vnutrennikh del snova pytaiut (19.02.2001)
———. Beschinstva v kurchaloevskom raione prodolzhaiutsia (21.02.2001)
———. O situatsii v mestakh kompaktnogo razmeshcheniia vynuzhdennykh pereselentsev: Zima 2000–2001 g. (26.02.2001)
———. 5 fevralia okraine sela Tevzeni (Tevzana) Vedenskogo raiona (26.02.2001)
———. Vedenskii raion: Ianvar' 2001 g. (26.02.2001)
———. Dachnyi poselok pod Khankaloi: Opoznany tri cheloveka (1.03.2001)
———. Trupy u Khankaly—neoproverzhimoe dokazatel'stvo voennykh prestuplenii federal'nykh sil (6.03.2001)

———. Persons detained in Chechnya by military and internal affairs agents become victims of summary executions (19.03.2001)
———. Pravozashchitnomu tsentry "Memorial" stala izvestna eshche odna zhertva vnesudebnykh kaznei, sovershavshikhsia na Khankale (26.03.2001)
———. Sobytiia v poselke Novogroznenskoe 15 Marta 2001 goda (2.04.2001)
———. Po povodu soobshchenii o 17 telakh ubitykh liudei, obnaruzhennykh na territorii Vremennogo otdela vnutrennikh del v Oktiabr'skom raione g. Groznogo (12.04.2001)
———. Four inhabitants of Argun are arrested during a "cleansing" operation in the town and are later found dead (14.04.2001)
———. Groznyi, "zachistki" tsentral'nogo rynka 29 Aprelia–2 maia 2001 g.: Pogromy, grabezhi, ubiistva (14.04.2001)
———. Otkrytoe obrashchenie initsiativnoi gruppy "Obshchee Deistvie" k Presidentu RF (24.04.2001)
———. Sovmestnoe obrashchenie Pravozashchitnogo Tsentra "Memorial" i Mezhdunarodnoi Federatsii Lig Prav Cheloveka k Chlenam Parlamentskoi Assamblei Soveta Evropy (25.04.2001)
———. On the passing by the UN Human Rights Commission of a resolution on the situation in the Chechen Republic (3.05.2001)
———. Appeal from Achkhoi-Martan (15.05.2001)
———. Open appeal of the president of the Chechen Republic of Ichkeriya to the Russian National Anti-War Committee for a peaceful resolution in Chechnya (31.05.2001)
———. A second civilian burial site discovered near the military base at Khankala (1.06.2001)
———. Umer Viktor Alekseevich Popkov (2.06.2001)
———. Letter to the UN High Commissioner for refugees concerning attempts to forcefully return refugees to Chechnya (13.06.2001)
———. Situation of internally displaced persons in the Republic of Ingushetia, spring 2001 (13.06.2001)
———. Otkrytoe obrashchenie chlenov Rossiiskogo obshchenatsional'nogo komiteta "Za prekrashchenie voiny i mirnoe uregulirovanie v Chechne" k lideram Velikobritanii, Germanii, Italii, Kanady, SSHA, Frantsii i Iaponii (14.06.2001)
———. Appeal from the citizens of the town of Argun (18.06.2001)
———. Rally near the village of Koshkeldy (21.06.2001)
———. Refugees conduct hunger strike (22.06.2001)
———. O popytkakh vozvrashcheniia bezhentsev na territoriiu Chechenskoi Respubliki (26.06.2001)
———. The hunger-strike of Chechen refugees temporarily living in Ingushetia continues (26.06.2001)
———. How people in Chechnya "disappear" (2.07.2001)
———. Mirnye massovye aktsii protesta v Chechne: Vesna- nachala leta 2001 goda (2.07.2001)
———. The "cleansing" operations in Sernovodsk and Assinovskaia were punishment operations (5.07.2001)
———. Cleansing operations in the Kurchaloyevskii region (9.07.2001)
———. The status of investigations into crimes against civilians committed by representatives of federal forces in the Chechen Republic from 1999–2001 (10.07.2001)
———. Cleansing operation in the village of Chernorech'e (10.07.2001)
———. Appeal from the doctors of the hospital in the village of Starye Atagi (19.07.2001)
———. Resoliutsiia kruglogo stola: Prekratit' zachistki (23.07.2001)

———. "Cleansing operations" in the village of Chiri-Iurt: May–June 2001 (30.07.2001)
———. Cleansing operation in the village of Tsotsin-Iurt (6.08.2001)
———. Cleansing operation in the village of Starye Atagi (12.08.2001)
———. Cleansing operation in the village of Goiskoe, Urus-Martan Region (28.08.2001)
———. Cleansing operation in the village of Alleroi (2.09.2001)
———. The level of illegal extortion at checkpoints in Chechnya is growing (14.09.2001)
———. The "cleansing operation" in the village of Mairtup, September 1–9, 2001: Cleansing by the rules? (19.09.2001)
———. Special operation in the village of Raduzhnoe on 18 July 2001 (21.09.2001)
———. Ob usloviiakh raboty mezhdunarodnykh i zarubezhnykh gumanitarnykh organizatsii na territorii Chechenkoi Respubliki (21.09.2001)
———. Sobytiia v Gudermese 17 sentiabria 2001 goda (30.09.2001)
———. O rabote sudov v Chechenskoi Respublike (15.10.2001)
———. "Zachistki" v predgornykh selakh (23.10.2001)
———. V poselke Kataiama (G. Groznyi) s 10 po 17 oktiabria 2001 goda byli ubity vosem' mirnykh zhitelei (24.10.2001)
———. "Zachistka" sela Alkhazurovo 8–11 oktiabria 2001 goda (26.10.2001)
———. Sobytiia v Argune: Resul'tat oprosov zhitelei Arguna sotrudnikami Pravoshchitnogo Tsentra "Memorial" (14.11.2001)
———. Press-konferentsiia na temu: "Navstrechu grazhdanskomu forumu; imena, iavki, familii; Otkrytoe pis'mo prezidentu rossii" (19.11.2001)
———. "Zachistka" sela Avtury (7.12.2001)
———. "Zachistka" v universitete g. Groznogo 12 noiabria 2001 g. (7.12.2001)
———. Istoriia s ischeznoveniem zhitelei sela Avtury poluchila razvitie (20.12.2001)

Year 2002

———. "Clean-up" operations in the village of Tsotsin-Iurt: October to November 2001 (8.01.2002)
———. Na dvore zima: O polozhenii bezhentsev v Ingushetii, ianvar' 2002 g. (11.01.2002)
———. Kommiunike o vstreche predstavitelei nepravitel'stvennykh pravozashchitnykh organizatsii i predstavitelei gosudartvennykh organov vlasti Chechenskoi Respubliki (15.01.2002)
———. Myths and truths about Tsotsin-Iurt: December 30, 2001–January 3, 2002 (16.01.2002)
———. To the Council of Europe Commissioner for Human Rights, Alvaro Gil-Robles (18.01.2002)
———. "Zachistki" v selakh Chechen-Aul, Starye Atagi, Tsotsin-Iurt i gorode Argun (dekabr' 2001–ianvar' 2002 g.) (23.01.2002)
———. Sluchai izcheznovenii ili ubiistv liudei, zaderzhannykh predstaviteliami federal'nykh sil (dekabr' 2001–ianvar' 2002 g.) (23.01.2002)
———. The tragic events in Shatoiskii region (23.01.2002)
———. Mopping up in Tsotsin-Iurt, February 12–13, 2002 (23.01.2002)
———. "Mopping-up" operation in Argun, January 3–7, 2002 (23.01.2002)
———. "Mopping-up" operation in the village of Chechen-Aul: 24–26 December 2001 (23.01.2002)
———. K sobytiiam v Starykh i Novykh Atagakh (4.02.2002)
———. Trevozhnye soobshcheniia iz Starykh Atagov (4.02.2002)
———. Tragicheskii sluchai v lagere "Bart," g. Karabulak (6.02.2002)

———. Mopping up in Tsotsin-Iurt, February 12–13, 2002 (14.02.2002)
———. Stennogramma vstrechi predstavitelei nepravitel'stvennykh pravozashchitnykh organizatsii i predstavitelei gosudarstvennykh organov vlasti Chechenskoi Respubliki (Chechenskaia Respublika, s. Znamenskoe, 12.01.2002) (18.02.2002)
———. Vtoraia vstrecha predstavitelei NPO i predstavitelei gosudarstvennykh organov vlasti CR (26.02.2002)
———. Communiqué on the second meeting of non-governmental human rights organizations and representatives of state authorities of the Chechen Republic (4.03.2002)
———. Kuda v Chechne "ischezaiut" liudi? (7.03.2002)
———. "Zachistka" v sele Starye Atagi, 12–19 fevralia 2002 goda (11.03.2002)
———. Dvadtsat' vtoraia "zachistka" s sele Starye Atagi, 6–11 marta 2002 goda (13.03.2002)
———. Republic of Chechnya, Argun: "Disappearances" of detainees; "disappeared" found in unmarked graves (14.03.2002)
———. Informatsionnaia spravka o polozhenii vynuzhdennykh pereselentsev v Dagestane na 15 fevralia 2002 goda (18.03.2002)
———. Sotsial'naiia situatsiia v Chechne (18.03.2002)
———. Appeal to the UN Commission for Human Rights, 59th Session, 2003 (27.03.2002)
———. Concerning the order of the commander of the United Group Forces in the Chechen Republic Number 80 (29.03.2002)
———. "Mopping-up" in the village of Tsotsin-Iurt: 25 March–1 April 2002 (8.04.2002)
———. "Mopping-up" in the village Alkhan-Kala: 11–15th April 2002 (19.04.2002)
———. Letter to the commanding OGV in the Chechen Republic, General-Lieutenant V. I. Molentskoi, to the prosecutor of the Chechen Republic, V. G. Chernov, and to the Commandant of the Chechen Republic, A. D. Pavlenko (25.04.2002)
———. Communiqué on the third meeting of non-governmental human rights organizations and representatives of state authorities of the Chechen Republic (30.04.2002)
———. Soveshchanie v MCHS Respublili Ingushetii, 29 marta 2002 goda (7.05.2002)
———. Polozhenie vynuzhdennykh pereselentsev v Ingushetii, Vesna 2002 goda (7.05.2002)
———. Poselok Kirova—izcheznoveniia i ubiistva, 27 aprelia–3 maia 2002 goda (13.05.2002)
———. "Mopping-up" in the village Alkhan-Kala, 25–30 April 2002, order number 80—only empty words?! (14.05.2002)
———. Komitet protiv pytok OON o sobliudenii Rossiiskoi Federatsiei "konventsii protiv pytok, zhetokikh, beschelovechnykh i drugikh unizhaiushchikh dostoinstvo vidov obrashcheniia i nakazaniia" (16.05.2002)
———. Kniga chisel: Demografiia, poteri naseleniia i migratsionnye potoki v zone vooruzhennogo konflikta c Chechenskoi respublike, kritika istochnikov (31.05.2002)
———. Several examples of the many occasions in May 2002 where order No. 80 of the OGV(s) commander has been deliberately flouted (6.06.2002)
———. Zachistka c. Mesker-Iurt (so slov vyshedshikh iz sela) (7.06.2002)
———. Punkty vremennogo razmeshcheniia vynuzhdennykh migrantov na territorii Chechenskoi Respubliki (10.06.2002)
———. Ingushetiia: Polozhenie bezhentsev iz Chechni; Leto 2002 goda (18.06.2002)
———. Priroda ne terpit pustoty: Nekotorye problemy otsenki pravovoi situatsii i pravoprimenitel'noi praktiki v zone vooruzhennogo konflikta v Chechenskoi respublike (9.07.2002)
———. Soobshchenie pravozashchitnogo tsentra "Memorial" o prekrashchenii uchastiia nepravitel'stvennykh organizatsii v zasedanniiakh postoiannoi rabochei gruppy (12.07.2002)

———. "Zachistka" v sele Chechen-Aul (11–24 iiunia 2002 goda) (12.07.2002)
———. "Zachistka" v sele Mesker-Iurt (21 maia–11 iiunia 2002 goda (18.07.2002)
———. "Zachistka" v groznenskoi priemnoi "Memoriala" (19.07.2002)
———. Recommendation of the Commissioner for Human Rights, Council of Europe, concerning certain rights that must be guaranteed during the arrest and detention of persons following "cleansing" operations in the Chechen Republic of the Russian Federation (25.07.2002)
———. "Zachistka" v sele Tsotsin-Iurt: 25–29 iiulia 2002 goda (9.08.2002)
———. Sobytiia v sele Tevzeni (Tevzana) avgust 2002 g. (26.08.2002)
———. On the return of IDPs from the camps of Ingushetia to Chechnya, August 2002 (6.09.2002)
———. On the readiness of forced migrants to move to Chechnya from different regions of the RF, July 2002 (6.09.2002)
———. Novoe zakhoronenie v Chechne (Ingushetii) (9.09.2002)
———. Obstrel punkta vremennogo razmeshcheniia v Groznom (12.09.2002)
———. Chechnia, tri goda spustia: Zhivye i mertvye (5.10.2002)
———. Otkrytoe pis'mo prezidentu Rossii V. V. Putinu (29.10.2002)
———. Zachistka v sele Tsotsin-Iurt (1–8 sentiabria 2002 goda) (1.11.2002)
———. Mezhdunarodnaia Konferentsiia "Za prekrashchenie voiny i ustanovlenie mira v chechenskoi Respublike" (6.11.2002)
———. Mir—eto i est' udar no terrorizmu (10.11.2002)
———. Vortolet Sbit: Ot otvetnykh deistvii postradali mirnye zhiteli (3–6 noiabria 2002 goda) (14.11.2002)
———. Ulozhenie o voennom upravlenii: Kommentarii k ukazu Prezidenta RF No. 1120 (14.11.2002)

Year 2003

———. Novoe massovoe zakhoronenie zhertv vnesudebnykh kaznei (13.01.2003)
———. Groznyi: ischeznoveniia zaderzhannykh, grabezhi, aktsii protesta (14.01.2003)
———. Strasburgskii sud prinial k rassmotreniiu pervye shest' zhalob zhitelei Chechni (21.01.2003)
———. On the situation with human rights violations in the Chechen Republic, September 2002–February 2003 (11.02.2003)
———. Open letter to the Commissioner for Human Rights of the Council of Europe, Mr. Alvaro Gil-Robles (14.02.2003)
———. Open letter to the Commissioner for Human Rights of the Council of Europe, Mr. Alvaro Gil-Robles (15.02.2003)
———. O provedenii referenduma v Chechenskoi Respublike (27.02.2003)
———. Appeal to the UN Commission for Human Rights, 59th Session, 2003 (March 2003)
———. Novoe zakhorenie v Chechne (Kapustino, 8 fevral'ia 2003 goda) (03.03.2003)
———. Beznakannost' prestupnnikov delaet neobkhodimym sozdanie Mezhduharodnogo tribunala (06.03.2003)
———. Sluchai nezakonnogo zaderzhaniia, pokhishcheniia, "izcheznoveniia" i ubiistv zaderzhannykh v Chechenkoi Respublike (07.03.2003)
———. PTS "Memorial": Provel opros zhitelei Chechenskoi Respubliki ob ikh otnoshenii k referendumu (25.03.2003)

———. Situatsii v den' provdeneiia referenduma v Shatoiskom i Urus-Martanovskom raionakh (10.04.2003)

———. Appeal to the UN Commission for Human Rights (21.04.2003)

———. Statement on behalf of the NGOs: 59th Session of the UN Commission on Human Rights, agenda item 9 (21.04.2003)

———. Reports of human rights organizations are supported by evidence from other sources (25.04.2003)

———. Letter to Sergei Kovalev from S. N. Fridinsky, Office of the Prosecutor General of the Russian Federation (25.04.2003)

———. Zaiavlenie mezhduharodnogo obshchestva "Memorial" po povodu terakta v Znamenskom (13.05.2003)

———. Ob amnistii, ob'iavliaemoi v sviazi s priniatiem Konstitutsii Chechenskoi Respubliki (20.05.2003)

———. Political crime in the Kalinovskaia settlement (29.05.2003)

———. Mirnym peregovoram v Chechne net razumnoi al'ternativy (05.06.2003)

———. "Deceptive justice: Situation on the investigation on crimes against civilians committed by members of the Federal Forces in the Chechen Republic during military operations 1999–2003 (updated in May 2003)" (10.06.2003)

———. Spravka: Polozhenie vnutrenie peremeshennykh lits v g. Groznyi Chechenskoi respubliki (24.06.2003)

———. "Normalizatsiia" v Chechne, "stabil'nost'" v Ingushetii: Materialy press-konferentsii (26.06.2003)

———. "Zachistka" v sele Alkhazurovo Urus-Martanovskogo raiona (25.07.2003)

———. Nespokoinaiia obstanovka sokhraniaetsia na territorii unichtozhennogo v kontse noiabria-nachale dekabria 2002g: Lageria "Iman" v p. Aki-Iurt (14.08.2003)

———. Prodolzhaiut postupat' trevozhnye signaly iz palatochnogo largeria "Bela" (st. Slepstovskaiia) (14.08.2003)

———. Spetsoperatsiia v slepstovskoi raionnoi bol'nitse (21 avgusta 2003 goda) (21.08.2003)

———. Respublika Ingushetiia: Palatochnyi lager' "Bella": 16–17 sentiabria 2003 goda (19.09.2003)

———. Respublika Ingushetiia: Palatochnyi lager' "Bella": 22 sentiabria 2003 goda (22.09.2003)

———. Zaiavlenie ot bezhentsev p/l "Bella" (22.09.2003)

———. Deputy prosecutor of Chechnya refutes official data (31.10.2003)

———. A. Cherkasov, "Voina v Chechne i mir v Rossii: Nekotorye aspekty vliianiia vooruzhennogo konflikta v chechne na vnutrenniuiu polituku Rossiiskoi Federatsii—i chto s etim delat?" (08.11.2003)

———. Zakliuchitel'nyie zamechaniia Komiteta po pravam cheloveka OON (izvlecheniia) (14.11.2003)

———. Kak v Chechne ubivaiut "pomoshchnikov arabskikh terroristov" (16.11.2003)

———. Pytki i nezakonnye tiur'my: Chechnia, 2003 god: Vystuplenie Olega Orlova, predsedatelia Soveta PTS (03.12.2003)

———. Pokhishcheniia, izcheznoveniia za ianvar'-noiabr' 2003 goda v Chechenskoi Respublike: Po dannym "Khornika nasiliia" Pravozashchitnogo tsentra "Memorial" (03.12.2003)

———. Regional'nyi operativnyi shtab po upravleniiu kontrterroristicheskoi operatsiei na Severnom Kavkaze zapisal ubitykh mirnykh zhitelei v boeviki (10.12.2003)

———. Pravozashchitnyi Tsentr "Memorial": O vozvrashchenii bezhentsev iz Ingushetii v Chechniu (situatsiia na osen' 2003 g.) (17.12.2003)

Year 2004

———. "Voina Palatkam" prodolzhaetsia: Ingushetiia, ianvar' 2004 goda (18.01.2004)
———. Pokhishcheniia, ischeznoveniia za 2003 god v Chechenkoi Respublike: Po dannym "Khroniki Nasiliia" Pravozashchitnogo Tsentra "Memorial" (20.01.2004)
———. Vnutriperemeshchennye litsa iz Chechenskoi Respubliki v palatochnykh lageriakh Respubliki Ingushetiia i v punktakh vremennogo razmeshcheniia posle vozvrashcheniia (10.02.2004)
———. Otkrytoe pis'mo prezidentu Rossiiskoi Federatsii V. V. Putinu ot zhitelei Chechni (12.02.2004)
———. "Siloviki" okazyvaiut davlenie na inostrannykh zhurnalistov, rabotaiushchikh na Severnom Kavkaze, i na mestnikh zhitelei, obshchaiushchikhsia s zhurnalistami (13.02.2004)
———. A. Cherkasov, Kniga chisel; Kniga utrat; Kniga strashnogo suda (26.02.2004)
———. "Dobrovol'naiia sdacha" Magomeda Khambieva (10.03.2004)
———. Aktsiia ustrasheniia v lagere "Sputnik" (30.03.2004)
———. Istoriia likvidatsii lageria "Sputnik" (05.04.2004)
———. Joint statement by Amnesty International, Human Rights Watch, the Medical Foundation for the Care of Victims of Torture, and Memorial: "The situation in Chechnya and Ingushetia deteriorates: New evidence" (08.04.2004)
———. Mother and five small children dead after aerial attack on civilian house in Chechnya (14.04.2004)
———. Detainment and murders of 8 Shalinskii region residents of the village of Duba-Iurt (15.04.2004)
———. Chechnya, Vesna—2004: Podrobnosti "Normalizatsii" (20.04.2004)
———. Refugees in Ingushetia: Reinstatement to the list; only through court? (07.05.2004)
———. Vnutriperemeshchennye litsa v punktakh vremennogo razmeshcheniia Chechenskoi Respubliki: Aprel' 2004 (07.05.2004)
———. Evropeiskii sud po pravam cheloveka provedet slushaniia po shesti zhalobam iz Chechni (15.06.2004)
———. Bezhentsev iz Ingushetii perevezli v Chechniu: Bor'ba za vyzhivanie prodolzhaetsia vdali ot dosuzhikh glaz (16.06.2004)
———. Kak prokuratura i sudy sposobstvuiut beznakazannosti v Chechne (20.06.2004)
———. Ocherednaiia "zachistka" v lagere bezhentsev v Al'tievo (24.06.2004)
———. Ingushetiia: Lager' bezhentsev iz Chechne v Altievo zakryvaiut (24.06.2004)
———. "Zachistka" v lagere bezhentsev iz Chechni v Al'tievo (molochno-tovarnaia ferma) (24.06.2004)
———. From the conflict zone (28.06.2004)
———. Ingushetiia: Situatsiia v mestakh kompaktnogo prozhivananiia vynuzhdenno pereselennykh lits. 3–5 iiulia 2004 goda (06.07.2004)
———. O polozhenii peremeshchennykh vnutri strany lits (VPL) iz Chechenskoi Respubliki v Respublike Ingushetiia i situatsii v puntktakh vremennogo razmeshcheniia v Chechenskoi Respublike (konets iiunia-iiul' 2004 g.) (12.07.2004)
———. Sotrudniki FSB pytaiut i ubivaiut (13.07.2004)

———. Osvobozhdeny vse bezhentsy iz Chechni, zaderzhannye v khode "zachistki" v Al'tievo (23.07.2004)
———. O polozhenii zhitelei Chechni v Rossiiskoi Federatsii (iiun' 2003 g.–mai 2004 g.) (01.08.2004)
———. Polozhenie vynuzhdennykh pereselentsev prozhivaiushchikh v lagere "Uchkhoz" Iandere (20.08.2004)
———. Presidentskie vybory v Chechenskoi Respublike (31.08.2004)
———. Beslan: Zakhvat zalozhnikov v shkole (spravka PTS "Memorial" po resul'tatam monitoringa i oprosov naseleniia) (05.09.2004)
———. Beslan: The hostage-taking at the school (05.09.2004)
———. Prokuratura Respublika Ingushetiia pytaetsia zakryt' nepravitel'stvennuiu pravozashchitnuiu organizatsiiu (07.09.2004)
———. Beslan: Otvestvennost' za zlodeianiia; zaiavlenie Pravozashchitnogo Tsentra "Memorial" (10.09.2004)
———. Situatsiia vokrug mest kompaktnogo prozhivaniia vnutriperemeshchennykh lits (VPL) iz Chechni v Ingushetii: Leto 2004 goda (20.09.2004)
———. Strasburgskii Sud rassmotril pervye zhaloby ot zhitelei Chechenskoi Respubliki (14.10.2004)
———. O predlozheniiakh general'nogo prokurora po bor'be s terrorizmom: Obrashchenie Mezhdunarodnogo Obshchestva "Memorial" k Prezidenty Rossii V. V. Putinu (29.10.2004)
———. Vpered v proshloe: Initsiativy genprokurora vozvrashchaiut Rossiiu vo vremena Bol'shogo terrora (Tezisy vystupleniia A. Cherkasov na press-konferentsii v Natsional'nom institute pressy) (03.11.2004)
———. Power agencies assault the mosque in Sleptsovsk (04.11.2004)
———. Poteri grazhdanskogo naseleniia v Chechenskikh voinakh (10.12.2004)
———. Poteri voennosluzhashchikh v chechenskikh voinakh (10.12.2004)

Year 2005

———. In December 2004 A. Maskhadov's eight relatives have been abducted in the Chechen Republic (12.01.2005)
———. Chechnya: Who is behind human abductions? (14.01.2005)
———. Zaiavlenie K. M. Maskhadovoi na imia generalnogo prokurora RF o pokhishchennykh rodstvennikakh (20.01.2005)
———. Open letter from seven Russian and international human rights NGOs concerning the creation of a round table in the framework of the PACE Political Affairs Committee regarding human rights, democracy and law in the CR (24.01.2005)
———. Zumsoi: Civilians are forced to flee their native village (04.02.2005)
———. Chechnia, 2004 god: Pokhishcheniia i ischeznoveniia liudei (07.02.2005)
———. The whereabouts of 7 relatives of Maskhadov remain unknown (08.02.2005)
———. Abducted rights defender is free again (14.02.2005)
———. FSB i Prokuratura Respubliki Ingushetiia po-prezhnemu pytaiutsia zakryt' nepravitel'stvennuiu pravozashchitnuiu organizatsiiu (16.02.2005)
———. Mesta kompaktnogo poseleniia (MKP), predlozhennye byvshim zhiteliam palatochnykh lagerei v Ingushetii kak al'ternativa vozvrashcheniiu v Chechenkuiu Respubliku, likvidiruiutsia (21.02.2005)
———. Ubiistvo piaterykh zhitelei Kurchaloevskogo raiona (22.02.2005)

———. Bomdardirovka bezhentsev s sela Shaami-Iurt byla ne edinichnym sluchaem (12.03.2005)
———. Chechnya 2004: "New" methods of anti-terror; hostage taking and repressive actions against relatives of alleged combatants and terrorists (17.03.2005)
———. Mopping-up operation in the village of Katayma in the city of Grozny (06.04.2005)
———. Views of Russian NGOs—Human Rights Center "Memorial" and center "demos" regarding the PACE roundtable on Chechnya (14.04.2005)
———. Prodolzhaiutsia pokhishcheniia i ubiistva zhitelei Chechni, osmelivshikhsia podat' zhalobu v Evropeiskii sud po pravam cheloveka (25.05.2005)
———. Rodstvenniki pokhishchennykh piketiruiut kompleks pravitel'stvennykh zdanii v g. Groznom (30.05.2005)
———. Osvobozhdeny rodstvenniki A. Maskhadova, pokhishchennye v dekabre 2004 goda (31.05.2005)

Interviews

Interviews cited with numbers were conducted in confidentiality, and the names of interviewees are withheld by mutual agreement.

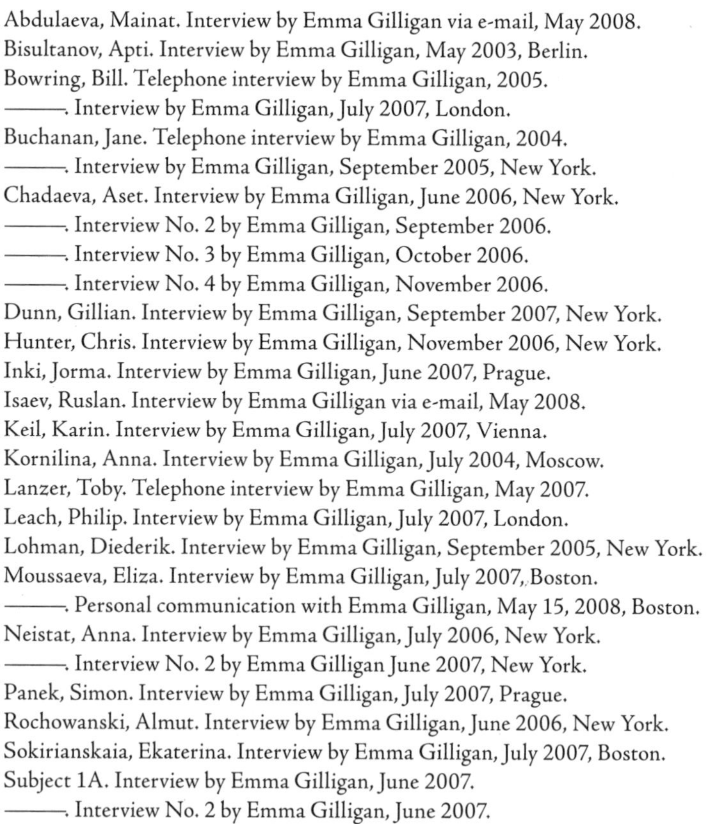

Abdulaeva, Mainat. Interview by Emma Gilligan via e-mail, May 2008.
Bisultanov, Apti. Interview by Emma Gilligan, May 2003, Berlin.
Bowring, Bill. Telephone interview by Emma Gilligan, 2005.
———. Interview by Emma Gilligan, July 2007, London.
Buchanan, Jane. Telephone interview by Emma Gilligan, 2004.
———. Interview by Emma Gilligan, September 2005, New York.
Chadaeva, Aset. Interview by Emma Gilligan, June 2006, New York.
———. Interview No. 2 by Emma Gilligan, September 2006.
———. Interview No. 3 by Emma Gilligan, October 2006.
———. Interview No. 4 by Emma Gilligan, November 2006.
Dunn, Gillian. Interview by Emma Gilligan, September 2007, New York.
Hunter, Chris. Interview by Emma Gilligan, November 2006, New York.
Inki, Jorma. Interview by Emma Gilligan, June 2007, Prague.
Isaev, Ruslan. Interview by Emma Gilligan via e-mail, May 2008.
Keil, Karin. Interview by Emma Gilligan, July 2007, Vienna.
Kornilina, Anna. Interview by Emma Gilligan, July 2004, Moscow.
Lanzer, Toby. Telephone interview by Emma Gilligan, May 2007.
Leach, Philip. Interview by Emma Gilligan, July 2007, London.
Lohman, Diederik. Interview by Emma Gilligan, September 2005, New York.
Moussaeva, Eliza. Interview by Emma Gilligan, July 2007, Boston.
———. Personal communication with Emma Gilligan, May 15, 2008, Boston.
Neistat, Anna. Interview by Emma Gilligan, July 2006, New York.
———. Interview No. 2 by Emma Gilligan June 2007, New York.
Panek, Simon. Interview by Emma Gilligan, July 2007, Prague.
Rochowanski, Almut. Interview by Emma Gilligan, June 2006, New York.
Sokirianskaia, Ekaterina. Interview by Emma Gilligan, July 2007, Boston.
Subject 1A. Interview by Emma Gilligan, June 2007.
———. Interview No. 2 by Emma Gilligan, June 2007.
Subject 2A. Interview by Emma Gilligan, June 2007.

———. Interview No. 2 by Emma Gilligan, June 2007.
Subject 3A. Interview by Emma Gilligan, July 2007.
Subject 4A. Interview by Emma Gilligan, July 2007.
Subject 5A. Interview by Emma Gilligan, July 2007.
Subject 6A. Interview by Emma Gilligan, June 2007.
Subject 7A. Interview by Emma Gilligan, June 2007.
Subject 8A. Interview by Emma Gilligan, May 2003.
Young, Mike. Interview by Emma Gilligan, September 2007, New York.

Documentary Films

Assassination of Russia. Documentary based on NTV footage and produced by Transparences Productions. France, 2000.
Chechen Lullaby. Documentary film by Nino Kirtadze. France, 2002.
Coca—The Dove from Chechnya. Documentary film by Eric Bergkraut. Switzerland, 2005.
Murder with International Consent. Documentary film by POLSAT-TV. Poland, 2003.
Terror in Moscow. HBO documentary film, produced and directed by Dan Reed. 2003.
The Three Comrades. Documentary film by Masha Novikova. Netherlands, 2006.

International Statutes

Convention on the Prevention and Punishment of the Crime of Genocide, 1948. http://www.hrweb.org/legal/genocide.html (accessed March 2009).
Convention on Prohibitions or Restrictions on the Use of Certain Conventional Weapons Which May Be Deemed to Be Excessively Injurious or to Have Indiscriminate Effects. Geneva, October 10, 1980. http://www.un.org/millennium/law/xxvi-18-19.htm (accessed March 2009).
European Convention on Human Rights, 1950. http://www.hri.org/docs/ECHR50.html.
Geneva Conventions of August 12, 1949. Convention (I) for the Amelioration of the Condition of the Wounded and Sick in Armed Forces in the Field. Geneva, 12 August 1949. http://www.icrc.org/ihl.nsf/FULL/365?OpenDocument.
———. Convention (II) for the Amelioration of the Condition of Wounded, Sick and Shipwrecked Members of Armed Forces at Sea. Geneva, 12 August 1949. http://www.icrc.org/ihl.nsf/FULL/370?OpenDocument.
———. Convention (III) relative to the Treatment of Prisoners of War. Geneva, 12 August 1949. http://www.icrc.org/ihl.nsf/FULL/375?OpenDocument.
———. Convention (IV) relative to the Protection of Civilian Persons in Time of War. Geneva, 12 August 1949. http://www.icrc.org/ihl.nsf/FULL/380?OpenDocument.
Protocol Additional to the Geneva Convention of 12 August 1949 and Relating to the Protection of Victims of Non International Armed Conflicts (Protocol II). June 8, 1977. http://www.unhchr.ch/html/menu3/b/93.htm (accessed March 2009).
Rome Statute of the International Criminal Court, 1998. http://untreaty.un.org/cod/icc/statute/romefra.htm (accessed March 2009).

INDEX

HUMAN RIGHTS AND CRIMES AGAINST HUMANITY

Eric D. Weitz, Series Editor

THIS SERIES PROVIDES a forum for publication and debate on the most pressing issues of modern times: the establishment of human rights standards and, at the same time, their persistent violation. It features a broad understanding of human rights, one that encompasses democratic citizenship as well as concerns for social, economic, and environmental justice. Its understanding of crimes against humanity is similarly broad, ranging from large-scale atrocities like ethnic cleansings, genocides, war crimes, and various forms of human trafficking to lynchings, mass rapes, and torture. Some books in the series are more historically oriented and explore particular events and their legacies. Others focus on contemporary concerns, like instances of forced population displacements or indiscriminate bombings. Still others provide serious reflection on the meaning and history of human rights or on the reconciliation efforts that follow major human rights abuses. Chronologically, the series runs from around 1500, the onset of the modern era marked by European colonialism abroad and the Atlantic slave trade, to the present. Geographically, it takes in every area of the globe. It publishes significant works of original scholarship and major interpretations by historians, human rights practitioners, legal scholars, social scientists, philosophers, and journalists. An important goal is to bring issues of human rights and their violations to the attention of a wide audience and to stimulate discussion and debate in the public sphere as well as among scholars and in the classroom. The knowledge that develops from the series will also, we hope, help promote human rights standards and prevent future crimes against humanity.